T0205666

THEORETICAL AND COMPUTATIONAL RESEARCH IN THE 21ST CENTURY

THEORETICAL AND COMPUTATIONAL RESEARCH IN THE 21ST CENTURY

Edited by
Nazmul Islam, PhD

Apple Academic Press

TORONTO   NEW JERSEY

Apple Academic Press Inc. | Apple Academic Press Inc.
3333 Mistwell Crescent | 9 Spinnaker Way
Oakville, ON L6L 0A2 | Waretown, NJ 08758
Canada | USA

First issued in paperback 2021

Exclusive worldwide distribution by CRC Press, a member of Taylor & Francis Group
No claim to original U.S. Government works

ISBN 13: 978-1-77463-348-9 (pbk)
ISBN 13: 978-1-77188-033-6 (hbk)

Library of Congress Control Number: 2014947476

Library and Archives Canada Cataloguing in Publication

Theoretical and computational research in the 21st century/edited by Nazmul Islam, PhD.

Includes bibliographical references and index.
ISBN 978-1-77188-033-6 (bound)

1. Research. 2. Science. I. Islam, Nazmul, author, editor

Q180.A1T54 2014   507.2   C2014-905512-9

ABOUT THE EDITOR

Nazmul Islam, PhD

Nazmul Islam, PhD, is now working as an assistant professor in the Department of Basic Sciences & Humanities at Techno Global-Balurghat (now Techno India-Balurghat),Balurghat, D. Dinajpur, India. He has published more than 60 research papers in several prestigious peer-reviewed journals and has written many book chapters and research books. In addition, he is the editor-in-chief of *The SciTech, Journal of Science and Technology; The SciTech, International Journal of Engineering Sciences*; and the *Signpost Open Access Journal of Theoretical Sciences*. He also serves as a member on the editorial boards of several journals.

Dr. Islam has been selected for inclusion in the 2011 and 2012 (11th and 12th) editions of *Who's Who in Science and Engineering* by the publisher of *Who's Who in America*. He has also been included in *2000 Outstanding Intellectuals of the 21st Century* in 2011 and selected as a member of IBC Top 100 Scientists in the year 2012 by International Biographical Centre, Cambridge, England.

Dr. Islam's research interests are in theoretical chemistry, particularly quantum chemistry, conceptual density functional theory (CDFT), periodicity, SAR, QSAR/QSPR study, drug design, HMO theory, biological function of chemical compounds, quantum biology, nanochemistry, and more.

CONTENTS

LIST OF CONTRIBUTORS

Blanca E. Carvajal-Gámez
Unidad Profesional Interdisciplinaria de Ingeniería y Tecnologías Avanzadas (Professional Unit Engineering and Advanced Technologies), Av. IPN 2580, Barrio La Laguna, Ticoman, CP 07740 México DF. Email: becarvajalg@gmail.com

Hernando Efrain Caicedo-Ortiz
Grupo de Ingeniería y Tecnologías Cuánticas, Corporación Universitaria Autónoma del Cauca, Calle 5 No. 3-85, Popayán, Colombia; Facultad de Ingeniería, Área de Ciencias Básicas Universidad Anahuac; Av. Universidad Anáhuac núm. 46, Col. Lomas Anáhuac, C.P. 52786, Huixquilucan, Estado de México, México; Instituto de Educación Media Superior del Distrito Federal—IEMS, San Lorenzo No. 290, Col. Del Valle Sur, C.P. 03100, Del. Benito Juárez, Ciudad de México, México. Email: hecaicedo@gmail.com

J. H. Caltenco Franca
ESIME-Zacatenco, Instituto Politécnico Nacional, Edif. 5, 1er. Piso, Col. Lindavista, México DF, CP 07738, Email: jcaltenco@ipn.mx

Rafael G. Campos
Facultad de Ciencias Físico-Matemáticas,Universidad Michoacana, 58060, Morelia, Mich., México. Email: rcampos@umich.mx

R. Cruz-Santiago
ESIME-Zacatenco, Instituto Politécnico Nacional, Edif.5, 1er. Piso, Col. Lindavista CP 07738, México DF. Email: rcruzs@ipn.mx

Dulal C. Ghosh
Department of Chemistry, University of Kalyani, Kalyani-741235, India. Email: dcghosh1@rediffmail.com

Francisco J. Gallegos-Funes
Escuela Superior de Ingeniería Mecánica y Eléctrica (Mechanical and Electrical Engineering Higher School), Av. IPN s/n, ESIME SEPI-Electrónica, Lindavista, 07738, México DF. Email: fgallegos@ipn.mx

A. Hernández-Galeana
Escuela Superior de Física y Matemáticas, Instituto Politécnico Nacional (IPN), Edif.9, Col. Lindavista, CP 07738, México DF. Email: albino@esfm.ipn.mx

Adolfo Huet
Facultad de Ciencias Físico-Matemáticas,Universidad Michoacana, 58060, Morelia, Mich., México. Email: ahuet@fismat.umich.mx

Laurian Ioan Piscoran
Department of Mathematics and Computer Science, North Univ. Center of Baia Mare, Victoriei 76, 430 122 Baia Mare, Romania. Email: plaurian@yahoo.com

Nazmul Islam
Department of Chemistry, University of Kalyani, Kalyani-741235, India; Theoretical and Computational Chemistry Research Laboratory, Techno Global-Balurghat, Balurghat, D. Dinajpur 733103, India. Email: nazmulislam@tgbtechno.com;nazmul.islam786@gmail.com

Sandip Kumar Rajak
Dumkal College, Basantapur, Dumakl, Murshidabad, WB, India; Department of Chemistry, University of Kalyani, Kalyani-741235, India. Email:sandip1ku@gmail.com

Ratan Kumar Bose
Department of Basic Science & Humanities, Techno Global Balurghat, Techno India Group, Balurghat, Dakshin Dinajpur-733103, West Bengal, India. Email: ratankrbose@gmail.com

J. López-Bonilla
ESIME-Zacatenco, Instituto Politécnico Nacional, Edif. 5, 1er. Piso, Col. Lindavista, CP 07738, México DF. Email: jlopezb@ipn.mx

J. Morales
Area de Física AMA, CBI, UAM-Azcapotzalco, Apdo. Postal 16-306, CP 02200 México DF. Email: jmr@correo.azc.uam.mx

G. Ovando
Area de Física AMA, CBI, UAM-Azcapotzalco, Apdo. Postal 16-306, CP 02200 México DF. Email: gaoz@correo.azc.uam.mx

J. M. Rivera-Rebolledo
Escuela Superior de Física y Matemáticas, Instituto Politécnico Nacional, Edif. 9, Col. Lindavista, CP 07738, México DF. Email: jrivera@esfm.ipn.mx

Elizabeth Santiago-Cortes
Grupo de Ingeniería y Tecnologías Cuánticas, Corporación Universitaria Autónoma del Cauca, Calle 5 No. 3–85, Popayán, Colombia. Email:elizabeth.santiago@uniautonoma.edu.co

NOTES ON CONTRIBUTORS

José Héctor Caltenco Franca was born in Mexico City in 1954. He received his BS degree in communication and electronics engineering and Master Science degree in electronics from ESIME-IPN in 1981 and 1996, respectively. He is currently working toward the PhD degree at ESIME-IPN. He is currently a professor in the same institution, and his research interests include EMC testing and measurements techniques, standardization and power line communications and some EMC aspects in Smart Grids. He is EMCS-IEEE member since 2004.

Rafael G. Campos is a professor at Universidad Michoacana and a member of the Mexican Academy of Sciences. He was born in Morelia, México. He has been teaching physics and mathematics since 1974 as lecturer-in-charge of more than 90 courses. He participated in the creation of the Institute of Physics and Mathematics and of the doctorate program in Physical Engineering at Universidad Michoacana. The research activity of Dr. Campos includes some topics in scientific computing and numerical analysis. In particular, signal processing, matrix representations of differintegral operators and numerical solutions of partial differential equations (PDEs).

Blanca E. Carvajal-Gámez was born in Mexico, D. F. She obtained the title in computer engineering in 2002 in the School of Computing. She has obtained a MSc in telecommunications engineering in 2008 at SEPI–IPN–ESIME. She obtained the degree of Doctor of Science in 2012 at SEPI–ESIME–CUALHUACAN. She is currently working as a research professor at the IPN.

Hernando Efrain Caicedo Ortiz holds his BSc degree in engineering physics from Universidad del Cauca (Unicauca) in Popayán, Colombia. He also holds an MSc in physical mathematics from Instituto Politécnico Nacional (IPN) in México City, México, and MSc Complexity from Universidad Autónoma de la Ciudad de México (UACM) in México City, México. He is currently Research Associate at the College of Engineering in Corporación Universitaria Autónoma del Cauca in Popayán, Colombia, Assistant Professor at the College of Engineering in Universidad Anahuac, Mexico State; Mexico, Professor and Research Associate at Instituto de Educación Media Superior del Distrito Federal, México City, México. His research interests focus on new models of computing, complex systems, astrophysics, and physics education.

R. Cruz-Santiago received his MSc in communications and electronics from National Polytechnic Institute of Mexico in 2004. He is currently Professor of

Computer Academy High School from the same institute. His areas of scientific interest are signal and image processing and filtering.

Francisco J. Gallegos-Funes received his PhD in communications and electronics from National Polytechnic Institute of Mexico in 2003. He is currently an associate professor in the Mechanical and Electrical Engineering Higher School from the same institute. His areas of scientific interest are signal and image processing, filtering, steganography, pattern recognition, and real-time applications.

Dulal C. Ghosh is currently an emeritus professor of UGC. He retired as a professor of the University of Kalyani. He also acted as a visiting professor of Assam University, BU, NBU. He is an ex-member of the Editorial Board of *International Journal of Molecular Science* (IJMS) and member of the Editorial Board of *International Journal of Chemical Modeling*, executive member of *The SciTech, Journal of Science and Technology* (TSTJST), and senior member of *International Journal of Environment Science* (IJES). He is working in the broad field of quantum chemistry. His main interest is to study the effect of symmetry on charge transfer and binding, origin of barrier, computation of environment dependent hybridization, density functional correlation of the physical processes of inversion and internal rotation, concepts and scales of atomic polarizability, electronegativity, hardness, electrophilicity and their interrelation, the fundamental charge equalization principles, and so on.

Albino Hernández-Galeana received his MSc degree in physics at the Center for Research and Advanced Studies of the National Polytechnic Institute, Mexico, 1985, and his PhD degree in elementary particle physics in 1989. At present, he is Titular Professor in the Physics Department of the Escuela Superior de Física y Matemáticas, Instituto Politécnico Nacional. His main scientific research is in Physics beyond the Standard Model.

Adolfo Huet was born in Mexico City and studied at the State University of Michoacan, Mexico (UMSNH). There, he earned his undergraduate degree in physics and mathematics in 2001 and his Master's degree in physics in 2003. Dr. Huet obtained his PhD in Physics from the University of Connecticut (UCONN) in 2010, where his worked focused on theoretical high energy physics. He has published several papers in quantum field theory. His current interests include theoretical physics, computational physics, and teaching. Dr. Huet currently resides in Querétaro, Mexico.

Ratan Kumar Bose is pursuing his PhD in applied mathematics and is working as Assistant Professor in the Department of Mathematics in Techno Global-Balurghat. Formerly, he was a lecturer in mathematics in N.S.O.U. Bose is currently associated as a Board Member of *The SciTech* Publishers, *Journal of Science and Technology*, editorial team member of *Signpost Open Access Journal of Theoretical Sciences*, and Editorial Board member of *International Journal of Applied Sciences and Engineering* (IJASE).His Research area is "Bio-Mechanics".

Sandip Kumar Rajak, MSc, PhD, is an assistant professor of chemistry in Dumkal College, Basantapur, Dumkal, Murshidabad, West Bengal, India, under the University of Kalyani. He has completed his PhD in the field of quantum chemistry under the supervision of Professor Dulal Chandra Ghosh (ex-professor), through University of Kalyani. He has published more than ten articles in international journals and in edited book chapters.

Piscoran Laurian-Ioan is a lecturer at Technical University of Cluj-Napoca, North University Center of Baia Marem, Romania. He obtained his PhD at "Babeş-Bolyai" University of Cluj-Napoca, Romania. He is an active researcher and has a 12-year teaching experience. He has more than 25 research articles; some of them published in reputed international journals. He is editor-in-chief at two International Journal of Geometry and also a reviewer of Mathematical Reviews and Zentralblatt für Mathematik. His topics of interest are in Geometry: curves and surfaces, Riemannian geometry, Finsler geometry, hyperbolic geometry, Euclidean geometry, projective geometry, and noncommutative geometry.

J. López-Bonilla obtained his PhD in theoretical physics (1982) by National Polytechnic Institute (IPN), Mexico City. He is professor of mathematical methods applied to engineering in the "Higher School of Mechanical and Electrical Engineering," IPN, and an Editorial Board member of *The SciTech, Journal of Science and Technology, Palestine Journal of Mathematics, Global Engineers and Technologist Review, Journal of Interpolation and Approximation in Scientific Computing, International Journal of Chemoinformatics and Chemical Engineering, International Journal of Special Functions and Applications, Global Jorunal of Advanced Research on Classical and Modern Geometries*, and *Information Science and Computing*.

J. Morales is physicist from the National Autonomous University of Mexico. He obtained his master and PhD degrees from the Louis Pasteur University, Strasbourg, France. In reality, he is working as professor/researcher at the Metropolitan Autonomous University-Azc. Mexico. His subject of interest is theoretical physics, especially mathematical physics. His work has been published in *IJQC, PhysicaScripta, JMP, JMCh, Phys Rev. Lett*,and others. He has been recognized by the National Council of Science and Technology, México, as National Researcher Level II.

Gerardo Ovando obtained his PhD in theoretical physics in 2008 from the National Polytechnic Institute (NPI), Mexico City. He has published 60 international scientific papers in the areas of general relativity, electrodynamics and quantum mechanics. He worked at the NPI during the period 1989–1998, and after he incorporated to "Universidad Autónoma Metropolitana-Azcapotzalco" where now he realizes his academic and scientific activities. He is member of the National System of Researchers, Conacyt, Mexico.

J. M. Rivera-Rebolledo received his MSc degree in physics at the National Polytechnic Institute, Mexico, 1976, and his PhD degree in elementary particle physics from the University of Trieste, Italy, 1980. At the present time, he is Titular Professor in the Department of Physics of the Escuela Superior de Física y Matemáticas, Instituto Politécnico Nacional. His main scientific research is in neutrino physics.

Elizabeth Santiago Cortés holds a BSc degree in experimental biology from Universidad Autónoma Metropolitana—Iztapalapa (UAM) in México City, México, and an MSc Complexity from Universidad Autónoma de la Ciudad de México (UACM) in México City, México. She is currently Associate Research at the College of Engineering in Corporación Universitaria Autónoma del Cauca in Popayán, Colombia. Her research interests focus on bioinformatics, complex systems and complex networks, and popularization of science.

LIST OF ABBREVIATIONS

AC	angular correlation
AS	adaptive steganography
BHCP	backward heat conduction problem
CC	cross-correlation
CD	Czekanowski distance
CDFT	conceptual density functional theory
CFSE	crystal field stabilization energy
CLCES	color local complexity-estimation-based steganographic
DCT	discrete cosine transform
DFT	density-functional theory
DWT	discrete wavelet transform
FERMO	frontier effective-for-reaction molecular orbital
FMO	frontier molecular orbital
FT	Fourier transform
GAP	gross atom population
GOP	gross orbital population
HA–HB	hard acid–hard base
HC	hiding capacity
HF-SCF	Hartree–Fock self-consistence field
HMO	Hückel molecular orbital
HOMO	highest occupied molecular orbital
HPF	high-pass filter
HSAB	hard and soft acid and base
HSV	hue, saturation, value
HVS	human visual system
IDWT	inverse discrete wavelet transform
IF	image fidelity
IQM	image quality measures
LFSE	ligand field stabilization energy
LPF	low-pass filter
LSB	least significant bit
LUMO	lowest unoccupied molecular orbital

MAE	mean absolute error
MBSP	median of block spectral phase
MHD	magnetohydrodynamic
MRA	analysis of multiresolution
MSE	mean square error
MWBSD	median of weighted block spectral distortion
NCC	normalized cross-correlation
NCD	normalized color difference
NMSHVSE	normalized mean square HVS error
PM	perceptual masking
PMH	principle of maximum hardness
PSNR	peak signal-to-noise ratio
Q	quality index
QC	quantum chemical
RGB	red, green, blue
SA–SB	soft acid–soft base
SA–SB	strong acid/strong base
SMD	spectral magnitude distortion
XFT	eXtended Fourier transform
YCbCr	luminance, chromatic blue, chromatic red
ZDO	zero differential overlap

LIST OF SYMBOLS

α	thermal diffusivity or diffusion coefficient
E	the diagonal matrix
C	positive constant
$U_a(\omega)$ and $G(\omega)$	Fourier transforms
f	function
k^r	propagation direction
τ_r	null vector

PREFACE

Theoretical science research is a prerequisite for all scientific, technical, and modern medical research. It is a prerequisite for concentrated future efforts within all high-technology research fields.

Advances in the theory of science may be considered as a symbiotic interaction between theory and experiment: the theory is seldom used to understand experimental results, and it may suggest to experimentalists to carry out new experiments; side by side, the experiments help theoreticians to test theoretical predictions and may lead to improved theories.

The common application of theoretical methods and concepts in all science disciplines enables a dialogue across research topics, and the branch of theoretical science is appointed a priority area in majority of colleges, research centers, and universities across the globe.

This research book focuses mainly on the recent developments of theoretical, mathematical and computational conceptions, modeling, and simulation of specific research themes covering all scientific and technical disciplines from mathematics, chemistry, physics, and engineering. The book contains timely reviews, research articles, and short communications covering all fundamental and applied research aspects in all disciplines of natural sciences including their historical representations and philosophical prospective.

The chapters of the book have been reviewed by individuals chosen for their diverse perspectives and technical expertise, in accordance with procedures approved by the Apple Academic Press.

CHAPTER 1: THE TIME EVOLUTION OF THE HARD AND SOFT ACIDS AND BASES THEORY

In this work, the authors reviewed an indispensable theoretical construct of conceptual chemistry—the hard–soft acid–base (HSAB) theory. The concept and efforts of its quantitative measurement evolved with time. The HSAB theory is much enhanced by the seminal work of Parr and coworkers within the scope of density-functional theory (DFT), such that it has been an important chapter of theoretical chemistry of present-day science. The hardness is neither an experimental observable nor a quantum mechanically measurable quantity. But still it is reified, modeled, and measured to quantify the HSAB principle.

CHAPTER 2: MAGNETO HYDRODYNAMIC EFFECTS ON AN ATHEROSCLEROTIC ARTERY: A THEORETICAL STUDY

This study provides an insight and detailed knowledge on the magnetohydrodynamics for the description of the non-Newtonian blood flow under the action of an applied magnetic field. This model is consistent with the principles of magnetohydrodynamics and takes into account magnetization. The ingrowths of tissue in the artery may lead to a fatal disease such as ischemic stroke, and coronary thrombosis, and hence, the investigations of blood flow through arteries are of considerable importance in many cardiovascular diseases, particularly atherosclerosis. This analytical study may provide a scope for estimating the role of various mechanical and rheological parameters involved in the investigation and to ascertain which of the parameters have the most dominating role in the formation and development of this arterial disease. The analytical expressions for axial velocity, volumetric flow rate, pressure gradient, resistance to blood flow, shear stress, and skin friction have been derived in presence of externally imposed magnetic field. These expressions reveal significant alterations in blood flow due to stenosis. It can be noted that magnetic field significantly controls the characteristics flow patterns.

CHAPTER 3: A FAST SOLVER FOR THE BACKWARD HEAT CONDUCTION PROBLEM IN UNBOUNDED DOMAINS

In this chapter, the authors solved the backward heat conduction problem in unbounded domains using a novel numerical technique. Since the solution of the initial value problem written in terms of the fundamental solution yields an integral transform, a weakly stable and accurate numerical solution to the inverse problem can be obtained by using the convolution theorem and a new fast method to compute the Fourier transform. With a slight modification, this method can also be applied to find inverse solutions in bounded domains.

CHAPTER 4: STEGANOGRAPHIC METHOD FOR COLOR IMAGES USING VARIANCE FIELD ESTIMATION AND SCALING FACTOR FOR ENERGY CONSERVATION

When images are processed for the implementation of steganographic algorithms, it is important to study the quality of the cover and retrieved images, because it typically uses digital filters, reaching visibly deformed images. When a steganographic algorithm is used, numerical calculations performed by the computer cause errors and alterations in the images. The authors applied a scaling factor depending on the number of bits of the image to adjust these errors. The embedding capacity of each pixel is determined by the local complexity of the cover image, allowing good visual quality as well as embedding a large amount of secret messages. They have classified the pixels using a threshold based on the standard deviation of the local complexity in the cover image to provide a compromise between the embedding capacity and the image visual quality. The experimental results demonstrated that the algorithm proposed produces insignificant visual distortion due to the hidden message. The proposed method in this work is attacked with various tests based on IQMs, demonstrating it can resist the image quality measures (IQMs).

CHAPTER 5: OVERVIEW OF QUANTUM COMPUTATION

Quantum computing is a new emerging branch that generalizes the concept of computation using quantum phenomena. In this chapter, the authors presented the basic elements that enable the processing of information in the context of quantum mechanics and information theory.

CHAPTER 6: CLASSICAL CHARGED PARTICLES IN ARBITRARY MOTION

The authors of the Chapter 6 provide an insight on the aspect of the electromagnetic field generated by a charge in arbitrary motion in Minkowski space. Particularly important is the deduction of the superpotential for the radiative part of Maxwell tensor.

CHAPTER 7: SECOND-ORDER LINEAR DIFFERENTIAL EQUATION IN ITS EXACT FORM

In Chapter 7, it is shown that an arbitrary second-order linear differential equation can be written such that two integrations are enough to obtain its general solution.

CHAPTER 8: ON THE OPERATOR EXP(2 λ (P + Q))

This work deals with the study of the realization of a factorization of the type: $\exp(2\lambda(P+Q)) = \exp(f(\lambda)Q)\exp(g(\lambda)P)\exp(h(\lambda)Q)$, and it is showed that if the operators P and Q satisfy the conditions $[[P,Q],P] = -2P$ & $[[P,Q],Q] = 2Q$, then it is valid the relation $\exp(2\lambda(P+Q)) = \exp(Q\tan\lambda)\exp(P\sin(2\lambda))\exp(Q\tan\lambda)$. This result is important in the study of the time evolution operator for the one-dimensional harmonic oscillator.

CHAPTER 9: QUANTUM COMPUTATIONAL STUDIES ON PORPHYCENE

Chapter 9 provides an insight and detailed knowledge on the various aspects of porphycene, a constitutional isomer of porphyrin. Porphycene and its derivatives display unique physical and optical properties, including strong absorptions in the red region of the UV-vis spectrum. These features have made porphycene and porphycene analogues molecules for use in biomedical applications and in the design of new materials. They are mainly used for photodynamic therapy, a promising treatment for cancer. Because of their high fluorescence yields, these compounds are widely used for tumor detection. This theoretical exercise was designed to provide more detailed information on the various binding sites of the porphycene. A theoretical study of the stability, reactivity, and site selectivity was carried out at the AM1 and Huckel method. Further, the author has made an attempt to compare the local reactivity indices of the DFT (Fukui function and local softness) and atomic charges. This study provides evidence that both the Fukui functions and local softnesses fail to explain the maximum reactive or more precisely the donor site of the molecule/ligand porphycene. But the pi charge density, ZDO and Mulliken charges show maxima on the trans-N atoms.

CHAPTER 10: THE EVALUATION OF PROTONATION ENERGY OF MOLECULES IN TERMS OF QUANTUM THEORETICAL DESCRIPTORS

In this chapter, based on the fundamental concept of protonation, the authors have explored that the proton affinities (PAs) of molecules have been used as the primary information of many chemicophysical processes and to characterize the reactivity surface of molecular sites. Protonation and/or deprotonation are the first step in many fundamental molecular rearrangements and in most of the enzymatic reactions. Protonation is also an essential step in certain analytical procedures such as electrospray mass spectrometry. The proton transfer reactions are of great importance in chemistry and in biomolecular processes of living organisms. The knowledge of the intrinsic basicity and the site of protonation of a compound in the gas phase are central to the understanding of its reactivity and mechanism of chemical reactions involving proton. In recent years, acid–base interactions are extensively studied so that experimental techniques could be devised to permit the quantitative study of the thermochemistry of the proton transfer reaction in the gas phase. The protonated form of the molecule is totally a new chemical species having different charge distribution of the atomic sites within the molecule, polarizability, dipole moment, bond length, and bond angle. Protonating or deprotonating a molecule or ion alters many chemical properties, in addition to the change in the charge and mass, hydrophilicity, reduction potential, optical properties among others. From the study of the vast literature on the determination of proton affinities and effect of protonation on molecules, it reveals that the physicochemical process of protonation is a complex phenomenon, and the determination of PA is not a simple procedure—both experimentally and theoretically. Therefore, there is enough scope of exploring some other methods—namely modeling and simulation—a well-known procedure for scientific study. Hope, this study will help each and every one associate with the study of protonation.

CHAPTER 11: ANALYSIS OF CASSON FLUID MODEL FOR BLOOD FLOW IN EXTERNALLY APPLIED MAGNETIC FIELD

In this chapter, the author proposed a Casson fluid model for blood rheology suitable for the description of the non-Newtonian blood flow under the action of an externally applied magnetic field. The author has demonstrated that his model is consistent with the principles of magnetohydrodynamics and takes into account of magnetization. A brief discussion and numerical simulation depending on the various biomaterials and flow variables (wall shear stress, velocity profiles, flow rate, effective velocity, and hematocrit) relevant in the present rheological model have also been discussed. The author opined that the study may provide a scope for estimating the role of various mechanical and rheological parameters involved in the investigation and to ascertain which of the parameters have the most significant role in the formation and development of this arterial disease. The analytical expressions for axial velocity, volumetric flow rate, pressure gradient, resistance to blood flow, shear stress, and skin friction have been derived in presence of externally imposed magnetic field considering the blood flow as Casson fluid model. In addition, the geometry of the different shapes of the stenosis assumed to be manifested in the arterial segment will be sought in this part. An extensive quantitative analysis is carried out by performing large-scale numerical computations of the above flow variables having physiological significance. The diagrammatic representation of the flow variables with the change of parameters are given with scientific discussion.

Finally, Dr. Nazmul Islam thanks the contributors, reviewers, and publishers for their valuable contributions.

CHAPTER 1

THE TIME EVOLUTION OF THE HARD AND SOFT ACIDS AND BASES THEORY

NAZMUL ISLAM and DULAL C. GHOSH

CONTENTS

1.1 INTRODUCTION

Our history says that the periodic table was written in Russian, the quantum mechanics was written in German, and our understandings were in English [1]. The present status shows that although the periodic table has the powerful chemical organizing power, it does not follow from the quantum mechanics. We are habituated in thinking and modeling in terms of many things that are mental constructs and do not occur in the real world, and hence do not follow from quantum mechanics. Or in other words, their measurement and evaluation in terms of quantum mechanics are ruled out because they are not the things of the real world, and hence have no quantum mechanical operators. They occur in mind and in the domain of hypothesis such as the unicorn of mythical saga [2]. They exist but cannot be seen. We can mention many such mental constructs in the domain of hypothesis. We mention here only two of such mythical objects. These are the "electronegativity" and the "hardness." If the meaning and purport and operational significance of these two legends are withdrawn from the pedagogy of chemistry, there will be a total chaos in the whole of the chemical and physical world. These two hypothetical and mental constructs are so important descriptors deep rooted in the thinking of chemistry and physics that scientists had to search method of their measurement through modeling. In fact, these are measured after reification [3], that is, suggesting and designing certain model and then evaluation was conceived. We may refer to the opinion of Parr et al. [4] who seem to have connected the construct of the hardness and the electronegativity with the noumenon of Kantian philosophy. The *noumenon* is an object knowable by the mind or intellect, but not by the senses. Thus, the hardness and/or electronegativity are objects of purely intellectual discourses. Scientists have designed scales of measurement of the electronegativity and hardness. Success lies in the fact that the results of semi empirically evaluated data are useful in correlation with chemical and physical behavior of atoms, molecules, and crystalline solids.

The improvement of basic structural thinking in chemistry was often based on empirical relations between some properties, which can be measured or can be found in the literature. The ultimate aim of chemists, till now, is to understand and correlate the naturally occurring phenomenon. For this purpose, chemists, rely upon the electronic structure of the fundamental gross building stones of the universe—the atoms.

Those concepts, which do not originate from a "strong" theory but clearly and vividly describe a series of relations among chemical phenomena, are immensely important. Because of the simplicity and clarity of these concepts, our structural thinking and the technical terms in scientific language are immensely enriched. Sometimes, they can be improved on the basis of some theories known later on. As a result, new concepts have been introduced in chemistry from time to time for rationalization and prediction and better elucidation of various physicochemical phenomena. The theory approaches a chemical experiment via selective approximations and simplifications, which then serves as bridge between the rigorous theory and experiment, the chemical reality. Two important concepts that have been highly successful in providing a better understanding of chemical binding and reactivity in a major class of molecular systems are the concepts of acids and bases. Acid and base are two diametrically opposite concepts such that when they are mixed in equivalent proportion, they destroy each other. It is very difficult to define an acid and a base in terms of their chemical composition or molecular structure [5].

This has been long recognized that acids and bases play a central role in any unified theory of chemical bonding. In this regard, their characterization has always been a conceptual challenge for chemists, with a rich and epistemological history. Literature [6] shows that since the beginning of seventeenth century, a growing interest to define acids and bases initiated with the pioneering works of Lémery and Boyle on the "Cartesian salt theory" and the associate principle of reactivity driven by the "struggle between acids and alkali" as well. Next, the major contribution comes from Rouelle in the eighteenth century, which consecrated the base concept as the complement of that of an acid, and that of Black, with his pneumatic theory of reactions. The effort of Rouelle and Black was being culminated by the Lavoisier's contribution according to which the oxygen is directly related to the acidic character of matter. At the beginning of the nineteenth century, further insight was brought by the physicochemical experiments of Volta, Gay–Lussac, and Liebig in elucidating the fact that acids have to contain hydrogen to be exchanged with a metal and a "radical" of different nature; they established the famous principle:

$$acid + base \leftrightarrow salt + water$$

The first unification of the acidic–basic character of a compound or solution was formulated by Arrhenius, Van't Hoff, and Ostwald in the

1880s, leading to a picture where acids and bases release hydrogen and hydroxide ions, respectively, and their interaction is responsible for the acid–base reactions. In the twentieth century, the acid and base definitions met considerable conceptual sublimation, paralleling the newly emerging quantum theory of atoms and molecules. This was achieved in three steps, however not necessarily chronologically.

It was in the year 1923, within several months of each other, that the famous Dutch scientist Johannes Nicolaus Brønsted and the British scientist Thomas Martin Lowry published [7(a), (b)] independently the same theory about the behavior of acids and bases.

Brønsted [7(b)] used the quotation to describe acid and base:

> ... acids and bases are substances that are capable of splitting off or taking up hydrogen ions, respectively.

One of the most important contributions of Lowry's theory is that he put forward the definition of acids and bases with the state of the hydrogen ion in solution, whereas Brønsted used free H^+ ion. Lowry, in his letter to the editor used the hydronium ion H_3O^+ that is commonly used today. Here is the quotation of Lowry [7(a)]:

> It is a remarkable fact that strong acidity is apparently developed only in mixtures and never in pure compounds. Even hydrogen chloride only becomes an acid when mixed with water. This can be explained by the extreme reluctance of a hydrogen nucleus to lead an isolated existence .... The effect of mixing hydrogen chloride with water is probably to provide an acceptor for the hydrogen nucleus so that the ionization of the acid only involves the transfer of a proton from one octet to another.

As such, the foreground theory belongs to Lowry and Brønsted theory, [7(a), (b)] which assumes the proton as the particle, never free, which intermediates between an acid (the donor) and a base (the acceptor) compounds during chemical reactions. Within this framework, the new acid–base interaction paradigm looks as follows:

$$\text{acid}_1 + \text{base}_2 \leftrightarrow \text{acid}_2 + \text{base}_1$$

But the Lowry and Brønsted theory [7(a), (b)] excessively enhanced the role of proton; fortunately, due to the Lewis' intuition, the *electron pair* was soon recognized as a more general conceptual entity in defining acids, bases, and their chemical interaction.

Many definitions and theories are put forward to define acid and base, but the Lewis [8] concept based on electronic structure appears to be the most convincing and enduring one. It is apparent that all other definitions of acid and base can be substituted by a single definition of Lewis. Lewis concept becomes a tool for systematizing reactive molecules and rationalizing reactive sites on the surface of molecules that provided insight into the nature of their reactivity. Considering acids and bases as chemical species susceptible to accept and donate a pair of electrons, there was a significant advance in this direction of understanding the intrinsic acid–base behavior and locating the site of acidity and basicity in the electronic structure of molecules. But soon, it was realized that Lewis concept was not sufficient to predict and systemize chemical facts relating to acid and base behavior, and a more sophisticated theory relating the acid–base property to the electronic structure and internal constitution of atoms and molecules was a just necessity.

Of the many efforts of systematizing and rationalizing the plethora of information accumulated on acid–base chemistry, the hard and soft acid and base (HSAB) principle propounded by Pearson [9] is undoubtedly the most promising and intriguing one. Pearson introduced a systematic way to classify the acids and bases into three categories—hard, soft, and borderline—on the basis of the polarizability of the species, not only the molecule but also the atoms and ions.

Pearson explains the fundamental question of the acid–base chemistry—why certain class of acid prefer to react with certain class of base by formulating a rule of thumb founded on the maxim "like prefers like" known as HSAB [9].

From now on, the molecular systems are recognized as hard and soft acids and bases, in the sense that each molecule can be conceived as hard–hard, soft–soft, hard–soft, or soft–hard bonding combinations between acids and bases. The associate HSAB principle of chemical reactivity was formulated on the maxim "hard acids prefer hard bases and soft acids prefer soft bases."

hard − soft + soft − hard ↔ hard − hard + soft − soft

After the introduction of HSAB theory and the subsequent works of the doyens of theoretical chemistry on the subject, the HSAB principle was placed on the edifice of sound theoretical architecture. The hardness along with the concept of electronegativity is the mainstream current theoretical research.

In this work, we shall follow the locus of the several attempts that were made to the refine and improve the qualitative HSAB principle growing to the pinnacle of present glory. However, we may point out that quantification of HSAB principle is still at large.

Attempts were made to develop theoretical models of HSAB principle in terms of the density functional theory [10, 11]. But, although many qualitative descriptors relating to HSAB principle could be quantified in terms of density functional theory, no satisfactory theoretical quantitative model that can unify the various facets of the principle into one and same principle is still at large. We are still after a grand theoretical model that can smoothly distinguish between the soft and hard character of acids and bases and their bonding. We propose to have a serious relook at the HSAB principle with an open mind. In order to find out a way to quantify the qualitative principle and place them on a sound quantitative platform, further attempts are required. This is just the main goal of the present work.

1.2 SUMMARY OF THE EARLY WORKS

1.2.1 HISTORY OF LEWIS ACID–BASE THEORY

Lewis acid–base concept [8] is one of the most useful schemes in conceptual chemistry. Based on this concept, almost entire chemistry was reformulated in terms of these so-called Lewis compounds. It is worth noting that the Lewis base definition seems to have consumed the Lowry –Brønsted theory [7(a), (b)] in its fold. A Lewis acid is an atom, ion, or molecule that has a tendency to act as an electron acceptor, whereas a Lewis base is an atom, molecule, or ion that tends to act as an electron donor. An acid and base interaction may be viewed as the lone pair electron donation from the base (B) to the acid (A) resulting in the formation of a coordinate covalent bond between an acid and a base creating an "acid–base adduct" (A:B).

$$A + B \rightarrow A{:}B \tag{1}$$

Thus, in brief, the Lewis theory is basically a theory of electron accountancy and magic numbers. Commonly, an acid–base interaction includes any degree of electron transfer of nonbonding, bonding, or antibonding electrons from the base to an unfilled nonbonding, bonding, or antibonding electronic state on the acid. The electronic states involved may be localized on a single atom or delocalized over several atoms in a molecule. Usually, only closed shells are considered to be involved in acid–base-type interactions, and usually a pair of electrons is involved in the process.

Although the strengths of acids and bases can be adequately described in terms of the relative dissociation constant (p^K) values of the acids and the bases within the Lowry–Brønsted acid–base theory, [7] there was no single scale of Lewis acidity and basicity, and also there was no whisper of measuring the acid–base strength and the ease of the reaction. The importance of the Lewis acid–base concept is that almost all inorganic compounds can be viewed as acid–base adducts or complexes, A:B. This is also true for organic compounds. Thus, the Lewis acid–base concept [8] covers almost the major area of chemical reactions and offers a grand unified model of that dissects any molecule mentally into parts: acid and base.

Moreover, there are numerous reasons that the Lewis theory has not replaced the Lowry–Brønsted model [7] for protic acids. Even when we try to classify the strength of Lewis acids qualitatively comparing their reactions with a common base, we find that it is impossible to come up with a single scale that encompasses all possible Lewis acids. Some Lewis acids (e.g., Al^{3+}, BF_3) act very much like H^+ when reacted with a base. Thus, we could use reactions with Al^{3+} to set up a scale of p^Ka's very similar to that using H^+. But, other Lewis acids, for example, Hg^{2+}, give an entirely different series of base strengths if the same procedure is followed for them. The origin of this strange behavior is believed to lie in the fact that the origin of protic acid strength is primarily electrostatic. But, when all Lewis acids are considered, a pure electrostatic model cannot be put forward. Many species react with bases using a significant amount of covalent bonding, and these cannot be directly related to the others that are compatible with an electrostatic model.

The scientists noticed forever that *mother nature* always shows a path to understand the naturally occurring facts and to reach at the core of the phenomenon. As for example, in nature, metal ions such as Mg^{2+} or Al^{3+} are observed as oxide and carbonate ores, whereas Cd^{2+}, Hg^{2+} and Pt^{2+} appear as sulphides and arsenide ores. It is also known that certain ligands formed their most stable complexes with metal ions such as Al^{3+}, Ti^{4+}, and Co^{3+}, whereas others formed stable complexes with Ag^+, Hg^{2+}, and Pt^{2+}.

The prediction of the reactivity of a generalized acid–base reaction and the stability of the acid–base adduct were very important. But at that time, there was no such theory that could explain the reactivity of such acids and bases.

The hard–soft concept was born nearly a half-century ago with the realization by a number of investigators that the strength of an acid or base is dependent on several factors—extrinsic to intrinsic. Prior to the seminal work of Pearson [9], the pioneering contribution to HSAB concept was made by Ahraland, Chatt, Davies, Schwarzenbach, Jorgenson, Hudson, Klopman, and Saville [12].

1.2.2 ORIGIN OF HARD AND SOFT CLASSIFICATION

In the earliest days of coordination chemistry, some basic trends concerning the stability of complexes in certain ligand-central atom combinations were discovered [13–16]. The main factors that affect the stability of complexes in the solution were broadly classified into the following two main types:

  (i) Enthalpic effects: This effect includes the variation of bond strength, steric and electrostatic repulsion between ligands in the complex, disolvation enthalpy of the metallic ion and ligands when the complex is formed, the conformation of the noncoordinated and the coordinated ligands, charge neutralization of the positive and negative ions; etc.

  (ii) Entropic effects: This effect includes the number and size of the chelate ring, number of the metal ions and ligands in solution, changes in solvation in the formation of the complex, entropy variations in noncoordinated ligands, changes in solvation in the formation of the complex, configuration entropy differences of the ligands in the complex; etc.

1.2.3 IRVING AND WILLIAM STABILITY SERIES

The idea of the hard–soft classification was initiated by Irving and William [17] *who assigned the relative stabilities of complexes formed by the metal ions with the ligands* in the form of stability series. Based on the stability of the products of the metal ions with ligands, they classified metal cations into two classes. As a consequence, ligands were also classified into two types on the basis of reactions with the two types of cations.

When the stability constants of the high-spin octahedral $[ML_6]^{2+}$ complex cations are studied, an increase in complex stability is found as follows:

$$Ba^{2+} < Sr^{2+} < Ca^{2+} < Mg^{2+} < Fe^{2+} < Co^{2+} < Ni^{2+} < Cu^{2+} > Zn^{2+}$$

This series refers to the Irving–Williams series, and basically it is the stability sequence of high-spin octahedral metal complexes for the replacement of water by other ligands.

The series can be explained in terms of (i) the ionic radius of the metal cations, (ii) the crystal field stabilization energy (CFSE) values, and (iii) the John–Teller effect [18].

We may point out, from the series of the stability constants of the metal ions in octahedral environment, that the ionic radius decreases from left to right, that is, the ratio "charge/radius" or simply the polarizing power of the cations increases. Similarly for ions of different charge and similar radius, the polarizing power is essential.

However, if we study the Irving–Williams series for different ligand types, we can see that the stability of complexes cannot be explained exclusively as a charge density effect. If we consider the first transition series, for example, we can observe that beyond Mn^{2+}ion there is an abrupt increase in the first step-wise stability constant (K_1) for the rest of the divalent cations and a sharp decrease for Zn^{2+} ion. We know that these ions possess additional ligand field stabilization energy (LFSE) when moving from d^5 to d^9. If we consider the complexes that are obtained from the aqueous solutions, we can easily understand that to have a positive LFSE, the ligand (L) needs to have a greater octahedral field stabilization energy (Δ_0) than that created by H_2O, as occurs with ethylenediamine and oxalate. If the situation is reversed, the LFSE would be negative with regard to water as occurs with F^-. Cu^{2+} complexes with chelate ligands present an additional stabilization energy when compared with those of Ni^{2+}despite the supplementary electron placed in an antibonding orbital. This anomaly is due to the stabilizing influence of the John–Teller effect, which increases the first step-wise stability constant, K_1 value. In a tetragonally distorted complex, there is a strong bond with the four ligands in the plane. For this reason, the value of K_1 and second step-wise stability constant K_2 follow this order. By contrast, the third step-wise stability constant, K_3 for Cu^{2+} with three chelate ligands is much smaller, because it is formally impossible to place the three ligands in C is positions.

1.2.4   THE "CLASS (A)" AND "CLASS (B)" CLASSIFICATION OF THE METAL IONS AND LIGANDS BY AHRLAND, CHATT, AND DAVIES

The classification of acceptors and donors in chemical reactions according to their ability to accept/or donate, especially in inorganic reactions, is a very old and intriguing problem [13–16]. Aquated metal ions tend to group into two categories in their reactions with halides ions. One class favors reactions with small, unpolarizable bases such as fluoride ion and other favors reactions with lag, polarizable bases such as iodide ion. Swarzenbeach [15] referred to these classes of metal ions as class A acceptors and class B acceptors, respectively. In 1958, Ahrland et al. [19(a), (b), (c)] extended the categories of metal ions through consideration of reactions with ligands other than halides. They [19(a)] correlated the preference of certain metal ions to react with certain ligands with the electron acceptance tendencies of the metal ions from the ligands and classified electron pair acceptors into two types—class (a) acceptor and class (b) acceptor—and as a consequence electron pair donors are also classified into two types: class (a) and class (b).

Class (a) acceptors or class (a) acids are those that can form the most stable complexes with the first ligand atom of each group. Class (a) acceptors include the following:

1. Alkali metal cations: Li^+ to Cs^+
2. Alkaline earth metal cations: Be^{2+} to Ba^{2+}
3. Lighter transition-metal cations in higher oxidation states: Ti^{4+}, Cr^{3+}, Fe^{3+}, Co^{3+}
4. The proton, H^+

Proton and most metals in their common valence states belong to class (a) and, therefore, the affinities of ligand for class (a) acceptors tend to run nearly parallel to their basicities, except when steric and other factors intervene.

The affinity toward the donor ligands of a class (a) acceptor follows the following trend:

(i)   For group 15: $N > P > As > Sb > Bi$
(ii) For group 16: $O > S > Se > Te$
(iii) For group 17: $F > Cl > Br > I$

The class (b) character appears to depend on the availability of electrons from the lower d-orbitals of the metal for dative pi-bonding. The acceptors of class (b) are less numerous. They are almost all derived from a number of neighboring elements occupying an area of more or less triangular shape in the periodic table. The base of this triangle stretches, in the sixth period, from about tungsten to polonium and its apex is at copper, Cu (I) being a definite class (b) acceptor and Cu (II) on the border between the classes. The most prominent class (b) acceptors are formed by elements in the central part of this area. Generally, the class (b) acceptors include heavier transition-metal cations in lower oxidation states, for example, Cu^+, Ag^+, Cd^{2+}, Hg^+, Ni^{2+}, Pd^{2+}, Pt^{2+}, etc. The class (b) acceptors form their most stable complexes with the last ligand of each group. Thus, the affinity of class (b) acceptors toward the donors follows the following order:

(i)   For group 15: $N < P < As < Sb < Bi$
(ii) For group 16: $O < S < Se < Te$
(iii) For group 17: $F < Cl < Br < I$

Ahrland et al. [19] classified the donor ligands as class (a) or class (b) depending on whether they formed more stable complexes with class (a) or class (b) metals.

From this analysis, a principle can be derived as *class (a) acceptors prefer to bind to class (a) donors or ligands, and class (b) acceptors prefer to bind to class (b) donors or ligands.*

Ahrland and his coworkers proposed Π-bonding theory to explain the metal ligand interactions [19].

1.2.5   PEARSON'S "HARD" AND "SOFT" CLASSIFICATION OF "ACIDS" AND "BASES"

It is widely known that the HSAB concept of Pearson [9] is an acronym for hard–soft Lewis acids and Lewis bases. The concept is widely used in chemistry for explaining the stability of compounds, reaction mechanisms, and reaction pathways. The term "hard" applies to the chemical species that are small, have high charge states, and are weakly polarizable. The term "soft" applies to the chemical species that are big, have low-charge states, and are strongly "polarizable".

The general idea of Ahrland et al. [19] was extended by Pearson [9] to explain the general acid–base reactions. In 1962, Edwards and Pearson [20] noticed that some substrates such as acyl halides or phosphate esters react rapidly with strongly basic nucleophiles, such as OH^-, but not with polarizable nucleophiles, such as I^- or thiourea. But other substrates such as hydrogen peroxide (H_2O_2) or Pt (II) complexes react rapidly with I^- or thiourea, but very slowly with OH^-.

Pearson [9] reviewed and analyzed the rate data for the generalized nucleophilic displacement reactions of the following types, Eqs. (2) and (3), published by Edwards and Pearson [20].

$$A^{/} + A{:}B \rightarrow A + A^{/}{:}B \qquad (2)$$

$$B^{/} + A{:}B \rightarrow B + A{:}B^{/} \qquad (3)$$

where A and $A^{/}$ are electrophilic substrates (Lewis acids) and B and $B^{/}$ are nucleophilic ligands (Lewis bases).

He [9] observed that for certain substrates, A-B, the rate of the above reaction was influenced predominantly by the basicity of the nucleophile, and other substrates had rates that depended chiefly on the polarizability of the nucleophile.

Pearson [9] arrived at the conclusion that the relative strengths of a series of bases will be compared for various acids provided the reference base is constant for each comparison. The coordinate bond energy, $-\Delta H$ for the generalized acid–base reaction largely depends on the properties of A and B. This is, no doubt, a thermo dynamical property, and thus the relative strength of an acid and base can be operationally defined using the displacement reactions, Eqs. (2) and (3). If the reactions, Eqs. (2) and (3),are favorable ($\Delta G < 0$ or $\Delta H < 0$), then it can be said that $A^{/}$ is a stronger acid than A and $B^{/}$ is a stronger base than B.

Although there are several factors that might affect the strength of the hard–hard and soft–soft interactions, it is probable that these factors may have different effects depending on the particular situation. Although the foregoing discussion is sketchy, it touches on most of the factors, which seem likely to be important in controlling the nature of hard–hard and soft–soft interactions. Because of the complexity of these factors, a more detailed discussion would scarcely be justified.

The idea [13–17, 19–20] of HSAB theory was initiated from a consideration of the thermodynamic strength of the interaction of acids with halides ions, which can form adducts with most of the elements in the periodic table. It is long recognized that the chemical properties of the elements varies periodically. There are periodic parameters, such as atomic radius, electronegativity, polarizability, global hardness, and most recently the electrophilicity index, etc., using which we can rationalize the variation of chemical properties of the elements. The parameters are known as fundamental parameters. Based on a fundamental atomic parameter, polarizability, Pearson [9], in an attempt to systematize and rationalize the intrinsic property of atoms, ions and molecule, classified them into three classes: —hard, soft, and borderline. It should be noted that by polarizability, Pearson [9] meant the ease of deforming the valence electron cloud of a chemical species. Division into these two categories is not absolute and intermediate cases occur, which was termed as "borderline."

(1) **Hard acid**—those that bind strongly to bases which bind strongly to the proton, that is, basic in the usual sense; the acceptor atom is of high positive charge, small size, and has no easily polarized outer electrons.

(2) **Soft acid**—those that bind strongly to highly polarizable or unsaturated bases, which often have negligible proton basicity. The acceptor atom is of low positive charge, large size and has polarizable outer electrons.

(3) **Soft base**—the donor atom is of low electronegativity, easily oxidized, highly polarizable, and with low-lying empty orbitals.

Some hard–soft and borderline Lewis acids and bases are presented in Tables (1.1) and (1.2), respectively.

(4) **Hard base**—the donor atom is of high electronegativity, hard to oxidize, of low polarizability, and with only high energy empty orbitals.

TABLE 1.1   Classification of Lewis acids

Hard acid or class (a) acid	Borderline	Soft acid or class (b) acid
$H^+,Li^+,Na^+,K^+,Be^{2+},Mg^{2+}$, $Ca^{2+},Sr^{2+},Sn^{2+},Al^{3+},Se^{3+}$, $Ga^{3+},In^{3+},La^{3+},Cr^{3+},Co^{3+}$, $Fe^{3+},As^{3+},Ir^{3+},Si^{4+},Ti^{4+},Zr^{4+}$, $Th^{4+},Pu^{4+},VO^{2+},UO_2^{2+}$,($CH_3)_2Sn^{2+}$, $BeMe_2,BF_3$, $BCl_3,B(OR)_3,Al(CH_3)_3$, Ga $(CH_3)_3,In(CH_3)_3RPO_2^+,RSO_2^+,ROSO_2^+$, $SO_3,I^{7+},I^{5+},Cl^{7+}$, R_3C^+,RCO,CO_2,NC^+,HX(H-bonding molecules)	$Fe^{2+},Co^{2+},Ni^{2+},Cu^{2+},Zn^{2+}$, $Pb^{2+},B(CH_3)_3$, SO_2,NO^+	$Cu^+,Ag^+,Au^+,Tl^+,Hg^+,Cs^+$, $Pd^{2+},Cd^{2+},Pt^{2+},Hg^{2+},CH_3Hg^+$ $Tl^{3+},Tl(CH_3)_3$, RH_3, RS^+, $RSe^+,RTe^+,I^+,Br^+,HO^+$, RO^+,I_2,Br_2,INC, etc, $C_6H_3(NO_2)_3$, 2,3,5,6-Tetra chloro-p-benzoquinone(chloranil), Tetracyanoethylene(C_6N_4) O,Cl,Br,I,R_3C, neutral metal ions(M^0), Bulk metals

TABLE 1.2   Classification of Lewis bases

Hard base or class (a) base	Borderline	Soft base or class (b)base
H_2O, OH^-,F^-,CH_3COO^-,PO_4^{3-},SO_4^{2-}, Cl^-,CO_3^{2-},ClO_4^-,NO_3^-,ROH,RO^-,R_2O,NH_3,RNH_2,N_2H_4	$C_6H_5(NH_2)$, C_6H_5N,N_3^-,Br^-, NO_2^-,SO_3^{2-},N_2	R_2S, RSH, RS^-, I^-, SCN^-,$S_2O_3^{2-}$,R_3P,R_3As, $(RO)_3P$, CN^-,RNC,CO,C_2H_4,C_6H_6,H^-,R^-

In the above classification, a large number of Lewis acids were put into one of two boxes, eventually labeled hard and soft by Pearson [9]. The same was done for a number of common bases. Due to the shortage of data, all of one kind, a variety of criteria was used [9] such as bond energies, equilibrium constants, rates of reaction, and the existence or non-existence of certain compounds. Pearson opined that the HSAB classification can be extended using the two groups of acids to group the bases into hard and soft categories as well, using the principle that "hard acids tend to bind hard bases; soft acids tend to bind soft bases."

It should be noted that this statement is not an explanation or theory, but it is a simple rule of thumb, which enables the chemists to predict qualitatively the relative stability of acid–base adducts and such qualitative description did not allow us for the quantification of the hard and soft behavior of acids and bases. Empirically, acids and bases were put into one of two categories, but there was no way of rank ordering them within the boxes. The main advantages of Pearson's classification [9] are its wide applicability and its ability to generalize certain chemical phenomena.

From polarizability consideration, Pearson had chosen to label class (a) as hard and class (b) as soft. This parallelism was questioned by Williams and Hale [21]. They felt that it cannot be convincingly shown that classes (a) and (b) are related to polarizability. Further, it is not clear that such definitions as hard and soft really refer to the same physical properties in neutral acceptors as in ions. Such controversy is justified since A and B refers to the classification of the metal ions in the aqueous medium and Pearson's classification applies in the gas phase.

Further, the various thermodynamic and bond energetic aspects of the class (a) and class (b) types of behavior were critically examined in 1966 by Williams and Hale [21].

The hard–soft classification of acid and bases has been popularized to the scientist because, on the basis of hard–soft classification, it is easier to say harder or softer than more class (a) character or more class (b) character. Moreover, the borderline classification can easily distinguish the acids or bases, for example, among the halides, fluoride, and chloride are "hard"; bromide is "borderline"; and iodide is "soft." Pearson's hard–soft classification is very popular in the scientific community. For example, Hudson [22] applied the HSAB concept to explain a wide variety of nucleophilic displacement reactions.

Pearson [9] noted that "the bonding between hard acids and bases is dominated by electrostatic interactions. This is shown by the fact that a strong interaction correlates with (1) small size and (2) high electronegativity of the base. These are purely electrostatic parameters, and this implies that the bonding is essentially ionic" and "the bonding between soft acids and bases seems to be primarily covalent in nature. Thus, a strong interaction occurs between large metal ions with high electronegativity and the most polarizable bases."

The hardness and/or softness of the acids and bases depend on several factors, such as the following:

1. The electronegativity and the hardness of the acids and bases
2. Number of donor and acceptor atoms and/or molecules
3. Electrophilic and nucleophilic behavior of the acids and bases
4. Polarity and polarizability of the acids and bases
5. The group contributions for electronic, magnetic, thermodynamic, and other properties (symbiosis)

SYMBIOSIS

In a landmark work, Jorgenson [23] pointed out that the hard and soft behavior of an acidic site and basic site is not an inherent property of the particular atom at that site, but the behavior can be influenced by the substituent atoms. The addition of soft, polarizable substituent(s) can soften an otherwise hard center and the presence of electron withdrawing substituents can reduce the softness of a site. Jorgenson [23] referred this tendency of a group or ligand (substituent) to increase or decrease the hard–soft behavior of a center as "symbiosis."

Thus, one the one hand, the hard metal ions have little electron density to share with a ligand. Hard ligands do not readily give up their electron density, thus the combination of the hard acid and hard base is stabilized by simple electrostatic force of attraction. On the other hand, soft metal ions and ligands are more prone to sharing electron density with a greater degree of covalency in the bonding and form a mutually stabilized complex.

If a hard metal is combined with a soft ligand, the metal does not readily accept the electron density being offered by the ligand, and therefore the resulting complex is less stable. In practice, the HSAB principle has proved remarkably useful in indicating favorable combinations of ligands and metal ions. A close inspection of the Tables (1.1) and (1.2) will provide with many useful examples that demonstrate the general validity of this approach. It is clear from Pearson's hard–soft classification scheme that there are some inherent properties of the acids and the bases that govern their relative strength toward a chemical reaction. Later, one very important inherent property of the acids and the bases that governs the relative strength of an acid toward a base and vice versa in a chemical reaction was identified as hardness [24(a), (b)].

We shall discuss the concept of hardness in the following section [vide infra].

1.2.6 THE HSAB CLASSIFICATION IN TERMS OF THE CONCEPT OF ELECTRONEGATIVITY

The concept of electronegativity provides a measure of the intrinsic strength of an acid or base [3, 25, 26]. A strong Lewis acid is a good electron acceptor and has high electronegativity/low chemical potential. A weak Lewis acid has a lower electronegativity than a strong Lewis acid, but it has a higher electronegativity than a Lewis base. A strong Lewis base readily donates electrons and has a lower electronegativity than a weak Lewis base. These relations are summarized by Ayers [3] as follows:

$$\chi(\text{strong acid}) > \chi(\text{weak acid}) > \chi(\text{weak base}) > \chi(\text{strong base}) > 0 \quad (4)$$

The perfect electron donor has $\chi = 0$. One can reify the electron-accepting abilities of real molecules by imagining how they would react with a perfect electron donor.

The HSAB concept was basically an empirical one. The dependence of relative strength of acids and bases on each other was not explained in this principle. There are also a number of extrinsic influences, and the concept of hard and soft concerns itself with these influences, such as the reference base used to determine the strength of acids and the reference acid used to determine the strength of bases. This particular extrinsic influence is called hardness, and its compliment and softness were coined by Pearson.

Reed, using a simple orbital model, recently explored the structural origin of hard–soft behavior in atomic acids and bases [27].

He discussed the physical basis of hard–soft behavior in terms of the set of atomic orbitals and the properties that have been associated with them. These properties are atomic size, orbital energy, energy gap, absolute hardness, relaxation energy, atomic charge, absolute electronegativity, polarizability, ionization energy, and electron affinity.

Among the relevant sets of atomic orbitals are the frontier orbitals, the responding electrons, and the whole valence shell. Associated with each of these structures are properties that have over the years been linked to hard–soft behavior.

The size of the species, its frontier orbital energy, and its frontier orbital energy gap are among the relevant properties of the frontier orbitals. The importance of frontier electrons and frontier orbitals is implied in the Lewis definition; thus, frontier orbitals were among the first electronic structures to be identified with acid–base behavior. The size of the occupied frontier orbital dictates the size of an atom. A reasonable and simple indicator of the relative size of an atom or ion is provided by the average distance of this electron from its nucleus. This may be obtained for a hydrogenic atomic orbital and is found to be inversely related to ε_r. Pearson [9] has also associated the gap in the energies of the occupied frontier orbital and the unoccupied frontier orbital, $\Delta \varepsilon_p$, which is the difference in the energy of the frontier electron and the lowest-energy virtual electron, with the absolute hardness.

Reed [27] pointed out that there have been several interpretations of hard–soft behavior, and among them one interpretation has considered hard and soft to involve two different properties: one of which dominates in a hard acid or base and the other in a soft acid or base. Thus, according to the HSAB principle, a correct matching of the hardness or its inverse, softness, between an acid and a base gives rise to an extra stability of the acid–base adduct. He further pointed out that in some cases, hard–soft is considered to be a property of the acid or base; and in others, it is a property of the acid–base interaction.

THE PEARSON–PAULING PARADOX

It is interesting to point out that Pearson [28] has called attention to an interesting anomaly between the HSAB rule and Pauling's original methods of defining electronegativity [29]. In Pauling method, the ionic resonance energy is considered as proportional to the square of the difference in electronegativity of the constituent atoms. This implies that the most stabilization occurs when the bonds are formed between the constituents furthest apart in electronegativity. Thus, the ionic resonance energy suggests writing the following reaction, in the forward direction as follows:

$$CsI + LiF \rightarrow LiI + CsF \qquad (5)$$
$$s–s \ h–h \ h–s \ s–h$$

Here, s and h stands for harder and softer, respectively.

But, experimentally it is found that the reverse reaction, which follows the HSAB rule, is energetically favorable.

$$LiI + CsF \rightarrow CsI + LiF(\Delta H \approx -63kJ/mol) \qquad (6)$$

This paradox is popularized in the text book of chemistry as Pearson–Pauling paradox.

1.2.7 LOCAL HSAB PRINCIPLE

Ayers and Parr [30] recently pointed out the ignored contribution from the Pearson's work [9(a)] is the local HSAB principle. The local HSAB principle [30] was stated as follows:

An ambidentate reagent with a hard reactive site and a soft reactive site tends to react with hard molecules at the hard site and soft molecules at the soft site.

This proposition introduced the concept of "local hardness"—the idea that different atoms and functional groups within a molecule have different hardnesses.

We shall discuss the local hardness in the following section (vide infra).

1.2.8 THE FRONTIER ORBITAL INTERPRETATION OF HSAB PRINCIPLE: KLOPMAN

Despite its empirical nature, it is still possible to summarize a great deal of diverse chemical information summarized by the HSAB principle. This usefulness of the HSAB principle mainly attracts chemists to study further on it. Klopman and Hudson [31] in an attempt to look more deeply into the physical implications of the HSAB principle showed that the polyelectronic perturbation treatment of chemical reactivity leads to a reasonable definition of hardness and softness including a general interpretation of ambident reactivity.

In his landmark paper, Klopman [24(b)] opined that when two reactants approach each other, a mutual perturbation of the molecular orbitals of both reactants occurs. The resulting change in energy can be estimated from SCF–MO calculations. When the bonds are completely formed and when the systems are simple enough, then good accuracy can be obtained for the calculations of the heats of formation.

Klopman [24(b)] considered two systems; R and S interact through their atomic site labeled r and s, respectively. The total perturbation energy (ΔE_{total}) is produced by two distinct effects: (i) the neighboring effect, which accounts for the interaction due to the formation of an ion pair without any charge or electron transfer and (ii) the partial charge transfer, which is usually accompanied by covalent bonding.

$$R^-_{(solv)} + S^-_{(solv)} \overset{(i)}{\rightarrow} R^-_{(solv)} + S^+_{(solv)} \overset{(ii)}{\rightarrow})(R^{\delta-} - S^{\delta+})_{(solv)} \tag{7}$$

This treatment of chemical reactivity was based on the limits of total energy equation for small perturbations (β) as follows:

$$\Delta E_{total} = \Delta E(1) + \tfrac{1}{2}\sum_{mn}^{\Delta E_{mn}} \tag{8}$$

$$\text{or, } \Delta E_{total} = q_r q_s (\Gamma/\varepsilon)\Delta_{solv}(1) + \sum_{m}^{occupied} \sum_{n}^{occupied} \left[\frac{2(C_r^m)^2 (C_s^n)^2 \beta^2}{E_m^* - E_n^*} \right] \tag{9}$$

where E_m^* and E_n^* are the energy of the highest-occupied orbital of the electrophile or acceptor, and the nucleophile or donor, respectively, Ψ_m and Ψ_n, are the lowest empty orbital of the electrophile or acceptor, and the nucleophile or donor, respectively, q is the total charge, Γ is the coulomb repulsion term, ε is the dielectric constant of the medium, and Δ_{solv} is the partial disolvation produced by the partial transfer of electron from the atomic orbital Ψ_m to Ψ_n, or simply the solvation energy.

Klopman further pointed out that various types of interaction can well recognize in terms of the frontier orbitals, E_m^* and E_n^*.

1.2.8.1 CHARGE-CONTROLLED REACTION

When the difference between the frontier orbitals is much larger than $4\beta^2$, very little charge transfer occurs and small energy differences between the various molecular orbitals of each molecule can be neglected, and the total perturbation energy is primarily determined by the total charges on the two reagents. Klopman called the reaction as a "charge-controlled reaction." Such an effect reflects an ionic-type interaction. It is predominant between highly charged species, when E_m^* is very low, that is, when the donor is difficult to ionize or polarize, and when E_n^* is very high, that is, when the acceptor has a low tendency to accept electrons and when both reactants are strongly solvated, that is, are of small size. It is also enhanced by (i) small values of β which corresponds to the low tendency to form covalent bonds, (ii) high Γ value, (iii) small radius, and (iv) low polarizability of the two reactants (Figure 1.1).

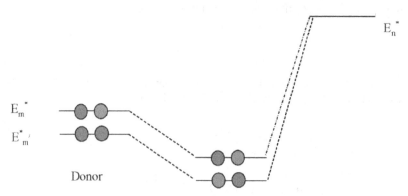

FIGURE 1.1   Charge-control effect.

1.2.8.2 FRONTIER-CONTROLLED REACTION

On the other hand, when the two frontier orbitals are nearly degenerate, that is, $\left| E_m^* - E_n^* \right| = 0$, then, their interaction becomes predominant, and strong electron transfer occurs between them. Klopman [24] called the reaction as a "frontier-controlled reaction."

It occurs only in reactions between nucleophiles of low electronegativity and electrophiles of high electronegativity with a good overlap of the interacting orbitals. Such an effect reflects to covalent bonding and can be associated with soft–soft interaction (Figure 1.2).

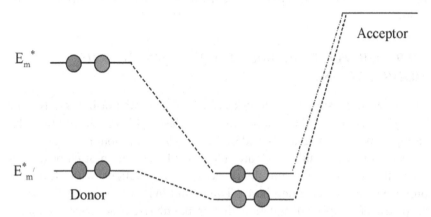

FIGURE 1.2   Frontier-control effect.

In brief, Klopman [24(b)] made an attempt to put the qualitative HSAB theory on a sound frontier orbital theory (FMO) and classified the donor and acceptor molecules into hard and soft categories on the basis of the difference in energy between the highest-occupied orbital of the nucleophile (donor), Ψ_m, and the lowest empty orbital of the electrophile or acceptor, Ψ_n, that is, the frontier orbitals. Klopman noticed that the hard acceptors will tend to form complex with the hard donors and soft acceptors will prefer soft donors. Thus, Klopman tried to justify the statement of Pearson in terms of frontier orbitals of the interacting molecules; hence, his paradigm was labeled as FMO theory of HSAB principle. Klopman [24(b)] concluded that "hard–hard interactions are charge controlled and depend mainly on the ionic interaction of the reagents, in addition to that the steric inhibition of solvation which may occur during the union of the ions further accentuates the endothermicity of the reaction characteristic of hard–hard interaction. On the other hand, in the case of soft-soft interaction are counterbalanced by the stabilization brought about by covalent bonding, and the reaction thus becomes exothermic."

Here, it is important to mention the work of Berkowitz [32] who in 1987 obtained an expression for the amount of charge transfer for the description of the initial stages of the reaction between a Lewis acid, A and a Lewis base, B using the density functional theory (DFT) [10–11].

He showed that for the soft acid–soft base interaction, the amount of charge transfer is controlled by the frontier orbitals. Thus, the exclusive role that frontier orbitals play in chemical reactivity was confirmed by his work.

1.2.9 THE FOUR-PARAMETER EQUATION AND ITS MODIFICATIONS

The order of the strength of a series of Lewis acids and/or bases may vary with the variation of the Lewis acid and/or base, which is used to rank the strength of the Lewis acids and/or bases. Thus, the donor and acceptor properties of acids and bases are interrelated [33]. In an attempt to correlate the magnitude of the donor–acceptor interactions with electronic properties of the acids and bases, Drago and his coworkers [34] in 1965 proposed an empirical equation that is popularized as "four-parameter equation" or double-scale equation. Recognizing the interdependence of the donor and acceptor properties of acids and bases, they represented the enthalpy of interaction of donor–acceptor pairs in a poor solvating media as follows:

$$-\Delta H = E_A E_B + C_A C_B \tag{10}$$

Here, A and B represent the electron acceptor and donor, respectively, while E ("electrostatic") and C ("covalent") are empirically determined parameters. This relationship provides a useful means of predicting enthalpies for the formation of donor–acceptor complexes for which the experimental values are not available.

It relates the hard–soft principle as follows:

"For there to be a strong donor–acceptor interaction, the two molecules must match in the sense that both must have a large E parameter or a large C."

It goes beyond the hard–soft principle in that the E and C parameters are not exclusive so that both the E and C parameters for a given molecule might be either large or small.

The products $E_A E_B$ and $C_A C_B$ were roughly related to trends in the electrostatic and covalent contributions to the enthalpy.

The theoretical basis of the Drago's equation has been of some interest. Klopman [24(b)] has shown that Eq. (10) is consistent with his perturbation theoretical approach to intermolecular interactions with the E parameters corresponding to a charge-controlled contribution and the C parameters corresponding to frontier-controlled, or covalent binding.

A theoretical support for the four-parameter equation was given by Marks and Drago on the basis of charge-transfer formulation [35]. They [35] also gave support to relating the E parameters to ionic interactions and the C parameters to covalent. Drago and Kabler [36] opined that "the idea that some substances are just stronger acids or bases than others with regard to both covalent and electrostatic interactions are invariably ignored in HSAB principle," and suggested to employ the terms "large C property" or "frontier controlled" for soft and "large E property" or "charge controlled" for hard. Substances can then be considered to have both a large C and a large E *relative* to some other substance. Large size, low ionization energy, and other properties leading to softness' often contribute to a large C, whereas small size and high charge, etc., contribute to a large E.

Pearson [37] as a reply to the comment of Drago and Kabler [36] proposed a possible quantitative statement of HSAB as follows:

$$\log K = S_A S_B + \sigma_A \sigma_B \qquad (11)$$

This is a typical four-parameter equation, two independent parameters for both the acid and base. It is most closely related to the equation proposed by Edwards and Pearson [20].

$$\log K = \alpha E_n + \beta H \qquad (12)$$

with $\alpha = \sigma_A$, $E_n = \sigma_B$, $\beta = S_A$, and $H = S_B$.

Pearson [37] again correlated Eq. (11) to the Drago's four-parameter equation and found that the most consistent interpretation would be $C_A = \sigma_A$, $C_B = \sigma_B$, $E_A = S_A$, and $E_B = S_B$.

Pearson commented that the hardness and softness parameters are quite different from Drago and Kabler's [36] mysterious suggestion that C is softness and E is hardness.

As a reply to the Pearson's comment, Drago [38] stated that the hard–soft model has its basis in arguments that are related to the strength of bonding. It is then applied and offered as an explanation for observations on systems in which kinetic control, entropy of adduct formation, and enthalpic and entropic effect such as solvation effects, ion-pairing effects, and/or lattice energy effects are large and could even dominate the observation. Drago [38] further commented "when HSAB considerations are employed on these systems, one is implying that the soft-soft or hard-hard interactions, which supposedly influence the bonding, dominate the chemistry."

According to Drago [38], the double-scale approach (E and C approach) predicts the strength of interaction quantitatively on systems in which the data used are related to the strength of binding. If the HSAB ideas are correct models for the strength of bonding, it must be capable of being expressed in a mathematical form and do well on data related to the strength of interaction. If it does not, it should be discarded and replaced by a more correct interpretation of the strength of binding. Drago [38] again stated that knowledge of the factors influencing the strength of interaction is important in correlating trends in reactivity and in suggesting new syntheses or experiments. This has been amply demonstrated by the wide acceptance and utilization of the HSAB ideas. The more correct model should be even more powerful in this kind of application.

Pearson [37] took issue with Drago's quantitative statement of the rule that "hard acids prefer to bind to hard bases and soft acids prefer to bind to soft bases" with the equation:

$$-\Delta H = H_A H_B + (K - H_A)(K/H_B) \tag{13}$$

This rather obvious mathematical translation of the above rule was criticized because Drago et al. [34–36] failed to incorporate intrinsic strength.

Again, Pearson [37] stated that the matter has never been clearly defined; it is difficult to see how his quantitative statement of HSAB can possibly work. The terms $-\Delta H$ and log K can be interchangeably used in HSAB; he proposed to write Eq. (10) as follows:

$$-\Delta H = S_A S_B + -\sigma_A \sigma_B \tag{14}$$

An equation of this form must fit the enthalpy data as well as the E and C equation:

$$-\Delta H = C_A C_B + -E_A E_B \tag{15}$$

Drago [38] further commented that the equalities, $C_A = \sigma_A$ $C_B = \sigma_B$, $E_A = S_A$, and $E_B = S_B$ and the statement is made that hardness or softness is σ_A or σ_B are incorrect. The consideration of Pearson [9(b)] and Klopman [24(b)] that hardness and softness are related to the C/E ratio is not always informative [39]. Further, no simple transformation of E and C parameters exists, which allows Eq. (6) to produce a set of parameters whose interpretation is consistent with the HSAB equation proposed by Pearson [9], that is, the correlation, $\alpha = \sigma_A$, $E_n = \sigma_B$, $\beta = S_A$, and $H = S_B$ have no physical sense.

Drago [38] opined that "if σ_A were a large number for a hard acid and σ_B a large number for a soft base, the product would be large in violation of the hard prefers hard and soft prefers soft rule. The only way around this problem is to call one positive and the other negative. If hardness were negative, stabilization would result from a hard acid and hard base, but now a destabilization as large as the soft–soft or hard–hard stabilization would result when a hard acid and a soft base are brought together."

But this does not make much physical sense in the theoretical explanations of HSAB rule. The claim of Pearson [9] that "even hard substances have some soft character and vice versa" cannot be accommodated with the sigma product ($\sigma_A \sigma_B$). Further, if hardness is negative and softness is positive, then intermediate acids and bases must be near to zero; therefore, $\sigma_A \sigma_B$ would be near zero and there would be practically no hard–hard or soft–soft contribution to adducts with intermediate acids (or bases) reacting with hard or soft bases (or acids). The only remaining possibility that can be considered for the Eq. (6) is that σ is zero for a hard substance and appreciable for a soft substance. If σ is zero for a hard acid or base, the hardness has an important effect.

The HSAB principle is very good in predicting the sign of ΔH correctly, but not its magnitude. It is not perfect, however, if we try to compare acids or bases of quite different intrinsic strengths. Steric factors and solvation energies can also be complicating effects. Thus, Drago and coworkers [40] modified the four-parameter equation by introducing two new parameters. They proposed an equation for computing enthalpies of solution-phase neutral molecule as follows:

$$-\Delta H = C_A C_B + -E_A E_B - W \qquad (16)$$

where W is a constant used for an energy always associated with a particular reactant, such as the enthalpy of dissociation of a dimer allowing it to react as a monomer. In the extension of Eq. (16) to cation base systems, the transfer energy is accommodated by adding an $R_A T_A$ term:

Thus, Eq. (16) becomes

$$-\Delta H = C_A C_B + -E_A E_B + R_A T_A \qquad (17)$$

where "the receptance" R_A identifies the Lewis acid as the receptor of the transferred electron density, as being related to the enthalpic stabilization of the cation per increment of electron density transferred to it. The term T_B is called "the transmittance," which determines the extent of the transfer from the base and the product represents the enthalpic stabilization that accompanies the electron transfer into the cation from the base. Thus, T_B relates to the ease of removing electron density from the base in the presence of the cation.

The four-parameter equation and its modified versions seem to give excellent agreement with experiment and compares very favorably with that suggested by Pearson. However, its empirical nature and the number of independent parameters involved in the calculations make it very impractical to use. In addition, no physical reason or explanation for hard and soft behavior is provided by such an approach.

1.2.10   THE DENSITY FUNCTIONAL UNDERPINNING OF THE HSAB PRINCIPLE

The HSAB principle remained qualitative for predicting the nucleophilic displacement reactions for a very long time. Although the strengths of acids and bases can be adequately described in terms of the relative PK values of the acids and the bases within the Lowry–Brønsted acid basetheory, there was no single scale of Lewis acidity and basicity and also there was no measure of the acid–base strength and the ease of the reaction.

In 1980, Jenson [41] used a relation between second ionization potentials versus z/r, where z is the atomic number and r is the radius of atom, to classify divalent metal ions into three broad categories: hard, soft, and borderline. Although this classification was not that acceptable by scientific community, this graphical classification was used by Williams [42] as an input of his work.

The scientific world had to wait till the seminal work of Parr and coworkers who, using the DFT as basis, placed the qualitative HSAB principle on a sound quantum mechanical platform [11]. The Hohenberg and Kohn [10], the founders of DFT pointed out that the total energy E for N electron system, is a functional of electronic density, $E(r)$.Given the electron density function $\rho(r)$ in a chemical system (atom or molecule) and the energy functional $E(\rho)$, the chemical potential, μ of that system in equilibrium has been defined as the derivative of the energy with respect to the number of electrons at fixed molecular geometry.

Parr et al. [43] showed that the slope, $[\partial E(r)/\partial N]_v$, of the energy $E(r)$ versus the number of electrons (N) curve (Figure 1.3) at a constant external potential(v), is the chemical potential, μ, and this property such as thermodynamic chemical potential [44] measures the escaping tendency of electrons in the species.

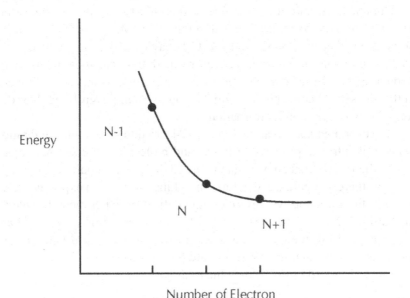

FIGURE 1.3   Plot of total electronic energy (all are negative) of a system in positive (+1), neutral (0), and negative (−1) state as a function of number of electrons (N).

The chemical potential, μ is given by [45]

$$\mu = [\delta E(\rho)/\delta\rho]_v \tag{18}$$

The differential definition more appropriate to atomic system is

$$\mu = [\partial E / \partial N]_v \tag{19}$$

Here, E is expressed as the function of the number of electrons, N i.e., functional of N, $E(N)$.

Then, following Iczkowski and Margrave [45], Parr et al. [43] defined the electronegativity as the additive inverse of the chemical potential.

$$\chi = -\mu \tag{20}$$

$$\text{or, } \chi = -\mu = - [\partial E / \partial N]_v \tag{21}$$

In 1983, the qualitative HSAB principle was placed on sound quantum mechanical basis by the seminal work of Parr and Pearson [46].

The chemical hardness, η is one of the oldest concepts of chemistry. The notion of hardness was first introduced by Mulliken [47] when he pointed out that the "hard" and "soft" behavior of various atoms, molecules, and ions can be conceived during acid–base chemical interaction. Soon after Mulliken's classification, the terms *hardness* and *softness* were in the glossary of conceptual chemistry and implicitly signifying their deformability under small perturbation.

However, Pearson [9] and Klopman [24] tried to systematize and rationalize this intrinsic property of atoms and molecules; one serious objection to the HSAB concept was that no exact definition of hardness existed. Nor was there an operational definition linking hardness to experiment. As a result, there was no way to give a theoretical or experimental value to the hardness for any chemical system. But after the seminal work of Parr and Pearson [46], the definition of hardness and theoretical value to the hardness for any chemical system could be assigned.

Parr and Pearson [46] defined the term *hardness* η as

$$2\eta = [\partial \mu / \partial N]_v = -[\partial \chi / \partial N]_v = [(\partial^2 E / \partial N^2)]_v \tag{22}$$

The chemical hardness fundamentally signifies the resistance toward the deformation or polarization of the electron cloud of the atoms, ions, or molecules under small perturbation of chemical reaction. Thus, the hardness as conceived in chemistry signifies the resistance toward the deformation of charge cloud of chemical systems under small perturbation encountered during chemical processes. Thus, the general operational significance of the hard–soft chemical species may be understood in the following statement. If the electron cloud is strongly held by the nucleus, the chemical species is "hard," but if the electron cloud is loosely held by the nucleus, the system is "soft" [9, 24].

Parr and Pearson [46] invoked the calculus of finite difference approximation to suggest an approximate and operational formula of hardness and electronegativity as under:

The energy (E) of a chemical system having N number of the valence electrons can be written in the form of the quadratic approximate equation as follows:

$$E = aN + bN^2 \qquad (23)$$

where 'a' is a constant, and it is a combination of core integral and a valence shell electron pair repulsion integral and 'b' is half of the average valence shell electron–electron repulsion integral.

Now differentiating Eq. (23) with respect to N at constant external potential, v we obtain

$$(\partial E/\partial N)_v = -a - 2bN = (I + A)/2 \qquad (24)$$

where I and A are the first ionization potential and electron affinity of the chemical species.

The right-hand side of the equation is the Mulliken [47] electronegativity (χ_M).

$$(\partial E/\partial N)_v = (I + A)/2 = \chi_M \qquad (25)$$

It is interesting to note that Putz [48], using finite difference approximation, showed that the Mulliken electronegativity definition can be recovered from the Parr electronegativity (χ_p) definition [43].

$$\chi_M = (I + A)/2 = \{(E_N - E_{N+1}) + (E_{N-1} - E_N)\}/2 = (-E_{N+1} + E_{N-1})/2 \qquad (26)$$

$$\chi_p = -\mu = -(\delta E/\delta N)_v = (-E_{N+1} + E_{N-1})/2 = \chi_M \qquad (27)$$

Now, second derivative of Eq. (24) is

$$\tfrac{1}{2}(\partial^2 E/\partial N^2)_v = b = (I - A)/2 \qquad (28)$$

This expresses the hardness (η) of the corresponding system [46]

$$\eta = \tfrac{1}{2}(\partial^2 E/\partial N^2)_v = (I - A)/2 \qquad (29)$$

It is important to mention here that Huheey [49] identified the parameter 'b' as inverse charge capacitance. The capacitance (C) of a spherical condenser is equal to $4\pi\varepsilon_0$. Komorowski [50] proposed hardness as inverse of capacitance, that is,

$$\eta = 1/C = (4\pi\varepsilon_0)^{-1} \qquad (30)$$

Pearson [51] proceeded further to evaluate I and A in terms of orbital energies of the highest-occupied molecular orbital, HOMO and the lowest unoccupied molecular orbital, LUMO by connecting it with Hartree–Fock SCF theory and invoking Koopmans' theorem,

$$\eta = (-\varepsilon_{HOMO} + \varepsilon_{LUMO})/2 \qquad (31)$$

and

$$\chi = -(\varepsilon_{HOMO} + \varepsilon_{LUMO})/2 \qquad (32)$$

It is transparent from Figure (1.4) that a soft molecule has a small HOMO–LUMO energy gap and a hard molecule has a large HOMO–LUMO energy gap.

The soft acids and bases have the properties that guarantee that the HOMO is relatively high in energy while the LUMO is relatively low in energy. Hard acids and bases have the opposite characteristics.

On the basis of the quantum theory of polarizability, Pearson [9(c)] pointed out that, in the presence of an 'electric field, exited states of a system are mixed with the ground state in such a way as to lower the energy. The smaller the excitation energy, the greater the effect. Thus, a small energy gap, (I–A) means high polarizability and soft acids and bases will be easily polarized.

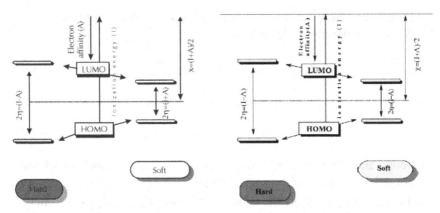

FIGURE 1.4 Correlation of the HOMO–LUMO gap, the hardness, and the electronegativity with the hard and soft behavior of chemical species.

Pearson [9(c)] further correlated the phenomenon that "unsaturation increases softness" with the HOMO–LUMO energy gap that usually defines the lowest-energy absorption band. Soft acids and bases should absorb light closer to the visible light than hard acids and bases. The chromophoric groups always correspond to relatively high energy HOMOs and low energy LUMOs.

Thereafter, in 1988, Pearson [52] has evaluated methods to rank the various Lewis acids and bases according to their local hardness derived from hemolytic bond dissociation data.

The details of the concepts of the electronegativity and hardness, their origin, and their physcochemical behavior will be explained in the later section.

1.2.11 THEORETICAL DEDUCTION OF THE HSAB PRINCIPLE

In their landmark paper, Parr and Pearson [46], based on the assumption that the energy of a chemical system is quadratic function of the number of electrons, suggested a theoretical formalism of the HSAB principle. In order to do so, they proposed a two-step mechanism for the formation of the A:B adduct from its constituents: acid (A) and base (B).

(i) The first step involves shift of some charge, ΔN from B to A.

(ii) The second step involves the formation of the actual chemical bond between the acid, A and the base, B.

Focusing initially on the first effect, they wrote the energy expression for A and B in the molecule as follows:

$$E_A = E_A^0 + \mu_A^0(N_A - N_A^0) + \eta_A(N_A - N_A^0)^2 \tag{33}$$

and

$$E_B = E_B^0 + \mu_B^0(N_B - N_B^0) + \eta_B(N_B - N_B^0)^2 \tag{34}$$

where E_A^0 and E_B^0, μ_A^0 and μ_B^0, and N_A^0 and N_B^0 are the energies, the chemical potentials, and the total number of electrons of the chemical species A and B, respectively, before the adduct formation; E_A and E_B are the energy of the chemical species A and B, respectively, after the adduct formation; and E_A and E_B, μ_A and μ_B, N_A and N_B are the energies, the chemical potentials, and the number of electrons present on A and B, respectively, after the formation of chemical bond between A and B, that is, in the adduct A:B and η_A and η_B are the hardness of A and B, respectively.

The electron numbers, N_A and N_B are as follows:

$$N_A = N_A^0 + \Delta N \tag{35}$$

and

$$N_B = N_B^0 - \Delta N \tag{36}$$

Now, with the physical process of charge transfer during chemical reaction leading to bond formation, the charge density kernel of atoms change and in the process, it would increase somewhere and decrease elsewhere so that the chemical potential of the chemical species or fragments will equalize to some intermediate values common to all. This principle is known as chemical potential equalization principle [53]. Thus, applying the chemical potential equalization principle on the acid–base formation reaction, Eq. (1) we obtain the following:

$$\mu_A = \mu_A^0 + 2\eta_A\Delta N = \mu_B = \mu_B^0 - 2\eta_B\Delta N \tag{37}$$

The shift of charge or the electron transfer can be easily calculated from Eq.(37) as follows:

$$\Delta N = (\mu_B^0 - \mu_A^0)/2(\eta_A + \eta_B) \tag{38}$$

Now, as $\chi = -\mu$

Hence,

$$\Delta N = (\chi^0_A - \chi^0_B)/2(\eta_A + \eta_B) \qquad (39)$$

The corresponding energy change, ΔE was calculated by Pearson as follows:

$$\Delta E = (E_A - E^0_A) + (E_B - E^0_B)$$

$$= -\tfrac{1}{2}(\mu_B{}^0 - \mu_A{}^0)\Delta N \qquad (40)$$

Putting $\chi = -\mu$,

$$\Delta E = -(\chi^0_A - \chi^0_B)^2/4(\eta_A + \eta_B) \qquad (41)$$

As the acid (A) must be more electronegative than base (B), $(\chi^0_A - \chi^0_B)$ is always positive, and hence an energy lowering results from electron transfer process.

1.2.12 EXPLANATION OF THE HSAB PRINCIPLE

Equation (41) reveals that the difference in absolute electronegativity drives the electron transfer, and the sum of the hardness parameter acts as a drag or resistance. In other words, the differences in electronegativity drive the electron transfer and the sum of the absolute hardness parameters inhibits electron transfer.

If both acid and base are soft, $(\eta_A + \eta_B)$ is a small number; and for a reasonable difference in electronegativities, ΔE is substantial and stabilizing. This explains the HSAB principle; meanwhile, it seems safe to say that it explains a part: soft prefers soft.

But, if both acid and base are hard, there is little electron transfer and energy stabilization from electron transfer, for a given difference in electronegativities. Parr and Pearson [46] commented "*This result seems paradoxical,*" and there is the need of the second effect—the formation of the chemical bond.

Parr and Pearson [46] further pointed out that in the molecule AB, similar to the electronegativity (chemical potential) equalization, the ionization potential of A,I_A and the ionization potential B, I_B are also equalized.

Using the condition $\mu_A = \mu_B$ and the Eq. (37), it can be shown that

$$I_A + A_A = I_B + A_B \tag{42}$$

and

The ionization potential effect: $I_B - I_A = \eta_B - \eta_A$ \hfill (43)

where A_A and A_B are the electron affinity of the A and B, respectively.

Thus, if both η_B and η_A are small, and/or if they are equal, then A and B have the same ionization potential in the molecule AB, that is, equalization of ionization potential occurs. In orbital language, this means that the one-electron energies of atomic orbitals on A and B have been made equal, or nearly equal. In both molecular orbital theory and valence bond theory, if orbital sizes are not too disparate, equal orbital energies always favor strong covalent bonding [46].

Parr and Pearson [46] further added that

(i) **Soft–soft interactions are largely covalent:** In soft acid–soft base adduct formation process, the two bonding electrons have comparable probabilities of being on A or B. Again this combination is favored by the ionization potential effect ($I_B - I_A = \eta_B - \eta_A$). These two combined effects show that the covalent bonding is dominant in soft–soft combinations and that good bonding will result.

(ii) **Hard–hard interactions are largely ionic:** In hard acid–hard base combinations, since there is little electron transfer from B to A, the bonding electrons must, on the average, remain on B resulting ionic bond formation. The chemical potential equalization is still favored that if both η_B and η_A are large, they might cancel each other. But this does not necessarily produce strong covalent bonding. The characteristics of a hard acid are high positive charge and small size of the cation which favor electrostatic interaction with B, which retains most of its negative charge, and which presents a favorable dipole interaction with a lone pair of electrons pointing at A.

(iii) **Hard–soft combinations are unfavorable:** For a hard–soft combination, on the contrary, stability is enhanced neither by the charge transfer nor by the condition favoring covalent bonding.

Parr and Pearson [46] also opined that the consideration that the soft–soft interactions are largely covalent, and that hard–hard interactions are largely ionic is not always novel.

1.2.13 THE CONCEPT OF DOUBLE BONDING

Pearson [54] explained the adduct formation between a neutral acid and a neutral base. Provided that η_A and η_B are both small, the stabilization of A:B adduct can be explained by double bonding. The concept of double bonding resembles the π-bonding theory of Chatt and his coworkers [19] who used the concept of π-bonding for explaining various metal ion-ligand preferences. During the adduct formation between a hard acid and a hard base, normally little two-way electron transfer occurs. If η_A and η_B are large, Pearson [9] also showed that there will be a one-way transfer from B to A. The probability of double bonding is greatly reduced for cationic acids. The main source of bonding that involves cationic acids will come from ionic bonding or ion-dipole bonding. Neutral molecules are the most likely to have two-way electron transfer. The unbiased values of $(\chi^0_A - \chi^0_B)$ for the neutral molecule determine the direction of net electron transfer. The total amount of electron transfer is governed by the sum of hardnesses of the acid and the base, $(\eta_A + \eta_B)$, and a small value of the summation is favorable for maximum covalent bonding.

Pearson [54] further commented that Eq. (39) measures the initial effects of bringing A and B into interaction with each other, and Eq. (39) is not that successful/suitable for calculating the net charges on the acid A and the base B.

Considering the above effects and using semiempirical molecular orbital theory, including ionic bonding and covalency. Pearson [54] derived an equation for ΔN as follows:

$$\Delta N = (\chi_A \sim \chi_B)/[2(\eta_A + \eta_B) - (1/R) - \{2\beta/(N_A N_B)^{1/2}\}] \tag{44}$$

Where β is the one-electron exchange integral, and hence is always negative; R is the inter nuclear distance between A and B; and N_A and N_B are the final numbers of electrons on A and B atoms, respectively.

1.2.14   QUANTIFICATION OF HSAB PRINCIPLE

Pearson [55], in order to refine HSAB principle that originally refers to the bond dissociation energy (ΔE) of the generalized acid–base reactions, Eq. (1) stated that the misinterpretation often made of the HSAB principle is the use of a single parameter (hardness or its inverse, softness) to determine the acid-base interaction, and this single-parameter assumption leads to the failure of the HSAB principle describing many chemical reactions. Moreover, the linear free-energy relationships that have been used to describe and predict the strengths of acid and base interactions require two parameters rather than one parameter for each the acid and the base, suggesting that at least one extrinsic influence on acid–base strength is in evidence. Thoughtful examination of these parameters and their interrelationships has suggested the existence of the HSAB principle [56].

Pearson [9(b), 57] in an attempt to head off this erroneous perception, assumed that the other entire factors, except softness, that determine the bond energy in a acid–base interaction may be considered as intrinsic strength (S) that depends on (i) the charge and (ii) the size of the interacting acid and base. He [57] assumed that the acid and base strength is singly ordered, and the acid-base interaction reaction (Eq. (1)) was given by him as follows:

$$S_A S_B = -\Delta E \tag{45}$$

As the reaction depends not only on the intrinsic strength but also on the softness parameter (σ), then the actual interaction reaction represented by Pearson is as follows:

$$S_A S_B + \sigma_A \sigma_B = -\Delta E \tag{46}$$

He [57] also pointed out that σ is positive for soft species and σ is negative for hard species, and this attempt gives extra stabilization of HSAB principle.

Equation (46) reveals that this equation resembles to the well-known four-parameter equation, Eq. (1.10), of Drago et al. [34].

Based on the experimental data, Pearson opined that for an exchange reaction of the type, Eq. (47), the only requirement is the relative hardness of the reactants to predict theoretically the preferred direction of the chemical reaction:

$$A:B+A':B'=A:B'+A':B \quad \Delta E > 0$$
$$\text{H–S} \quad \text{S–H} \quad \text{H–H} \quad \text{S–S} \tag{47}$$
$$[\text{H} = \text{harder}, \ \text{S} = \text{softer}]$$

Gazquez et al. [58] showed that the feasibility of the above reaction may be studied in terms of the energy change in a simple quadratic model as follows:

$$\Delta E = N\Delta\mu - (1/2)N^2\Delta\eta \tag{48}$$

(approximated up to second order of energy change)

where N is the number of electrons, and $\Delta\mu$ and $\Delta\eta$ are the changes between the reactants and products. If μ were constant, then ΔE would decrease if $\Delta\eta$ were positive.

For a very small amount of electron transfer (ΔN) from base to acid during the acid–base adduct formation, it is better to use the following equation:

$$\Delta E = (\partial E/\partial N)_v \, \Delta N + (1/2) \, (\partial^2 E \partial N^2)_v \, (\Delta N)^2 \tag{49}$$

Now, we obtain

$$\Delta E = \Delta N\mu - (1/2) \, \eta \, \Delta N^2 \tag{50}$$

This hard–soft classification is based on the relative hardness of the interacting species. Feasibility of a reaction can be explained by a fundamental rule of nature. Pearson first studied that a reaction proceeds to the direction that produced the hardest molecule. Thus, apart from the celebrated HSAB principle, Pearson proposed "there is a rule in nature that every system tries to be as hard as possible" a rule of thumb known as the principle of maximum hardness (PMH) [59].

1.2.15   THE FUKUI FUNCTION

Parr and Yang [60] connected DFT with the frontier orbital theory of chemical reactivity of Fukui. Although electronegativity and hardness are global properties of the system, the electron transfer between two molecules involves the electron transfer from a definite filled orbitals on the donor orbital, usually the highest-occupied molecular orbital, HOMO to an empty acceptor orbital usually the lowest unoccupied molecular orbital,

LUMO. The normalized electron densities of these frontier orbitals are called the frontier function or the Fukui function, $f(r)$.

The Fukui function, $f(r)$ describes the sensitivity of chemical potential to local change in external potential and is considered as the measure of reactivity at a local point(r) and defined by Parr and Yang [60] as follows:

$$f(r) = (\delta\rho(r)/\delta N)_{v(r)} \tag{51}$$

In order to point out the preferred direction of attack of a reagent (R) approaches to S, Parr and Yang [60] assumed that "the preferred direction is the one for which the initial $|d\mu|$ for the species S is a maximum."

They considered three cases:

For governing nucleophilic attack, the positive Fukui function was given by the following equation:

$$f^+(r) = (\delta\rho(r)/\delta N)^+_{v(r)} \text{ when } \mu_S > \mu_R \tag{52}$$

the negative Fukui function for governing electrophilic attack was given as

$$f^-(r) = (\delta\rho(r)/\delta N)^-_{v(r)} \text{ when } \mu_R > \mu_S \tag{53}$$

and the neutral Fukui function for governing the radical attack was given by the following equation:

$$f^0(r) = (\delta\rho(r)/\delta N)^0_{v(r)} \text{ when } \mu_S \approx \mu_R \tag{54}$$

where μ_S and μ_R are the chemical potentials of R and S, respectively.

A "frozen core" approximation now gives $d\rho = d\rho_{valence}$, and the above equations can be approximated to

$$f^+(r) = \rho_{HOMO} \text{ for donor molecule} \tag{55}$$

$$f^-(r) = \rho_{LUMO} \text{ for acceptor molecule} \tag{56}$$

$$f^0(r) = \tfrac{1}{2}(\rho_{HOMO} + \rho_{LUMO}) \text{ for both donor and acceptor molecule} \tag{57}$$

$f^0(r)$ is for the case where there is electron transfer in both direction as found in $(\sigma + \pi)$ bonding. The magnitude of the Fukui functions at the several sites of a molecule determines which atom will form the coordinate covalent bonds. This leads to the local HSAB principle.

1.2.16 LOCAL HARDNESS AND SOFTNESS

The hardness is not restricted to be constant everywhere, unlike the chemical potential. Therefore, local hardness can be assigned. Although Pearson [9] made first contribution to the concept in early 1963, the notion of local hardness was first introduced by Berkowitz et al. [32].

Berkowitz et al. [32] have derived the expression for local softness that reveals its relation to its reciprocal property, local hardness.

The idea is to define the appropriate two-variable kernels for hardness and softness, and then to generate local hardness and local softness from the corresponding kernel equations.

Here, we consider a ground state, or change of one ground state to another for which $\rho(r)$ determines all properties; it determines μ and $v(r)$. Starting from the Hohenberg–Kohn theorem, the modified potential can be written as follows:

$$u(r) = v(r) - \mu = \delta F[\rho]/\delta\rho(r) \tag{58}$$

where $u(r)$ is a functional of $\rho(r)$, and the functional derivatives looks thus:

$$-2\eta(r, r) = \delta u[r]/\delta\rho(r') = \delta u[r']/\delta\rho(r) \tag{59}$$

where $\eta(r, r)$ is the hardness kernel.

The calculation of the local hardness is difficult; therefore, the local softness defined by Yang and Parr [60(b)] is as follows.

As $u(r)$ is a functional of $\rho(r)$, the reverse i.e., $\rho(r)$ is a functional of $u(r)$ and its functional derivative also exists.

The softness kernel is defined as follows:

$$-s(r, r') = \delta\rho [r]/\delta u(r') = \delta\rho [r']/\delta u(r) \tag{60}$$

Now, using Eqs. (59) and (60), we can identify the local hardness and softness terms as follows:

$$s(r) = \int s(r, r')dr' \tag{61}$$

$$\eta(r) = 1/N \int\eta(r, r')\rho(r')dr' \tag{62}$$

These two quantities are also local in nature, i.e.,

$$2 \int s(r) \, \eta(r) \, dr = 1 \tag{63}$$

They defined the term *local hardness*, $\acute\eta$ as the change in chemical potential with changing electron density in different parts of the molecule. Thus

$$\acute\eta = \tfrac{1}{2}(\delta\mu/\delta\rho)_v \tag{64}$$

$$s(r) = (\delta\rho/\delta\mu)_v = S f \tag{65}$$

Thus, the local softness depends on the one-electronic density function of the frontier orbital, f. If the global hardness and the frontier orbitals are known, the local softness can be calculated at each atom. In a chemical reaction, the most efficient interaction will be between the softest part of each molecule. This allows the maximum transfer of electrons for a given difference in chemical potentials.

By using the concept of electron density $\rho(r)$, one can define a descriptor of local softness [60].

The local softness at an orbital r is defined using the following equation:

$$s(r) = f(r)S \tag{66}$$

where $f(r)$ is known as the Fukui function

The condensed softness, or the softness of an atom in a molecule, may be derived through the chemical potential equalization principle that leads to define the Fukui function of the kth atom in a molecule A with N_A electrons, in the following form:

$$S^+_k = f^+_k S \text{ for nucleophilic attack} \tag{67}$$

and

$$S^-_k = f^-_k S \text{ for electrophilic attack} \tag{68}$$

Parr and Yang [60] approximated the f^+_k and f^-_k as follows:

$$f^+_k = \rho_{LUMO}(r) \tag{69}$$

and

$$f^-_k = \rho_{HOMO}(r) \tag{70}$$

Therefore,

$$S^+_k = \rho_{LUMO}(r)\ S \text{ for nucleophilic attack} \tag{71}$$

$$S^-_k = \rho_{HOMO}(r)\ S \text{ for electrophilic attack} \tag{72}$$

The condense softness or the softness of an atom in molecule was defined as the sum

$$S^\pm = \sum_{K=1}^{K} S \tag{73}$$

where K is the total number of atoms in the molecule.

The condense hardness or the hardness of an atom in molecule was given by the following equation:

$$\eta^\pm = 1/S^\pm \tag{74}$$

According to Fuentealba et al. [61], the condensed Fukui function can give, in general, valuable information of site selectivity in chemical reactions and systematization in a family of molecules. They have shown the selectivity toward protonations of anilines, and derivatives molecules can be correctly assessed by the electrophilic Fukui function. The solvent effects on the condensed Fukui function are negligible.

Although local hardness and local softness are related, one is not simply reciprocal of the other. There is a different method for the determination of the local hardness of atoms in a molecule. This method is based on the distribution of the electron density at each atom, leading to a net charge on the atom. The assumption is then made that the local hardness increases with the net positive charge. As it can be noted from the equations for the local quantities, the local softness is the measure of the response of the electron density to a perturbation in the chemical potential at constant external potential. Since, the chemical reaction is, in general, considered as a perturbation in the number of electrons, the local softness can be effectively used as an appropriate descriptor to probe the chemical reaction. In particular, this has direct implications to the area of catalysis where the fluctuation in charge density is shown to be very important.

It is important to point out the work of Garza and Robles [62] who clarified the definition of local hardness within the Kohn–Sham formulation of the DFT and derived exact equations for the local hardness of open- and closed-shell electronic systems. They found that the Kohn–Sham independent particle kinetic energy does not contribute to local hardness.

It should be noted that the definition of local hardness is not very clear and is defined in an ambiguous manner. It has been pointed out by Harbola, Chattaraj, and Parr [63] that the derivative is ambiguous for a ground state due to the Hohenberg–Kohn theorem. Pal et al. [64] observed that "while the definition of local hardness is ambiguous, the local softness has been defined clearly." Ayers and Parr [30] commented "In the density functional theory of chemical reactivity, the local hardness is known to be an ambiguous concept." Chattaraj et al. [65] gave a critical account on the present status of the local hardness and analyzed various sources of confusion and misunderstanding concerning the definition and working equation of local hardness. They analyzed the behavior of hardness-related global, local, and nonlocal properties and opined that although local hardness has become very useful in predicting the region selectivity of chemical reactions, the lack of a rigorous definition in the literature has shown that different approximations can yield different, and sometimes contradictory, conclusions.

1.2.17 THE LOCAL HARD–SOFT ACID AND BASE CONCEPT

Parallel to the global developments of the HSAB concept, the concepts of local softness and hardness have emerged. The local quantities describe atomic sites in the molecule. Several definitions of the local quantities have been proposed. Although the definition of local hardness is ambiguous, Ghosh and Berkowitz defined the local softness [66]. The definition assumes a DFT approach. The local softness has been related to the Fukui function, which has been associated with the reactivity of the local sites [60].

Apart from the celebrated HSAB principle, one more principle was proposed by Pal and his coworkers [64] to describe the hard–soft behavior of the atomic sites in the molecule is the local HSAB concept.

The fact that the reactivity of the different sites of a molecule toward electrophilic and nucleophilic attacks is not the same can be correlated through the corresponding electrophilic and nucleophilic definitions of local softness. In particular, the condensed definitions based on finite difference approximation of obtaining the derivatives have now been conveniently used. In general, it has been shown that for any individual molecule, the most reactive site is located at the atom with the largest value of local softness of Fukui function. However, Gazquez and Mendez have shown that the interaction between two molecules will not necessarily occur through their softest atoms but rather through those atoms whose Fukui functions are the same. This version of the local HSAB principle was proved by the minimization of the grand canonical potential. Assuming the global softnesses of the molecules to be similar, the local HSAB principle states that the local softnesses of the interacting atoms are same. It is interesting to investigate if the equality of local softnesses of the interacting atoms is a more general principle, that is, whether this holds even when the global softnesses of the two molecules have different values.

For a polyatomic system, the local softness $s(r)$ (s is the global softness) is proportional to the Fukui function $f(r)$ [11]. This function represents the sensitivity of the chemical potential of a system to an external perturbation applied locally, such as a magnetic or an electrostatic field. In this case, the HSAB principle is locally applied: "hard regions of a system prefer to interact with hard reagents whereas soft regions prefer soft species." In a chemical reaction, the most efficient interaction will be between the softest parts of each molecule. This allows the transfer of maximum electron from a base to an acid.

Gazquez and Mendez [58] showed that the energy of stabilization between the two reacting systems A and B is greater if the Fukui functions of the reacting atoms in A and in B are greater. However, they also showed that the interaction between A and B does not necessarily occur through the softest atoms of A and B, but through those atoms whose Fukui functions are roughly close to each other. That is,

$$f^k(A) \approx f^l(B) \tag{75}$$

In deriving the rule of the "equality of the Fukui functions" associated with chemical reaction, the global HSAB principle was proposed by Pal et al. [64] as the global softness of acid A (S_A) was assumed to be equal to that of the base B (S_B). Under these conditions, the local softness of atom k in A is also equal to that of atom l in B, that is

$$s_A^{\ k} \approx s_B^{\ l} \tag{76}$$

Gazquez and Mendez [58] made remarks that the general statement of equal local softnesses of the atoms participating in a reaction may be obtained directly by minimization of the grand canonical potential and without assuming $S_A = S_B$. This is a more general statement of their earlier definition of the local HSAB principle to determine the atoms through which the reaction between A and B takes place. The principle may also be viewed as a generalization of the global HSAB principle.

1.2.18 THE FUKUI FUNCTION VERSUS LOCAL HARD–SOFT CONCEPT

Li and Evans [67] demonstrated that the Fukui function plays a central role in the study of chemical reactivity and selectivity. Both the frontier molecular orbital (FMO) theory and the HSAB principle are intrinsically related to the Fukui function. By using an energy perturbation method within the framework of DFT, they showed that the FMO theory can be understood as a part of the HSAB principle. The selectivity of achemical reaction is determined by the nature of the reaction. Thus, for a hard reaction, the site of minimal Fukui function is preferred; for a soft reaction, the site of maximal Fukui function is preferred.

Chattaraj [68] made a critical analysis on the local HSAB principle and frontier orbital theory in order to study of chemical reactivity and site selectivity. He pointed out that the maximum Fukui function site is the best for the frontier controlled soft–soft reactions; whereas for the charge controlled hard–hard interactions, the preferred site is associated with the maximum net charge and not necessarily the minimum Fukui function.

1.2.19 PHYSICAL BASIS OF THE HSAB PRINCIPLE

The physical basis of HSAB principal was not properly elucidated until the landmark work of Ayers [3]. In this work, Ayers explored the interrelationship between several properties of molecules and their chemical hardness. To quantify the interaction energy between hard and soft acids and bases, Ayers relied on the fundamental periodic relationship between the chemical hardness, size, polarizability, charge, and electronegativity of the chemical systems.

The most interesting point to study the physical nature of HSAB is that it will help us understand why exceptions to the HSAB principle sometimes occur [3].

Pearson [9] invoked the concept of hardness to study the chemical properties of compounds, specifically, the tendency of hard acids to interact with hard bases and the tendency of soft acids to interact with soft bases. The physical properties of the compounds were not described at that time [9].

It is not worth mentioning that the physical properties and chemical properties of acids and bases are interrelated and follow each other.

Thus Ayers [3] commented thus: "Discovering the physical basis of a chemical principle requires relating the principle to one or more of the fundamental variational principles that govern chemical reactivity."

He [3] cited the examples of the electronegativity equalization principle [53] and the frontier-electron theory [24] based on the Fukui function both of them follow directly from the fundamental variational principle for the electron density.

1.2.20 UNDERSTANDING THE HSAB PRINCIPLE: THE DOUBLE-EXCHANGE REACTION

The double-exchange reaction between a hard acid–soft base adduct (A_hB_s), and a soft acid–hard base adduct (A_sB_h) was taken to theorize and understand the HSAB principle. Ayers et al. [69] have explored new approach based directly on acid- and base-exchange reactions and, especially, the double-exchange reaction:

$$A_hB_s + A_sB_h \leftrightarrow A_hB_h + A_sB_s \qquad (77)$$

where A_h is a hard acid, B_s is a soft base, A_s is a soft acid, and B_s is a soft base.

The electrostatic and electron-transfer contributions to the energy in the above double-exchange reaction make both the hard acid–hard base and soft acid–soft base products enormously favorable.

Ayers [3] commented thus: "for this reason, the double exchange reaction should almost always follow the HSAB principle."

It is now well established [69] that the electron transfer strongly favors the formation of the soft acid/soft base product, and the electrostatic interaction energies strongly favors the formation of the hard acid/hard base product.

It was Ayers [3] who opined that the HSAB principle does more than just make predictions about the double-exchange reaction and the corresponding acid- and the base-exchange reactions and proposed a general model that includes the electron transfer, the electrostatic effects and also the polarization effect.

$$A_h B_s + A_s \leftrightarrow A_h + A_s B_s \tag{78}$$

$$A_h + A_s B_h \leftrightarrow A_h + A_s B_h \tag{79}$$

$$B_s + A_s B_h \leftrightarrow B_h + A_s B_s \tag{80}$$

$$A_h B_s + B_h \leftrightarrow B_s + A_h B_h \tag{81}$$

Equations (78–79) and (80–81) are the corresponding acid-exchange reactions and the base-exchange reactions respectfully of the double-exchange reaction, Eq. (77).

The concept also makes predictions about the behavior of the reactive sites of the ambidentate ligands and also this leads to the introduction of the local hard/soft acid/base principle:

An ambidentate base (or acid) tends to bind to soft acids (or bases) through its soft reactive site and hard acids (or bases) through its hard reactive site.

Gazquez and Mendez [58] suggested that this rule could be explained using the local softness [60, 70] which is just the softness multiplied by the Fukui function:

$$s^+(r) = S f^+(r) \text{ for acids} \tag{82}$$

$$s^-(r) = S f^-(r) \text{ for bases} \tag{83}$$

Although, Ayers [3] has always been doubtful of the idea that "matching" the local softnesses of the acidic and basic reactive sites favors reactivity and pointed out some exceptions of the "matching" concept. "In spite of the value of the local softness at the site, it seems that hard acids usually prefer the most negatively charged reactive site on a base. Even when the two reactive sites have similar negative charges, a hard acid may prefer the site with the larger local softness [3]."

1.2.20.1 ELECTROSTATIC AND ELECTRON-TRANSFER EFFECTS

Ayers [3] explained the contribution of the physical properties of hard reagents to the chemical reaction energy between acids and bases, and he also observed that this consideration supports the HSAB principle. It was stated that the variation principle for the electron density also plays a role in the HSAB principle:

> when an acid and a base react, electron density moves from the base to the acid until the energy of the product is minimized.

In the case of such reaction, the electron-transfer process lowers the energy of the system (ΔE_{el}) by

$$\Delta E_{el} = -(\mu_B - \mu_A)^2/2(\eta_A + \eta_B) = -(\chi_B - \chi_A)^2/2(\eta_A + \eta_B) \quad (84)$$

Here μ, χ, and η denote the chemical potential, electronegativity, and the hardness of the acid (A) and the base (B) involved in the reaction, respectively.

The above Eq. (84) computes the contribution of electron transfer to the reaction energy between an acid and a base.

The preference for the hard acid/hard base and soft acid/soft base products in the double-exchange reaction, Eq. (77), can be easily explained by the electron-transfer effects if there were no other contributions to the reaction energy.

It was shown [69] that for the single-exchange reactions with a soft reagent, Eqs. (78) and (80), the electron-transfer contribution to the energy favors the soft acid—soft base product over the "mixed" hard acid/soft base or soft acid/hard base alternative. This is a support to the HSAB principle.

However, there is some contradiction to the HSAB principle. The electron-transfer contribution to the reaction energy also predicts that the "mixed" products in reactions, Eqs. (79) and (81), would be favored over the hard acid/hard base alternative[69].

Because the electron-transfer energy is inversely proportional to the hardness of the reagents, Eq. (41), electron-transfer effects have a propensity to be insignificant when hard acids react with hard bases. Hard acids and hard bases tend to be small and highly charged; therefore, the electrostatic interactions between a hard acid and a hard base have a propensity to dominate.

Now the electrostatic contribution to the reaction energy is given by the following equation:

$$\Delta E_{qq} = q_A q_B / (r_A + r_B) \tag{86}$$

here, q_A, q_B, r_A, and r_B represent the charges and radii of the acidic and basic reactive sites.

Just as the electron-transfer contribution to the reaction energy is determined using the fundamental variational principle for the density, the electrostatic contribution to the reaction energy is determined using the fundamental variational principle for the external potential:

when two reactants come together, their nuclei arrange themselves so that the energy of the 'supermolecule' is minimized [71].

Hence to proceed further Ayers [3] considered the double-exchange reaction including the electrostatic contribution to the reaction energy and by omitting the electron-transfer contribution, he showed that the hard–hard and soft–soft adducts are still favored. Moreover, in the single-exchange reactions with a hard reagents, Eqs. (79) and (81), the hard acid–hard base products are now favored over their mixed alternatives.

In the exchange reactions with a soft reagent, "mixed" compounds such as the hard acid/soft base are favored over the soft acid/soft base product that would be predicted based on the HSAB principle. This anomaly of mixed product formation was explained [3] in terms of the stability of electron-transfer contributions to the reaction energy, which favored over the soft acid/soft base product formation.

1.2.20.2   POLARIZABILITY EFFECTS

Ayers [3] noted that the soft reagents are not small or highly charged, but they are polarizable. Thus, he [3] further commented that "determining whether the enhanced polarizability of soft reagents supports the HSAB principle requires determining how the polarizability affects the interaction energy between acids and bases."

Now let us consider the mechanism of acid–base adduct formation. When an acid and a base approach each other, the charge on the acid polarizes the base, and vice versa. This is commonly known as charge-induced dipole interaction. The energy change due to this charge-induced dipole interaction was given by Ayers [3] as follows:

$$\Delta E_{q\alpha} = -\{(\alpha_B q_A^2)/2(r_A + r_B)^4\} - \{(\alpha_A q_B^2)/2(r_A + r_B)^4\} \tag{87}$$

where α_A and α_B denote the polarizability of acidic and basic reactive sites.

The charge-induceddipole is often the largest polarizability-dependent contribution to the reaction energy and is only significant when one or both of the reagents are highly charged. In such case, the charge–charge interaction or the electrostatic interaction will be the dominant factor.

On the other hand, in most cases where the charge-induced dipole interaction energy is large, the reactivity preferences will be determined by an even larger charge–charge interaction. Thus, while the charge-induced dipole interaction in Eq. (86) is not quantitatively small, it is usually qualitatively unimportant.

This is supportive because the charge-induced dipole contribution to the reaction energy is not especially favorable for the HSAB principle.

Now when neutral atoms react with each other, the reactive sites of the acid and base are uncharged, or at least small, the dominant electrostatic interaction is the London dispersion interaction:

$$\Delta E_L = -(3\varepsilon_A \varepsilon_B \alpha_A \alpha_B)/\{2(\varepsilon_A + \varepsilon_B)(r_A + r_B)^6\} \tag{88}$$

ε_A and ε_B arise from the closure approximation and represent the average excitation energy of the acid and the base, respectively. The chemical hardness is approximately equal to first excitation energy [72]; therefore, it is reasonable to infer that

$$\Delta E_L \approx -(3\eta_A \eta_B \alpha_A \alpha_B)/\{2(\eta_A + \eta_B)(r_A + r_B)^6\} \tag{89}$$

From the review of Ayers [3], we may concur with his comment that "the HSAB principle is a robust rule for predicting the products of chemical reactions" [3]. He also noted that the double-exchange reactions always do not follow the HSAB principle and pointed out some exceptions to the HSAB principle.

- **Case 1: When one of the acids and one of the bases is very strong:** In such case the surpassing stability of the strong acid/ strong base (SA–SB) product can overwhelm the preference for the hard acid–hard base (HA–HB) and the soft acid–soft base(SA–SB) products. Here, the intrinsic strength of acids and bases is measured using their electronic chemical potential. This exception occurs only when one acid is much stronger than the other acid and one base is much stronger than the other base.

- **Case 2: When one of the potential products of the double-exchange reaction is exceptionally stable:** If the stability is due to an orbital-specific interaction between one of the acids and one of the bases, then the HSAB principle may be violated. For example, a soft acid might be able to form a multiple bond to the hard base but not to the soft base. This would preferentially stabilize the soft acid–hard base product and an exception to the HSAB principle might result.

- **Case 3: If the entropy of one or more of the potential products is very high:** Then the maximum entropy products might be favored over the minimum energy products. Ayers's [3] analysis was based on the expectation that all the potential product molecules would have similar entropy. The fact that the HSAB principle seems to work across the broad range of temperatures of relevance to chemistry supports this assumption.

- **Case 4: If one or more of the potential products is preferentially solvated**: Then the favored product may be the molecule that with the largest frees energy of solvation. From the famous Le Chatelier's principle, we can say that if one or more of the potential products is insoluble, then the reaction will proceed to the direction of the insoluble product. Ayers [3] made an analysis where he assumed that the free energy of solvation was similar for all the potential product molecules. The fact that supports his assumption is "the HSAB principle seems to work not only in the gas phase, but across a broad range of solvents."

- **Case 5: When the interaction between the reactive sites of the acid and base is not driven by the dominant interaction between the acidic and basic reagents:** For multidentate ligands

where the dominant interaction between the acidic and basic reagents is not the interaction between their reactive sites, the Ayers
model based on the reactive-site interaction energy will not be
valid.

The single-exchange reactions are much more insightful to differences
in the intrinsic strength of the acids and bases. Ayers made the conclusion
that the HSAB principle is much less robust for single-exchange reactions
and isomerization reactions of ambidentate ligands.

This is due to the fact that in single-exchange reactions electron-transfer effects and electrostatic effects favor different products. The double-
exchange reaction follows the HSAB principle nicely because of the fact
that in such case the electron-transfer effects and electrostatic effects rein-
force each other.

For example, if electrostatic effects are more important than electron
transfer effects in the acid-exchange reaction with a soft base, Eq. (78),
then the reaction will favor the hard acid–soft base product. However, the
electron-transfer effects will ordinarily dominate in the case of the soft
reagent because the reagents are associated with small charges and large
amounts of electron transfer.

Ayers proved that the HSAB principle is a driven by simple electron
transfer effects and mathematically showed [73] that "for the exchange
reaction, wherein two molecules, one the product of reacting a hard acid
and a soft base and the other the product of reacting a soft acid with a hard
base, exchange substituents to form the preferred hard–hard and soft–soft
product."

It is very important to remember that the HSAB principle only applies when the strengths of acids and/or bases are similar/closer, and these
exceptions to the HSAB principle indicate interesting molecule-specific
properties that are not directly related to the chemical hardness of the reagents.

1.2.21 LIMITATION OF THE HOMO–LUMO CONCEPT OF CHEMICAL INTERACTION—THE FERMO CONCEPT TO THE HSAB PRINCIPLE

da Silva et al. [74, 75] opined that the HOMO–LUMO gap itself cannot
describe the hardness difference between the various binding sites in the
same molecules such as those formed by ambidentate ligands, such as

the thiocyanate anion, where more than one coordinating sites of different hardness are present. Hence, the HOMO–LUMO concept is not sufficient to explain the chemical reactivity for such compounds. To explain the chemical reactivity for such molecules, formed by ambidentate ligands, a new concept was introduced by da Silva et al. [74, 75] known as "frontier effective-for-reaction molecular orbital" (FERMO). This concept, using an intuitive statement based on the HOMO–LUMO approach to the hardness and softness, presented the FERMO–LUMO gaps. In the FERMO concept, MO composition and shape are taken into account to identify the MO that will actually be involved in a given reaction. A molecule could have as many FERMOs as it has reactions sites, and it could be the HOMO or any other FMO. da Silva et al. [74, 75] applied the FERMO concept to the HSAB principle [9] for ambidentate ligands and correctly described the soft and hard sites in case of the systems they studied.

1.2.22   PROOFS FOR HSAB PRINCIPLE

The Pearson's HSAB concept was basically formulated to explain the direction of an acid–base double-exchange reaction. The proof of HSAB principle requires a realization of the HSAB concept or some idea to demonstrate its feasibility, or a demonstration in principle, whose purpose is to verify that some concept or theory has the potential of being used. A proof of concept is usually small and may or may not be complete. However, it is not easy to theoretically establish the hard and soft acids and bases principle, Chattaraj et al. [76] offered two proofs for HSAB principle with a restriction "among potential partners of a given electronegativity, hard likes hard and soft likes soft."

Here, it is important to mention that using a heterolytic dissociative version of Pauling bond energy equation, Patra et al. [77] also made some attempts to provide qualitative and quantitative proof for the HSAB principle of Pearson.

1.3   CONCLUSION

The HSAB Theory is an Indispensable Theoretical Construct of Conceptual Chemistry. The Pearson's HSAB concept was basically formulated to explain the direction of an acid–base double-exchange reaction. The concept and efforts of its quantitative measurement evolved with time.

In this work, we sketched the time evolution of the HSAB theory. We see that the HSAB theory is much sublimated with the seminal work of Parr and coworkers within the scope of DFT such that it has been an important chapter of theoretical chemistry of present-day science. The hardness is neither an experimental observable nor a quantum mechanically measurable quantity. But still it is reified, modeled, and measured to quantify the HSAB principle.

The famous Pareto principle "Efficiency is highest when partners are both well satisfied," is appears in chemistry also, and that is the HSAB principle.

ACKNOWLEDGMENT

NAZMUL ISLAM thanks the management of University of Kalyani, Techno Global-Balurghat, and Techno India Group for providing research facility.

KEYWORDS

- **Conceptual density functional theory (DFT)**
- **Hard–soft acid–base theory**
- **Periodicity**
- **Time evolution of the HSAB theory**

REFERENCES

1. Scerri, E.; The Periodic Table: Its Story and Its Significance. Oxford [Oxfordshire]: Oxford University Press; **2007**.
2. Frenking, G.; and Krapp, A.; Unicorns in the world of chemical bonding models. *J. Comput. Chem.* **2007,** *28,* 15–24.
3. Ayers, P. W.; The physical basis of the hard/soft acid/base principle. *Faraday Discuss.* **2007,** *135,* 161–190.
4. Parr, R. G.; Ayers, P. W.; and Nalewajski, R. F.; What is an atom in a molecule? *J. Phys. Chem. A.* **2005,** *109,* 3957–3959.
5. Huheey, J. E.; Keiter, E. A.; and Keiter, R. L.; Inorganic Chemistry, Principles of Structure and Reactivity. New York: Addison-Wesley Publishing Company; 4th edition. **1993**.
6. Putz, M. V.; Maximum hardness index of quantum acid-base bonding. *MATCH Commun. Math. Comput. Chem.* **2008,** *60,* 845–868.

7. (a) Lowry, T. M.; The uniqueness of hydrogen. *Chem. Ind.* **1923**, *42*, 43–47.
   (b) Brønsted, J. N.; The acid-basic function of molecules and its dependency on the electric charge type. *J. Phys. Chem.* **1926**, *30*, 777–790.
8. (a) Lewis,G. N.; The atom and the molecule. *J. Am. Chem. Soc.* **1916**, *38*, 762–785.
   (b) Lewis, G. N.; Valence and the Structure of Atoms and Molecules. New York: Chemical Catalogue Co.; **1923**.
9. (a) Pearson, R. G.; Hard and soft acids and bases. *J. Am. Chem. Soc.* **1963**, *85*, 3533–3539.
   (b) Pearson, R. G.; Acids and bases. *Sci.* **1966**, *151*, 172–177.
10. Hohenberg, P.; and Kohn, H.; Inhomogeneous electron gas. *Phys Rev.* **1964**, *136*, 864–871.
11. Parr, R. G.; and Yang, W.; Density Functional Theory of Atoms and Molecules. Oxford University Press, USA; **1989**.
12. Pearson, R. G.; Hard and soft acids and bases—the evolution of a chemical concept. *Coord. Chem. Rev.* **1990**, *100*, 403–425.
13. Sidgwick, N. V.; Complex formation. *J. Chem. Soc.* **1941**, 433–443.
14. Bjerrum, J.; On the tendency of the metal ions toward complex formation. *Chem. Rev.* **1950**, *46*, 381–401.
15. Davies, J. A.; Synthetic Coordination Chemistry: Principles and Practice. World Scientific, Singapore; **1996**.
16. Gispert, J. R.; Coordination Chemistry. Wiley-VCH; **2008**. www.beck.de doi: 10.1002/aoc.1550
17. *Irving, H. M. N. H.; and Williams, R. J. P.; The stability of transition-metal complexes.* *J. Chem. Soc.* **1953**, *3192–3210.*
18. Jahn, H. A.; and Teller, E.; Stability of polyatomic molecules in degenerate electronic states. I. orbital degeneracy. *Proc. R. Soc. London A.* **1937**, *161*, 220–235.
19. (a) Ahrland, S.; Chatt, J.; and Davies, N. R.; The relative affinities of ligand atoms foracceptor molecules and ions. *Q. Reu. Chem. Sot.* **1958**, *12*, 265–276.
    (b) Chatt, J.; The stabilisation of low valent states of the transition metals: introductory lecture. *J. Inorg. Nucl. Chem.* **1958**, *8*, 515–531.
    (c) Ahrland, S.; Factors contributing to (b) behavior in acceptors. *Struct. Bonding (Berlin).* **1966**, *1*, 207–210.
20. Edwards, J. O.; and Pearson, R. G.; The factors determining nucleophilic reactivities. *J. Am. Chem. Soc.* **1962**, *84*, 16–24.
21. Williams, R. J. P.; and Hale, J. D.; The classification of acceptors and donors in inorganic reactions. *Struct. Bonding (Berlin).* **1966**, *1*, 249–281.
22. Hudson, R. F.; The concept of hard and soft acids and bases and nucleophilic displacement reactions. *Coord Chem. Rev.* **1966**, *1*, 89–94.
23. Jorgenson, C. K.; "Symbiotic" ligands, hard and soft central atoms. *Inorg Chem.* **1964**, *3*, 1201–1202.
24. (a) Klopman, G. A.; Semiempirical treatment of molecular structures. I. Electronegativity and atomic terms. *J. Am. Chem. Soc.* **1964**, *86*, 1463–1469.
    (b) Klopman, G.; Chemical reactivity and the concept of charge- and frontier-controlled reactions. *J. Am. Chem. Soc.* **1968**, *90*, 223–234.

25. Baird, N. C.; and Whitehead, M. A.; Ionic character. *Theor. Chim. Acta.* **1964,** *2,* 259–264.

26. Orsky, A. R.; and Whitehead, A. M.; Electronegativity in density functional theory: diatomic bond energies and hardness parameters. *Can. J. Chem.* **1987,** *65,* 1970–1979.

27. (a) Reed, J. L.; Hard and soft acids and bases: atoms and atomic ions. *Inorg. Chem.* **2008,** *47,* 5591–5600.
    (b) Reed, J. L.; Hard and soft acids and bases: small molecules. *Inorg. Chem.* **2009,** *48,* 7151–7158.

28. Pearson, R. G.; Failure of Pauling's bond energy equation. *Chem. Commun. (London).* **1968,** *2,* 65–67.

29. (a) Pauling, L.; The nature of chemical bond. IV. The energy of single bonds and the relative electronegativity of atoms. *J. Am. Chem. Soc.* **1932,** *54,* 3570–3582.
    (b) Pauling, L.; The Nature of Chemical Bond. 3rd edition. Ithaca, New York: Cornell University Press; **1960.**

30. (a) Ayers, P. W.; and Parr, R. G.; Local hardness equalization: exploiting the ambiguity. *J. Chem. Phys.* **2008,** *128,* 184108 (1–8).
    (b) Ayers, P. W.; and Parr, R. G.; Beyond electronegativity and local hardness: higher-order equalization criteria for determination of a ground-state electron density. *J. Chem. Phys.* **2008,** *129,* 054111(1–7).

31. Klopman, G.; and Hudson, R. F.; Polyelectronic perturbation treatment of chemical reactivity. *Theor. Chim. Acta.* **1967,** *8,* 165–174.

32. Berkowitz, M.; Density functional approach to frontier controlled reactions. *J. Am. Chem. Soc.* **1987,** *109,* 4823–4825.

33. Doglas, J.; and Kollman, P.; An analysis of the hard-soft Lewis acid-base concept and the Drago equation employing ab initio molecular orbital theory. *J. Phys. Chem.* **1981,** *85,* 2717–2722.

34. Drago, R. S.; and Wayland, B. B.; A double-scale equation for correlating enthalpies of Lewis acid-base interactions. *J. Am. Chem. Soc.* **1965,** *87,* 3571–3577.

35. Marks, A. P.; and Drago, R. S.; Justification for the E and C equation. *J. Am. Chem. Soc.* **1975,** *97,* 3324–3329.

36. Drago, R. S.; and Kabler, R. A.; Quantitative evaluation of the HSAB [hard-soft acid-base] concept. *Inorg. Chem.* **1972,** *11,* 3144–3145.

37. Pearson, R. G.; [Quantitative evaluation of the HSAB (hard-soft acid-base) concept]. Reply to the paper by Drago and Kabler. *Inorg. Chem.* **1972,** *11,* 3146–3146.

38. Drago, R. S.; Pearson's quantitative statement of HSAB [hard-soft acid-base] *Inorg. Chem.* **1973,** *12,* 2211–2212.

39. Beerbower, A.; and Jensen, B.; The HSAB principle and extended solubility theory. *Inorg. Chim. Acta.* **1983,** *75,* 193–197.

40. Drago, R. S.; Wong, N.; Bilgrien, C.; and Vogel, G. C.; E and C parameters from Hammett substituent constants and use of E and C to understand cobalt-carbon bond energies. *Inorg. Chem.* **1987,** *26,* 9–14.

41. Jensen, W. B.; The Lewis acid base concept. New York: Wiley-Interscience; **1980**.
42. Williums, R. J. P.; Changing Metal Cycles and Human Health. Ed. Nriagu, J. O.; Springer-Verlag Berlin; **1984**.
43. Parr, R. G.; Donnelly, R. A.; Levy, M.; and Palke, W. E.; Electronegativity: The density functional viewpoint. *J. Chem. Phys.* **1978,** *68,* 3801–3807.
44. Gyftpoulous,E.P.; Hatsopoulos, G.N.;Quantum-thermodynamic definition of electronegativity.*Proc. Natl. Acad. Sci.***1968,***60,*786–793.
45. Iczkowski, R. P.; and Margrave, J. L.; Electronegativity. *J. Am. Chem. Soc.* **1961,** *83,* 3547–3551.
46. Parr, R. G.; and Pearson, R. G.; Absolute hardness: companion parameter to absolute electronegativity. *J. Am. Chem. Soc.* **1983,** *105,* 7512–7516.
47. Mulliken, R. S.; Molecular compounds and their spectra II. *J. Am. Chem. Soc.* **1952,** *74,* 811–824.
48. Putz, M. V.; Systematic formulations for electronegativity and hardness and their atomic scales within density functional softness theory. *Int. J. Quantum. Chem.* **2006,** *106,* 361–389.
49. Huheey, J. E.; The electronegativity of groups. *J. Phys. Chem.* **1965,** *69,* 3284–3291.
50. Komorowski, L.; Electronegativity and hardness in the chemical approximation. *Chem Phys.* **1987,** *114,* 55–71.
51. Pearson, R. G.; Absolute electronegativity and hardness correlated with molecular orbital theory. *Proc. Natl. Acad. Sci.* **1986,** *83,* 8440–8441.
52. Pearson, R. G.; Chemical hardness and bond dissociation energies. *J. Am. Chem. Soc.* **1988,** *110,* 7684–7690.
53. Sanderson, R. T.; An interpretation of bond lengths and a classification of bonds. *Sci.* **1951,** *114,* 670–672.
54. Pearson, R. G.; Absolute electronegativity and absolute hardness of Lewis acids and bases. *J. Am. Chem. Soc.***1985,** *107,* 6801–6806.
55. Pearson, R. G.; The HSAB principle—more quantitative aspects. *Inorg. Chem. Acta.* **1995,** *240,* 93–98.
56. Reed, J. L.; Hard and soft acids and bases: atoms and atomic ions. *Inorg. Chem.* **2008,** *47,* 5591–5600.
57. Pearson, R. G.; Hard and soft acids and bases. *Chem. Br.* **1967,** *3,* 103–107.
58. Gazquez, J. L.; Martinez, A. M.; and Mendez, F.; Relationship between energy and hardness differences. *J. Phys. Chem.* **1993,** *97,* 4059–4063.
59. (a) Pearson, R. G.; Recent advances in the concept of hard and soft acids and bases. *J. Chem. Edu.* **1987,** *64,* 561–567.
(b) Pearson, R. G.; The principle of maximum hardness. *Acc. Chem. Res.* **1993,** *26,* 250–255.
60. (a) Parr, R. G.; and Yang, W.; Density functional approach to the frontier-electron theory of chemical reactivity. *J. Am. Chem. Soc.* **1984,** *106,* 4049–4050.
(b) Yang, W.; and Parr, R.G.; Hardness, softness, and the Fukui function in the electronic theory of metals and catalysis. *Proc. Natl. Acad. Sci.* USA. **1985,** *82,* 6723–6726.

61. Fuentealba, P.; Pérez, P.; and Contreras, R.; On the condensed Fukui function. *J. Chem. Phys.* **2000,** *113,* 2544–2551.
62. Garza, J.; and Robles, J.; Local hardness revisited: definition and the spin-polarized Kohn–Sham formulation of density functional theory. *Int. J. Quantum Chem.* **1994,** *49,* 159–169.
63. Harbola, M. K.; Chattaraj, P. K.; and Parr, R. G.; Aspects of softness and hardness concepts in density-functional theory. *Isr. J. Chem.* **1991,** *31,* 395–402.
64. Krishnamurty, S.; Roy, R. K.; Vetrivel, R.; Iwata, S.; and Pal, S.; The local hard–soft acid–base principle: a critical study. *J. Phys. Chem. A* **1997,** *101,* 7253–7257.
65. Chattaraj, P. K.; Roy, D. R.; Geerlings, P.; and Torrent-Sucarrat, M.; Local hardness: a critical account. *Theor. Chem. Acc.* **2007,** *118,* 923–930.
66. Ghosh, S.; and Berkowitz, M. A.; Classical fluid-like approach to the density-functional formalism of many-electron systems. *J. Chem. Phys.* **1985,** *83,* 2976–2983.
67. Li, Y.; and Evans, J. N. S.; The Fukui function: a key concept linking frontier molecular orbital theory and the hard-soft-acid-base principle. *J. Am. Chem. Soc.* **1995,** *117,* 7756–7759.
68. Chattaraj, P. K.; Chemical reactivity and selectivity: local HSAB principle versus frontier orbital theory. *J. Phys. Chem. A.* **2001,** *105,* 511–513.
69. Ayers, P. W.; Parr, R. G.; and Pearson, R. G.; Elucidating the hard/soft acid/base principle: a perspective based on half-reactions. *J. Chem. Phys.* **2006,** *124,* 194107(1–8).
70. Berkowitz, M.; and Parr, R. G.; Molecular hardness and softness, local hardness and softness, hardness and softness kernels, and relations among these quantities. *J. Chem. Phys.* **1988,** *88,* 2554–2557.
71. Ayers, P. W.; and Parr, R. G.; Variational principles for describing chemical reactions: the Fukui function and chemical hardness revisited. *J. Am. Chem. Soc.* **2000,** *122,* 2010–2018.
72. Nagy, A.; Hardness and excitation energy. *J. Chem. Sci.* **2005,** *117,* 437–440.
73. Ayers, P. W.; An elementary derivation of the hard/soft-acid/base principle. *J. Chem. Phys.* **2005,** *122,* 141102(1–3).
74. da Silva, R. R.; Santos, J. M.; Ramalho, T. C.; and Figueroa-Villar, J. D.; Concerning the FERMO concept and Pearson's hard and soft acid-base principle. *J. Braz. Chem. Soc.* **2006,** *17,* 223–226.
75. da Silva, R. R.; Ramalho, T. C.; Santos, J. M.; and Figueroa-Villar, J. D.; On the limits of highest-occupied molecular orbital driven reactions: the frontier effective-for-reaction molecular orbital concept. *J. Phys. Chem. A.* **2006,** *110,* 1031–1040.
76. Chattaraj, P. K.; Lee, H.; and Parr, R. G.; Principle of maximum hardness. *J. Am. Chem. Soc.* **1991,** *113,* 1854–1855.
77. Patra, G. K.; Hati, S.; and Dutta, D.; Proofs for Pearson's HSAB principle. *Ind. J. Chem.* **1999,** *38,* 1–3.

CHAPTER 2

MAGNETO HYDRODYNAMIC EFFECTS ON AN ATHEROSCLEROTIC ARTERY—A THEORETICAL STUDY

RATAN KUMAR BOSE

CONTENTS

2.1 INTRODUCTION

Among all the fatal diseases of the human body, circulatory disorders are still a major cause of death. The understanding of anatomy and physiology of an organic system depends much on the knowledge of blood flow through arteries. A systematic study on the rheological and hemodynamic properties of blood and blood flow could play a significant role in the basic understanding, diagnosis, and treatment of many cardiovascular, cerebrovascular, and arterial diseases. It is well known that stenosis (narrowing in the local lumen in the artery) is responsible for many cardiovascular diseases. When the degree of narrowing becomes significant enough to impede the flow of blood from the left ventricle to the arteries, heart diseases develop. Although the exact mechanism of the formation of stenosis in a conclusive manner remains somewhat unclear from the standpoint of physiology and pathology, the abnormal deposition of various substances such as cholesterol, fat on the endothelium of the arterial wall, and proliferation of connective tissues accelerates the growth of the disease. Plaques are thereby formed and lead to serious circulatory disorders. Plaque forms when cholesterol, fat, and other substances build up in the inner lining of the artery. This process is called *carotid circulatory disorders*. It greatly disturbs the normal blood flow leading to malfunction of the hemodynamic system (the flow of blood) and cardiovascular system. Carotid artery stenosis is a major risk factor for ischemic stroke (most common form of stroke usually caused by blood-clot plugging an artery).

The cause and development of many arterial diseases are related to the flow characteristics of blood and the mechanical behavior of the blood vessel walls. The abnormal and unnatural growth in the arterial wall thickness at various locations of the cardiovascular system is medically termed "Atherosclerosis." Its presence in one or more locations restricts the flow of blood through the lumen of the coronary arteries into the heart leading to cardiac ischemia. Once the constriction develops, it brings about significant alterations in the blood flow, pressure distribution, wall shear stress, and impedance (flow resistance). The fact that the hemodynamic factors play a commendable role in the genesis and growth of the disease has attracted many researchers to explore modern approach and sophisticated mathematical models for investigation on flow through stenotic arteries. To illuminate the effects of stenoses present in the arterial lumen, intensive experimental and numerical researches have been carried out worldwide for both normal and stenotic arteries. In most of the investigations relevant to the domain under discussion, the Newtonian behavior of blood (single-phase homogeneous viscous fluid) was accepted. This model of blood is acceptable for high shear rate in case of a flow through narrow arteries of diameter ≤1,000 μm; on the basis of the experimental observations, Bernett and Whitemore [1] suggested that blood behaves similar to a non-Newtonian fluid under certain conditions. H-B fluid model and Casson fluid models are used in the theoretical investigation of blood flow through narrow arteries. Investigations have mentioned that blood obeys H-B equation at low shear rates when flowing through a tube of diameter of 0.095 mm or less and represents fairly closely occurring flow of blood in arteries.

The laminar flow of blood in different arteries under certain conditions behaves like a visco-elastic fluid motion [2, 3]. Also, the blood flow affects the thermal response of living tissues, which depends on the geometric structure of artery (tapered artery) and flow variation of blood due to stenosis. It has been established that once a mild stenosis develops, the resulting flow disorder further influences the development of the disease and arterial deformity, and changes the regional blood rheology [3, 4]. Steady flow through an axi-symmetric stenosis has been investigated extensively by Smith using an analytical approach indicating that the flow patterns strongly depend on the geometry of the stenosis and the upstream Reynolds number (n) [5]. In recent years, some studies [6–10] have reported on the analysis of blood flow through single arteries in the presence of certain conditions [6–10]. Misra and Chakraborty [11] developed a mathematical model to study the unsteady flow of blood through arteries treating blood as a Newtonian viscous incompressible fluid paying due attention to the orthotropic material behavior of the wall tissues. The analysis explored the wall stress in the stenotic region and the shear stress at the stenotic throat. The tapered blood vessel segment having a stenosis in its lumen is modeled as a thin elastic tube with a circular cross-section containing a non-Newtonian incompressible fluid. Siddiqui et al. [12] presented a study of pulsatile flow of blood through stenosed artery by modeling blood as Herschel–Bulkley fluid with two parameters—the yield stress and the power index n. The variation of velocity with radial distance in different magnetic intensity, taking $n = 0.95$, is exhibited graphically. Also, the variation of wall shear stress and longitudinal impedance are shown taking different values of the parameters. Misra et al. [13, 14] presented a theoretical analysis of the problem of hematocrit reduction (due to plasma skimming) in a capillary emerging from the parent artery making an angle α with the parent artery. The study deals with both steady and pulsatile flow of blood treated as a non-Newtonian fluid of Herschel–Bulkley type. The study revealed that the velocity of blood in the parent artery reduces when the fluid index (n)/yield stress increases.

The same nature of variation was found for volumetric flow rate of blood in the capillary. Nanda and Basu Mallik [15] presented a theoretical study for the distribution of axial velocity for blood flow in a branch capillary emerging out of a parent artery at various locations of the branch. The results are computed for various values of r and the angle made by the branch capillary with the parent artery. Also, due attention was given to the variation of n (fluid index parameter). A theoretical estimate for the velocity of blood for various non-negative values of the fluid index parameter and the yield stress in different locations is presented. Mandal et al. [16] proposed that the most characteristic bio-magnetic fluid is blood, which behaves as a magnetic fluid, due to the complex interaction of the intercellular protein, cell membrane, and the hemoglobin, a form of iron oxides, which is present at a uniquely high concentration in the mature red blood cells, while its magnetic property is affected by factors such as the state of oxygenation. It is found that the erythrocytes orient with their disk plane parallel to the magnetic field and also that blood possesses the property of diamagnetic material when oxygenated and paramagnetic when deoxygenated. Abbas et al. [17] investigated two-dimensional magneto hydrodynamic (MHD) flow of upper convicted Maxwell fluid in a porous channel. Arterial wall shear stress is considered to be an important factor in the localization of atherosclerosis. A mathematical model to study the effect of porous parameter and height of stenosis on the wall shear stress has been studied by Misra and Verma [18]. A mathematical analysis of MHD flow of blood in very narrow capillaries in the presence of stenosis has been studied by Jain et al. [19]. It is assumed that the arterial segment is a cylindrical tube with time-dependent multistenosis. In the proposed investigation, an attempt will be made to deal with a problem, considering hemodynamic and cardiovascular disorders due to non-Newtonian flow of blood in multistenosed arteries. It gives us an opportunity to consider the problem of blood flow through a stenosed segment of an artery where the rheology of blood is described by Herschel–Bulkley fluid model. The dispensability of an arterial wall has been accounted for based on local fluid mechanics. Then an appropriate finite difference technique will be adopted to solve the unsteady non-Newtonian flow of blood with different boundary conditions in a cylindrical coordinate system. A quantitative analysis will be done based on numerical computations by taking the different values of material constants and other parameters. The variation of skin-friction with axial distance in the region of the stenosis is presented graphically with respect to externally applied magnetic field on stenosed arterial segment. The qualitative and quantitative changes in the skin-friction, shear stress, and volumetric flow rate at different stages of the growth of the stenosis have also been presented in presence of an applied magnetic field.

	Nomenclature		
τ	shear stress	z	axial coordinate
τ_H	yield stress	u	Axial average velocity of flow
τ_R	skin-friction	R_0	radius of the artery
M	Magnetization	$R(z)$	radius of the artery at stenosed portion
δ	stenosis height	L	length of the artery
λ	flow resistance	L_0	length of the stenosis
B	Applied Magnetic Field	p	pressure
Q	volumetric flow rate	k	viscosity coefficient
r	radial coordinate	n	fluid index

2.2   THE PROBLEM AND ITS SOLUTION

Consider the motion of blood following Herschel–Bulkley equation through an axially symmetric stenosed artery under the influence of an external applied uniform transverse magnetic field are shown in Figure 2.1 and Figure 2.2.

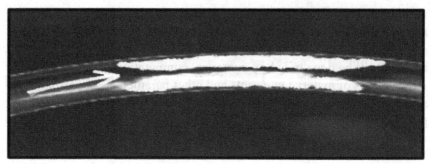

FIGURE 2.1   Atherosclerotic arteries.

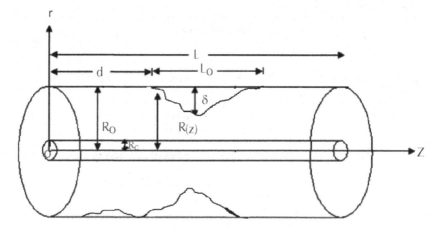

FIGURE 2.2   Considerable geometry of arterial stenosed segments and stenosis throat.

In such case, the radius of artery $R(z)$ can be written as

$$\overline{R}(z) = R_0\left[1 - A\left\{(\overline{l_0})^{(s-1)}(\overline{z} - \overline{d}) - (\overline{z} - \overline{d})^s\right\}\right], \text{ where } \overline{d} \leq \overline{z} \leq \overline{d} + \overline{l_0} \tag{1}$$

and radius of the artery is $R(z)$
= R_0; otherwise

where $A = \dfrac{\delta}{R_0 \overline{l_0}^s} \dfrac{s^{s/(s-1)}}{(s-1)}$

The Navier–Stoke equation is

$$-\frac{\partial \overline{p}}{\partial \overline{z}} + \frac{1}{r}\frac{\partial}{\partial r}(\overline{r}\overline{z}) + \mu_0 M \frac{\partial \overline{B}}{\partial \overline{z}} = 0 \tag{2}$$

Therefore, the constitutive equation according to Herschel–Bulkley fluid model

$$-\frac{\partial \overline{u}}{\partial \overline{r}} = \frac{1}{k}(\overline{\tau} - \overline{\tau_{H}})^{n} = f(\tau); \overline{\tau} \geq \overline{\tau_{H}}$$

$$k(-\frac{\partial \overline{u}}{\partial \overline{r}}) = (\overline{\tau} - \overline{\tau_{H}})^{n} = f(\tau); \overline{\tau} \geq \overline{\tau_{H}} \qquad (3)$$

$$and \frac{\partial \overline{u}}{\partial \overline{r}} = 0; \overline{\tau} \leq \overline{\tau_{H}}$$

Therefore, the boundary conditions pertaining to the problem

$$\overline{u} = 0 \text{ at } \overline{r} = \overline{R(z)} \qquad (4)$$

$$\overline{\tau} \text{ is finite at } \overline{r} = 0 \qquad (5)$$

And in the core region of artery $\overline{u} = \overline{u_{c}}$ and $\overline{r} = \overline{R_{c}}$, where $\overline{u_{c}}$ is the core velocity of blood.

Therefore, the nondimensional schemes are as follows:

$$r = \frac{\overline{r}}{R_{0}}, \quad z = \frac{\overline{z}}{l}, \quad R = \frac{\overline{R}}{R_{0}}, \quad p = \frac{\overline{p}}{\rho u_{0}^{2}}, \quad u = \frac{\overline{u}}{u_{0}}, \quad \tau = \frac{\overline{\tau}}{\rho u_{0}^{2}}, \quad d = \frac{\overline{d}}{l},$$

$$l_{0} = \frac{\overline{l_{0}}}{l}, \quad B = \frac{\overline{B}}{B_{0}} \qquad (6)$$

B_{0} is the external transverse uniform constant magnetic field; now the geometry is

$$R(z) = R_{0}\left[1 - A\left\{(l_{0})^{(s-1)}(z-d) - (z-d)^{s}\right\}\right]; \quad d \leq z \leq d + l_{0}$$

$$= 1; \text{ otherwise} \qquad (7)$$

where

$$A = \frac{\delta}{R_0 l_0^s} \frac{s^{s/(s-1)}}{(s-1)}$$

Now, Eqs. (2) and (3) reduce to

$$-\frac{\partial p}{\partial z} + \frac{1}{r}\frac{\partial}{\partial r}(r\tau) + (\frac{\mu_0 MB_0}{\rho u_0^2})\frac{\partial B}{\partial z} = 0 \qquad (8)$$

And $k(-\frac{\partial \bar{u}}{\partial \bar{r}}) = (\bar{\tau} - \bar{\tau_H})^n$ reduces in its non-dimensional form as

$$k(-\frac{\partial u}{\partial r})(\frac{u_0}{r_0}) = (\tau \rho u_0^2 - \tau_H \rho u_0^2)^n$$

$$(\tau - \tau_H)^n = \frac{k}{\rho^n u_0^{2n-1} R_0}(-\frac{\partial u}{\partial r}) \qquad (9)$$

Where considering $m_1 = (\frac{\mu_0 MB_0}{\rho u_0^2})$ and $m_2 = \frac{k}{\rho^n u_0^{2n-1} R_0}$

Now, the boundary conditions becomes

$u_0 = 0$ at $R(z) = r$ and τ is finite at $r = 0$

Again, from Eqs. (7) and (8)

$$-\frac{\partial p}{\partial z} + \frac{1}{r}\frac{\partial}{\partial r}(r\tau) + m_1 \frac{\partial B}{\partial z} = 0 \qquad (10)$$

$$(\tau - \tau_H)^n = m_2(-\frac{\partial u}{\partial r}) \qquad (11)$$

$$\frac{\partial u}{\partial r} = 0; \ \tau \leq \tau_H$$

We know that $\tau_R = -\dfrac{R}{2}\dfrac{\partial p}{\partial z}$ where $R = R(z)$

And the volumetric flow rate Q is given by the Rabinowitsch equation

$$Q = \frac{\pi R^3}{\tau_R^3}\int_0^{\tau_R}\tau^2 f(\tau)d\tau \tag{12}$$

where n is the fluid index parameter.

Now, substituting the values of $f(\tau)$ from Eq. (3) to Eq. (12),

$$Q = \frac{\pi R^3}{\tau_R^3}\int_0^{\tau_R}\tau^2 \frac{1}{k}(\tau - \tau_H)^n d\tau \tag{13}$$

(where n = fluid index parameter)

$$Q = \frac{\pi R^3 \tau_R^n}{k(n+3)}(1-\frac{\tau_H}{\tau_R})^{n+1}\left[1+(\frac{2}{n+2})\frac{\tau_H}{\tau_R}+\frac{2}{(n+1)(n+2)}(\frac{\tau_H}{\tau_R})^2\right] \tag{14}$$

When $(\frac{\tau_H}{\tau_R}) \leq 1$, the above equation reduces to

$$Q = \frac{\pi R^3}{k(n+3)}\left\{\tau_R - \left(\frac{n+3}{n+2}\right)\tau_H\right\}^n \tag{15}$$

Again, the boundary conditions (4) and (5) become

$$u = 0 \text{ at } R(z) = r \text{ and } \tau \text{ is finite at } r = 0 \tag{16}$$

Therefore, Eqs. (10) and (11) and the boundary condition (16) reduce to the velocity of blood

$$u = -\frac{1}{2^n m_2\left(\dfrac{\partial p}{\partial z}-m_1\dfrac{\partial B}{\partial z}\right)}\left[\left\{\left(\frac{\partial p}{\partial z}-m_1\frac{\partial B}{\partial z}\right)r-2\tau_H\right\}^{n+1}-\left\{\left(\frac{\partial p}{\partial z}-m_1\frac{\partial B}{\partial z}\right)R-2\tau_H\right\}^{n+1}\right] \tag{17}$$

The volumetric flow flux Q is thus calculated as

$$Q = 2\pi \int_0^{R(Z)} r u \, dr$$

$$Q = \pi \{R(z)\}^2 u \tag{18}$$

Therefore, Eqs. (17) and (18) reduces the form

$$Q = -\frac{\pi R^2}{2^n m_2 \left(\frac{\partial p}{\partial z} - m_1 \frac{\partial B}{\partial z}\right)} \left[\left\{ \left(\frac{\partial p}{\partial z} - m_1 \frac{\partial B}{\partial z}\right) r - 2\tau_H \right\}^{n+1} - \left\{ \left(\frac{\partial p}{\partial z} - m_1 \frac{\partial B}{\partial z}\right) R - 2\tau_H \right\}^{n+1} \right] \tag{19}$$

Again, Eqs. (15) and (19) reduces the form

$$Q = -\frac{\pi R^2}{2^n m_2 \left(\frac{\partial p}{\partial z} - m_1 \frac{\partial B}{\partial z}\right)} \left[\left\{ \left(\frac{\partial p}{\partial z} - m_1 \frac{\partial B}{\partial z}\right) r - 2\tau_H \right\}^{n+1} - \left\{ \left(\frac{\partial p}{\partial z} - m_1 \frac{\partial B}{\partial z}\right) R - 2\tau_H \right\}^{n+1} \right]$$

$$\tau_R = (-1)^{\frac{1}{n}} \frac{\{k(n+3)\}^{\frac{1}{n}}}{2\{Rm_2\left(\frac{\partial p}{\partial z} - m_1 \frac{\partial B}{\partial z}\right)\}^{\frac{1}{n}}} \left[\left\{ \left(\frac{\partial p}{\partial z} - m_1 \frac{\partial B}{\partial z}\right) r - 2\tau_H \right\}^{n+1} - \left\{ \left(\frac{\partial p}{\partial z} - m_1 \frac{\partial B}{\partial z}\right) R - 2\tau_H \right\}^{n+1} \right]^{\frac{1}{n}} + \left(\frac{n+3}{n+2}\right) \tau_H \tag{20}$$

Shear stress is considered as τ,

Thus,
$$\tau = -k \left(\frac{\partial u}{\partial r}\right)_{r=R} \tag{21}$$

where
$$k = \mu$$

Therefore,
$$\tau = -\mu \left(\frac{\partial u}{\partial r}\right)_{r=R} \tag{22}$$

Differentiating Eq. (17) with respect to r and substituting the value in Eq. (22) we obtain shear stress,

$$\tau = \mu \left\{ \frac{\partial}{\partial r} \left(\frac{1}{2^n m_2 \left(\frac{\partial p}{\partial z} - m_1 \frac{\partial B}{\partial z} \right)} \left[\left\{ \left(\frac{\partial p}{\partial z} - m_1 \frac{\partial B}{\partial z} \right) r - 2\tau_H \right\}^{n+1} - \left\{ \left(\frac{\partial p}{\partial z} - m_1 \frac{\partial B}{\partial z} \right) R - 2\tau_H \right\}^{n+1} \right] \right) \right\}$$

$$\tau = \left\{ \frac{\mu}{2^n m_2} \left\{ \left(\frac{\partial p}{\partial z} - m_1 \frac{\partial B}{\partial z} \right) R - 2\tau_H \right\}^n \right\}, \text{ since } r = R \qquad (23)$$

2.3 NUMERICAL RESULTS AND DISCUSSION

To have an estimate of the quantitative effects of the various parameters involved in the analysis, it is necessary to evaluate the analytical results obtained for dimensionless shear stress to flow, τ. It is based on area-axial average velocity of flow on constant tube diameter, where the constitutive coefficient index "n" for blood flow problems are generally taken to lie between 0.9 and 1.1 [20–21], and in this analysis, we have used the value 0.95 for $n < 1$ and stenosis height, $\frac{\delta}{R_0} = (0.1,0.2,0.3,0.4,0.5)$, velocity of blood $(u) = (0.5, 2.5, 4.5, 6.5, 8.5\,,)$, $\tau_H = 0.05$ then $k = 3$, when $\tau_H = 0.10$ then $k = 4$, because viscosity of blood at $37°C$ is $(3-4) \times 10^{-3}$ Pa.S. [22]. It is seen that the shear stress decreases as the velocity increases from 0.5 to 8.5 with respect to different increasing externally used magnetic intensity. Here, we have considered that the magnetic intensity assumed the values $B = (B_1 = 1.1 \times 10^4, B_2 = 2.1 \times 10^4, B_3 = 4.1 \times 10^4)$ [23–24] and $B_0 = 8$ tesla. Measurement has also been performed for the estimation of the magnetic susceptibility of blood, which was found to be 3.5×10^{-6} and -6.6×10^{-7} for the venous and arterial blood, respectively, considering the value of $M = -6.6 \times 10^{-7}$. [16] Due to velocity gradient, where independent predictor of hypertension improvement (odds ratio: 1.39; 95% confidence interval: 1.05–1.65; $p = 0.013$) is taken and therefore the severity of the stenosis significantly affects the shear stress characteristics [25]. Approximately considering the density of blood in stenosed artery is $\rho = 1$ (1.060 approx). It is also estimated in this study that the different increasing magnetic intensity and radial distance affect the volumetric flow rate of the nonsymmetric stenosed artery.

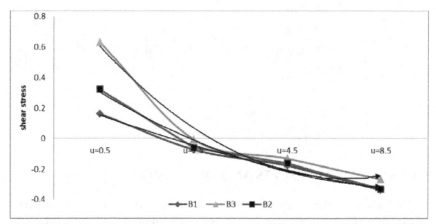

FIGURE 2.3 Variation of shear stress with respect to different increasing magnetic field intensity and flow velocity.

In above theoretical analysis in Figure 2.3, variation of shear stress with respect to different increasing magnetic field intensity and flow velocity is proposed, where we observe that an increasing magnetic field intensity decreases the shear stress of blood flow in a significant manner.

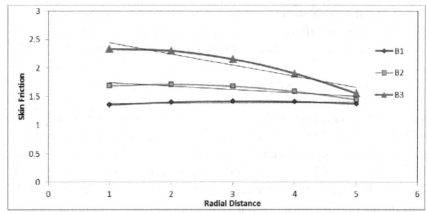

FIGURE 2.4 Variation of skin friction with respect to different increasing magnetic field intensity and radial distance of the stenosed artery.

And in Figure 2.4, variation of skin friction with respect to different increasing magnetic field intensity and radial distance of the stenosed artery is shown,

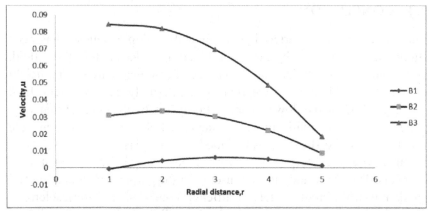

FIGURE 2.5   Variation of flow velocity of blood in stenosed artery with respect to different increasing magnetic field intensity and radial distance.

where Figure 2.5 denotes that increasing magnetic field intensity and radial distance affect the flow velocity of blood in an atherosclerotic artery enormously.

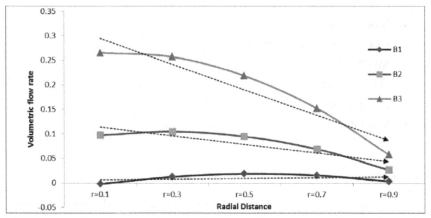

FIGURE 2.6   Variation of volumetric flow rate with respect to different increasing magnetic field intensity and radial distance of artery

Figure 2.6 shows that with respect to the different rheological parameters in Herschel–Bulkley fluid model, the different increasing magnetic field intensity and radial distance of artery affect the volumetric flow rate of blood in atherosclerosis significantly.

2.4   CONCLUSION

The blood flow in an arterial segment with multiple stenoses has been studied in this analysis by modeling blood as a Herschel–Bulkley fluid. The numerical simulation shows that the rheological parameters, height of stenosis, yield stress of the fluid, and externally used magnetic field strongly influence the flow characteristics qualitatively and quantitatively. Especially, the externally imposed magnetic field takes a commendable role to reduce the shear stress of blood with increasing flow velocity in an atherosclerotic artery. The flow of blood is sharper in the constricted channels. Thus, this study is more useful for the purpose of simulation and validation of different models in different conditions of arteriosclerosis. Thus, the model developed in this chapter will throw light on the clinical treatment of the obstruction of fluid movement due to the formulation of multiple stenoses in the arterial system and may reduce some of the major complications for the development of ischemia blood pressure, hypertension, and coronary thrombosis.

KEYWORDS

- **Blood flow**
- **Herschel Bulkely fluid model**
- **MHD effect**
- **Skin friction**
- **Shear stress**
- **Velocity**

REFERENCES

1. Whitmore, R. L.; Rheology of the Circulation. **xii +,** New York: Oxford Pergamon Press; **1968**.
2. Mondal, P. K.; An unsteady analysis of non-Newtonian blood flow through tapered arteries with a stenosis. *Int. J Non-Linear Mech.* **2005,** *40,* 151–164.
3. Nanda, S.; and Bose, R. K.; Mathematical analysis on blood flow through a flexible stenosed artery. *Int. J. Civil Mech. Eng.* **2012,** *2,* 17–30.
4. Walters, K.; Second Order Effects in Elasticity, Plasticity, and Fluid Dynamics. **xxii+.** New York: Oxford Pergamon Press; **1964**.
5. Smith, F.T.; The separation flow through a severely constricted symmetric tube. *J. Fluid Mech.* **1979,** *90,* 725–754.

6. Katiyar, V. K.; and Basavarajappa, K. S.; Blood flow in the cardiovascular system in the presence of magnetic field. *Int. J. Appl. Sci. Comput.* **2002,** *9,* 118–127.

7. Kinouchi, Y.; Yarnaguchi, H.; and Tenforde, T. S.; Theoretical analysis of magnetic field interactions with aortic blood flow. *J Bioelectromagnetics.* **1996,** *17,* 21–32.

8. Sud, V. K.; and Sekhon, G. S.; Blood flow through the human arterial system in the presence of a steady magnetic field. *Phys. Med. Biol,* **1989,** *34,* 795–805.

9. Tashtoush, B.; and Magableh, A.; Magnetic field effect on heat transfer and fluid flow characteristics of blood flow in multi-stenotic arteries. *Heat Mass Transfer.* **2008,** *44,* 297–304.

10. Tzirtzilakis, E. E.; A mathematical model for blood flow in magnetic field. *Phys. Fluids.* **2005,** *17,* 1–15.

11. Misra, J. C.; and Chakraborty, S.; Flow in arteries in the presence of stenosis. *J. Biomech.* **1986,** *19,* 907–918.

12. Siddiqui, S. U.; Mishra, S.; and Medhavi, A.; Blood flow through a composite stenosis in an artery with permeable wall. *Appl. Appl. Math.* **2011,** *6,* 1798–1813.

13. Misra, J. C.; Shit, G. C.; and Rath, H. G.; Flow and heat transfer of a MHD viscoelastic fluid in a channel with stretching walls: some applications to haemodynamics. *Comput. Fluids.* **2008,** *37,* 1–11.

14. Misra, J. C.; and Kar, B. K.; Momentum integral method for studying flow characteristics of blood through a stenosed vessel. *Biotechnol.* **1989,** *26,* 23–25.

15. BasuMallik, B.; and Nanda, S. P.; A non-Newtonian two-phase fluid model for blood flow through arteries under stenotic condition. *IJPBS.* **2012,** *2,* 237–247.

16. Mandal, P. K.; Ikbal, Md. A.; Chakravarty, S.; Wongb Kelvin, K. L.; and Mazumdar, J.; Unsteady response of non-Newtonian blood flow through a stenosed artery in magnetic field. *J. Comput. Appl. Math.* **2009,** *230,* 243–259.

17. Abbas, Z.; Sajid, M.; and Hayat, T.; Mhd boundary-layer flow of an upper-convected maxwell fluid in a porous channel. *Theor. Comput. Fluid Dyn.* **2006,** *20,* 229–238.

18. Mishra, B. K.; and Verma. N.; Effect of porous parameter and stenosis on the wall shear stress for the flow of blood in human body. *Res. J. Med. Med. Sci.* **2007,** *2,* 98–101.

19. Jain, M.; Sharma, G; and Singh, R.; Mathematical modeling of blood flow in a stenosed artery under mhd effect through porous medium. *Int. J. Eng.-Trans. B: Appl.* **2010,** *23,* 243–252.

20. Sankar, D. S.; Mathematical analysis of blood flow through stenosed arteries with body acceleration. January 28–29, 2010. *Nat. Conference Appl Math. (NCAM).* **2010.**

21. Sankar D. S.; and Lee, U.; Mathematical modeling of pulsatile flow of non-Newtonian fluid in stenosed arteries. *Commun. Non-Linear Sci. Numer. Simul.* **2009,** *14,* 2971–2981.

22. Nanda. S. P.; and Bose. R. K.; A mathematical model for blood flow through a narrow artery with multiple stenosis. *J. Appl. Math. Fluid Mech.* **2012,** *4,* 233–242.

23. Haik, Y.; Pai, V.; and Chen, C. J.; Biomagnetic Fluid Dynamics: Fluid Dynamics at Interfaces. Ed. Shyy, W.; Narayanan, R.; Cambridge: Cambridge University Press; **1999,** 439–452.

24. Motta, M.; Haik, Y.; Gandhari, A.; Chen, C. J.; High magnetic field effects on human deoxygenated hemoglobin light absorption. *Bioelectrochem. Bioenerg.* **1998,** *47,* 297–300.

25. Leesar, M. A.; et al., Prediction of hypertension improvement after stenting of renal artery stenosis: comparative accuracy of translational pressure gradients, intravascular ultrasound, and angiography. *J. Am. Coll. Cardiol.* **2009**, *53*, 2363–2371.

CHAPTER 3

A FAST SOLVER FOR THE BACKWARD HEAT CONDUCTION PROBLEM IN UNBOUNDED DOMAINS

RAFAEL G. CAMPOS and ADOLFO HUET

CONTENTS

3.1 INTRODUCTION

In technological and scientific applications related to heat transfer, it is often used to solve the inverse of the heat conduction problem: the so-called backward heat conduction problem (BHCP). This is also called retrospective heat conduction problem, and it is one of the cases in the general classification of inverse heat conduction problems [1]. It is the inverse of the initial boundary value problem for the heat equation; and for this reason, it is also called a final boundary value problem. This problem consists in finding the initial temperature distribution given the final distribution. It is an ill-posed problem since the solution does not have a continuous dependence on the data [2], and it may have no solution at all [3]. Besides this, it is a singular boundary value problem if the domain is unbounded as in the present case. Many methods of solving this problem in bounded domains can be found in the literature; regularization, mollification, and functional methods are popular techniques [4]. Some of these methods may be used together with additional special techniques to treat the case of unbounded domains [5–10].

In this chapter, we present a fast and easy-to-implement method for solving a BHCP in unbounded domains. This is a boundary element method that uses a new algorithm to compute the Fourier transform of quadratically integrable functions defined in R^n with no need of artificial boundary conditions imposed at the computational domain or regularized solutions that are frequently used; this algorithm is called extended Fourier transform (XFT) [11] and has complexity $O(N^m logN)$ in n dimensions when the same number of nodes N is taken for all dimensions. An accurate and weakly stable numerical solution of the BCHP in unbounded domains can be obtained by applying this algorithm, and the convolution theorem to the integral transform that gives the solution of the direct problem.

In Section 3.2, we first describe the basic tools by solving the BHCP in R^n. In Section 3.3, we restrict $n = 2, 3$ and give some examples of BCHPs. At the end of the section, we show how this technique can also be applied to other kind of inverse heat conduction problems.

3.2 THE PROBLEM AND SOLUTION

Consider the function $u(x, t)$ where $x \in \mathbb{R}^n$ and t is a real number. The inverse problem to solve is the following: given $f(x)$, find $u(x, 0)$ such that

$$\frac{\partial u(x,t)}{\partial t} = \alpha \nabla^2 u(x,t), \quad x \in \mathbb{R}^n, \quad 0 < t \le t_f$$

$$u(x,t_f) = f(x), \quad x \in \mathbb{R}^n, \tag{1}$$

where α is the thermal diffusivity or diffusion coefficient. Now, if $g(x)$ is a given bounded continuous function, the unique bounded solution of the direct problem, i.e., of the initial value problem:

$$\frac{\partial u(x,t)}{\partial t} = \alpha \nabla^2 u(x,t), \quad x \in \mathbb{R}^n, \quad t > 0$$

$$u(x,0) = g(x), \quad x \in \mathbb{R}^n \tag{2}$$

can be obtained by the using Green's functions [12, 13]

$$u(x,t) = \frac{1}{(4\pi\alpha t)^{n/2}} \int_{\mathbb{R}^n} e^{-\frac{\|x-y\|^2}{4\alpha t}} u(y,0) dy \tag{3}$$

The partial differential equation appearing in the inverse and direct problems is the same; however, these problems have some remarkable differences. In the direct problem, Eq. (2), a small change in the data always gives a small change in the solution. In the inverse problem, Eq. (1), this is not true.

The integral transform in Eq. (3) is known in the literature as Gauss or Weierstrass transform of the function $u(x, 0)$. Therefore, solving Eq. (1) is equivalent to find the inverse Gauss transform of Eq. (3). This can be done by using the Fourier transform and the convolution theorem. Taking into account that the Fourier transform of the kernel is

$$\int_{\mathbb{R}^n} e^{ik \cdot x} e^{\|x\|^2/4\alpha t} dx = (4\pi\alpha t)^{n/2} e^{-\alpha t \|k\|^2}$$

the convolution of Eq. (3) yields

$$U(k,0) = e^{\alpha t_f \|k\|^2} U(k,t), \tag{4}$$

where $U(k, t)$ is the Fourier transform of $u(x, t)$. Taking the inverse transform, we obtain the solution:

$$u(x,0) = \frac{1}{(2\pi)^n} \int_{\mathbb{R}^n} e^{-ik \cdot x} e^{\alpha t \|k\|^2} U(k,t) dk \tag{5}$$

of the final boundary problem (1), and the problem now is to obtain a reliable numerical approximation of $u(x,0)$.

3.2.1 NUMERICAL SOLUTION

To do this, we use the XFT, a new algorithm [11] based on the FFT for computing the Fourier transform:

$$U(k,t) = \int_{-\infty}^{\infty} e^{ik \cdot x} u(x,t) dx$$

where t is a parameter (time in this case). According to this,

1. consider the points $x_j = \frac{\pi}{2}\sqrt{2N}(2j - N - 1)$ of the real line measured in any system of units and compute the vector v according to the following relation:

$$v_i(t) = e^{-i\pi N - \frac{1}{N^j}} u_j(t), \ j = 1, 2, \ldots, N.$$

Here, the vector $u(t) = (u_1(t), u_2(t), \ldots, u_N(t))^T$ is considered to be formed with the values of the temperature $u(x, t)$ at the nodes x_j, that is, $u_j(t) = u(x_j, t)$.
2. Consider the points $\kappa_m = (\pi / 2\sqrt{2N})(2m - N - 1)$ measured in the system of units such that the product $x_j \kappa_m$ is dimensionless.
3. Then, the XFT gives an approximation [A scaled function by $a = 4/\pi$ is denoted by $\tilde{f}(y,t)$ i.e., $\tilde{f}(y,t) = f(ay,t)$ .Therefore, $\tilde{U}_J(t)$ denotes the approximation to $U(a\kappa_j,t)]\tilde{U}(t) = (\tilde{U}_1(t), \tilde{U}_2(t), \ldots, \tilde{U}_x(t))^T$ to the Fourier transform $U(k, t)$ evaluated at the points $a\kappa_j$ $(a = 4/\pi)$ according to the following relation:

$$\tilde{U}_J(t) = \frac{\pi}{\sqrt{2N}} e^{i\pi\left(\frac{(N-1)^2}{2N} - \frac{N-1}{N}(j-1)\right)} fft\left(v(t)\right)_j, \quad j = 1,2,\ldots,N$$

where $fft(v(t))$ stands for the output of any standard FFT algorithm applied to the vector $v(t)$.

Instead of approximating at the scaled points $a\kappa_j$, it is better in some cases to approximate just at the nodes κ_j. This can be done by scaling the function $u(x, t)$ to yield $\tilde{u}(x,t) = u(ax, t)$ and

$$U(k/a,\, t) = a \int_{-\infty}^{\infty} e^{ik \cdot x} \tilde{u}(x,t)\, dx$$

Since the XFT gives a scaled approximation, we have that

$$U(\kappa_j, t) \cong U_j(t) = a\, xft_1 \left[\tilde{u} \lim_{x \to \infty}(t) \right]_j, \quad j = 1,2,\ldots,N,$$

where $xft_1\left[\tilde{u}(t)\right]$ stands for the output of the one-dimensional XFT applied to $\tilde{u}(t)$. For the inverse transform, we have a similar result

$$u_j(t) = a\, ixft_1[U(t)]_j, \quad j = 1,2,\ldots,N, \tag{6}$$

where now $ixft_1\left[\tilde{U}(t)\right]$ stands for the output of the inverse XFT applied to $\tilde{U}(t)$.

This algorithm is based on the approximation of a square-integrable function by a linear combination of discrete Hermite functions [11]. Because of this, it gives accurate results for the computation of the Fourier transform of rapidly decreasing functions evaluated at the nodes κ_j.

The generalization of these results to more dimensions can be done straightforward, and the approximated and scaled version of Eq. (4) is found to be the vector of N^n components

$$\tilde{U}_q(0) = (e^{at\|a\kappa\|^2} \tilde{U}(t))_q,$$

ordered according to the following equation:

$$q = j_1 + (j_2 - 1) N + ... + (j_n - 1) N^{n-1}, \quad j_m = 1, 2, ..., N. \tag{7}$$

Here, $e^{\alpha t \, \|a \, \kappa\|^2}$ stands for the $N^n \times N^n$ diagonal matrix whose diagonal elements are given by the following equation:

$$e^{\alpha t \, a^2 \, (\kappa_{j_1}^2 + \kappa_{j_2}^2 + ... + \kappa_{j_n}^2)} \tag{8}$$

For simplicity, we have taken the same number of nodes N for all dimensions. Taking this and Eq. (6) into account, the numerical solution of the BHCP Eq. (1) is given by the following equation:

$$u_q (0) = a^n ixft_n \left[e^{\alpha t} a \kappa^2 \, xft_n \left[u(t) \right] \right]_q , \tag{9}$$

Where $xft_n[\cdot]$ and $ixft_n[\cdot]$ stand for the n-dimensional version of the XFT algorithm and its inverse, respectively.

3.2.2   STABILITY

Note that the ill-posedness nature of the discrete BHCP comes from the exponential term in Eq. (9), which becomes greater as the backward time t, N, or n are increased. Therefore, to compute a large time t, the number of nodes should be relatively small, according to the given number of dimensions n. In addition, note that for a given α, the product αt and the machine numerical precision define a characteristic backward time beyond which the method is unable to give a result.

Let F be the matrix associated to the n-dimensional XFT algorithm and F^{-1} its inverse. Then, F and F^{-1} can be written as the Kronecker product of the one-dimensional XFT matrices F_k:

$$F = F_n \bigotimes \, ... \otimes F_2 \otimes F_1, \quad F^{-1} = F_n^{-1} \bigotimes \, ... \otimes F_2^{-1} \otimes F_1^{-1} .$$

Therefore, the solution (9) can be written in matrix form as follows:

$$u(0) = a^n F^{-1} E F u(t), \tag{10}$$

where E is the diagonal matrix defined by Eq. (8), and the present solution is weakly stable since

$$| u(0) \leq Cu(t) ,$$

where C is a positive constant depending on N, n, α, and t, such that $\lim_{N\to\infty} C = \infty$. This is the condition of weak stability given in Eq. (1).

3.3 RESULTS

We test the numerical solution (9) in this section. To show the performance of this procedure, we take $n = 2$, 3 and three problems with known solution. The solution for the first one is a Dirac delta function; the second example consists of a homogeneous temperature distribution (which happens to be a nonsquare-integrable function); and for the third example, we use a volcano-shaped radially symmetric distribution with a nontrivial peak. In each of these examples, we use $\alpha = 0.0002$ m²/s, which corresponds to the thermal diffusivity of Helium. We also take the same number of nodes N for all dimensions.

In the following examples, the exact values of $u(x, 0)$ are known. Thus, in order to measure the error of our method, we define $\mathcal{E}_{\zeta_m}$ as the maximum absolute value of the differences between the exact and approximated initial values on the plane $x_3 = \zeta_m$, that is,

$$\mathcal{E}_{\zeta_m} = \max_{j,k} \left| u\left(\xi_j, \eta_k, \zeta_m, 0\right) - u_q(0) \right| , \tag{11}$$

where q is the index associated to (j, k, m) through Eq. (7) and ξ_j and η_k are nodes on the directions x_2 and x_3, respectively.

3.3.1 A DIRAC DELTA DISTRIBUTION

In this example, we take $x \in \mathbb{R}^2$ and a final temperature given by the following equation:

$$u(x,t) = \frac{1}{4\pi\alpha t} e^{-x^2/4\alpha t} , \tag{12}$$

so that the initial temperature is the distribution $u(x, 0) = \delta(x)$. The exact final temperature and approximate solution of the inverse problem (1) obtained by Eq. (9) at the time $t = 700$ s for this case, is given in Figures (3.1) and (3.2).

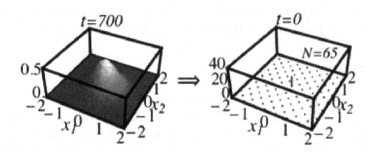

FIGURE 3.1   Numerical approximation of $u(x, 0) = \delta(x_1, x_2)$ obtained by Eq. (9) for the final function (12) at $t = 700$ s with $N = 65$. The values of $u(x_1, x_2, 700)$ and the corresponding approximated values $u_q(0)$ are given on the vertical axes of the left-hand and right-hand side figures, respectively.

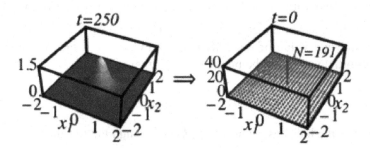

FIGURE 3.2   Numerical approximation of $u(x, 0) = \delta(x_1, x_2)$ obtained by Eq. (9) for the final function (12) at $t = 250$ s with $N = 191$. The values of $u(x_1, x_2, 250)$ and the corresponding approximated values $u_q(0)$ are given on the vertical axes of the left-hand and right-hand side figures, respectively.

In order to compute a solution for a long time, the value of N should be relatively small; for example, for $N = 65$, the attainable backward time is about 700 s. Beyond this value, the method is unable to render good results. Note that in this example, the number of nodes is odd. This is necessary to seize the nature of $\delta(x)$ because the origin is contained in the nodes for N odd.

3.3.2 A UNIFORM DISTRIBUTION

We now take $u(x, t) = 1$ for $x \in \mathbb{R}^3$. Therefore, the solution of the inverse problem (1) is $u(x, 0) = 1$. In other words, an initial uniform distribution of temperature will be maintained the same at any future time. The numerical solution of the inverse problem (1) for this case, obtained by Eq. (9) at the time $t = 1,000$ s, is given in Figure (3.3). We display the numerical results only on the x_3-planes: $x_3 = 0.0$ and $x_3 = 6.1$. For the displayed data on Figure (3.3), we have $E0.0 \doteq E6.1 = 10^{-11}$. Here, $x_3 = 6.1$ corresponds to the boundary upper z-plane.

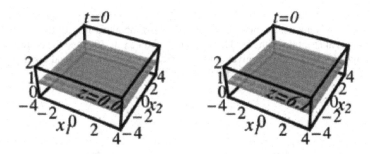

FIGURE 3.3   Numerical approximation of $u(x_1, x_2, z, 0) = 1$ for $z = 0.0$ and $z = 6.1$ obtained by Eq. (9) with the final function $u(x, t) = 1$ at $t = 1,000$ s with $N = 33$. The values of the approximated values $u_q(0)$ are given on the vertical axis. The error for this case is 10^{-11}.

3.3.3 A RADIAL DISTRIBUTION

As a third example, consider the distribution

$$u(x,t) = \frac{x_1^2 + x_2^2 + x_3^2 + 6\alpha t \ (1+4\alpha t)}{(1+4\alpha t)^{7/2}} e^{-(x_1^2 + x_2^2 + x_3^2)/(1+4\alpha t)} , \tag{13}$$

which has the solution

$$u(x,0) = \left(x_1^2 + x_2^2 + x_3^2\right) e^{-(x_1^2 + x_2^2 + x_3^2)} \tag{14}$$

The numerical solution obtained with $N = 33$ is displayed on Figures (3.4) and (3.5). Here, we take the planes $z = 0.0$ and $z = 0.7$, respectively. The resulting errors are $E_{0.0} = E_{0.77} = 10^{-7}$.

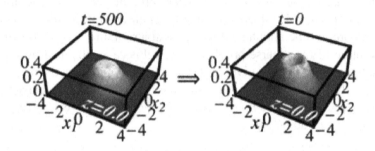

FIGURE 3.4 Numerical approximation of Eq. (14), obtained by Eq. (9) for the final function (13) at $t = 500$ s with $N = 33$. The values of $u(x_1, x_2, 0, 500)$ and the corresponding approximated values $u_q(0)$ are given on the vertical axes of the left-hand and right-hand side figures, respectively. The error for this case is 10^{-7}.

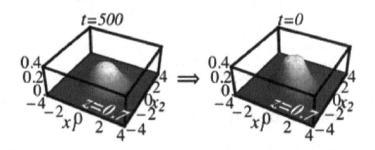

FIGURE 3.5 Numerical approximation of Eq. (14), obtained by Eq. (9) for the final function (13) at $t = 500$ s with $N = 33$. The values of $u(x_1, x_2, 0.7, 500)$ and the corresponding approximated values $u_q(0)$ are given on the vertical axes of the left-hand and right-hand side figures, respectively. The error for this case is 10^{-7}.

3.3.4 BOUNDED DOMAINS

In this subsection, we illustrate with an example how a slight modification of the present method can help in solving inverse heat conduction problems in bounded domains. Considerthefollowingone-dimensional problem in $(0, \ell)$, $\ell > 0$:

- Find the heat flux $\varphi(t)$ at the boundary $x = 0$, where there is a heat source, when the temperature $u_\ell(t)$ at $x = \ell$ is given and the initial condition is zero.

- Boundary element methods have been used in [14] for solving this problem with a discontinuous function $\varphi(t)$; thus, this example can also be used for benchmarking the performance of the present method against others. The temperature $u_\ell(t)$ and the flux $\varphi(t)$ are related by (see [14] for details)

$$u_\ell(t) = \frac{\int_0^t e^{-\ell^2/4(t-\tau)}}{\sqrt{\pi(t-\tau)}} \phi(\tau)d\tau = \int_{-\infty}^{\infty} g(t-\tau)q(\tau)d\tau, \qquad (15)$$

where $g(t) = e^{-\ell^2/4t} H(t)/\sqrt{\pi t}$, $q(t) = \varphi(t)H(t)$, and $H(t)$ is the Heaviside function. Therefore, convolving Eq. (15), we obtain the analog of Eq. (5):

$$q(t) = \frac{1}{2\pi} \int_{-\infty}^{\infty} e^{-i\omega t} U_a(\omega)/G(\omega)d\omega,$$

where $U_a(\omega)$ and $G(\omega)$ are the Fourier transforms of $u_\ell(t)$ and $g(t)$, respectively. Therefore, the numerical solution of this problem is

$$q_k = a \, ixft_1[xft_1[u_\ell(t)]/xft_1[g(t)]]_k \qquad (16)$$

which is the analog of Eq. (9). In this example, we take as data the temperature $u_\ell(t)$ obtained by a numerical integration of Eq. (15) where the function $\varphi(t)$ is known a priori and given by

$$\phi(t) = \begin{cases} 1, & t_1 \leq t \leq t_2, \quad t_3 \leq t \leq t_4 \\ 0, & otherwise \end{cases},$$

where $t_1 = 0.2$, $t_2 = 0.7$, $t_3 = 1$, and $t_4 = 1.5$. We take $\ell = 1/3$. In Figure (3.6), the numerical results are compared with the exact solution and a plot of the error $|q(t_k) - q_k|$ is given.

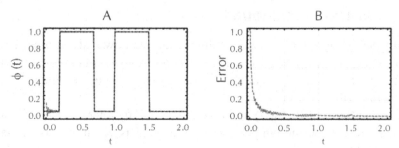

FIGURE 3.6   (A) Numerical solution for the heat flux as given by Eq. (15). The exact function (solid lines) is compared with the output of Eq. (16) with $N = 215$ (dashed lines). The boundary points are $x = 0$ and $x = 1/3$. (B) Plot of the error $|q(t_k) - q_k|$.

3.4   CONCLUSION

The present technique yields accurate numerical results whenever the Fourier transform can be applied to solve a particular problem. For instance, the standard Cauchy problem for the heat equation given in Eq. (2) can be solved by using this technique for a large number of values of t and α with numerical stability, and the inhomogeneous heat equation can be attempted to be solved in the same way with an extra dimension for the time integral corresponding to the inhomogeneous term. However, this is not the case for the inverse problem (1) since, as noted earlier, the exponential term in Eq. (9) becomes greater as the backward time t, N, or n are increased. A similar situation occurs in the last example of the previous section since $1/G(\omega) = \sqrt{\omega} \exp\left(\ell\sqrt{2|\omega|}\right)$ becomes greater as ℓ or N is increased. Therefore, in the cases where these parameters are large, the method is unable to give a result.

KEYWORDS

- **Boundary element method**
- **Fast Fourier transform**
- **Gauss transform**
- **Heat equation**
- **Inverse problems**
- **XFT**

ACKNOWLEDGMENT

This work was partially supported by ConsejoNacional de Ciencia y Tecnología, project 99006-CB-2008-01.

REFERENCES

1. Alifanov, O. M.; Inverse Heat Conduction Problems. Berlin: Springer-Verlag; **1994**.
2. Lavrent'ev, M. M.; Romanov, V. G.; and Shishatskii, S. P.; Ill-Posed Problems of Mathematical Physics and Analysis. Translations of Mathematical Monographs.American Mathematical Society USA; **1986,***64*.
3. Sobolev, S. L.; Partial Differential Equations of Mathematical Physics. New York: Dover Publications, Inc.; **1989**.
4. Hao, D. N.; and Gorenflo, R.; A noncharacteristiccauchy problem for the heat equation. *Acta Appl. Math.***1991,***24*, 1–27. DOI: 10.1007/BF00047360
5. Fu, Ch.; Xiong, X.; and Qian, Z.; Fourier regularization for a backward heat equation. *J. Math. Anal. Appl.* **2007,***331*, 472–480.
6. Xiong, X.; Fu, Ch.; and Gao, X.; Error estimates of a difference approximation method for a backward heat conduction problem. *Internat. J. Math. Math. Sci.* ID 45489, **2006,** 1–9. DOI 10.1155/IJMMS/2006/45489
7. Kirkup, S. M.; and Wadsworth, M.; Solution of inverse diffusion problems by operator-splitting methods. *Appl. Math. Modelling.***2002,***26*, 1003–1018.
8. Dang, D. T.; and Tran, N. L.; Regularization of a discrete backward problem using coefficients of truncated Lagrange polynomials. *Elect. J. Diff. Eq.* **2007**, *51*, 1–14.
9. Hao, D. N.; A mollification method for ill-posed problems. *Numer.Math.***1994,***68*, 469–506.
10. Showalter, R. E.; The final value problem for evolution equations. *J. Math. Anal. Appl.* **1974,***47*, 563–572.
11. Campos, R. G; Rico–Melgoza, J.; and Chávez, E.; A new formulation of the fast fractional Fourier transform. *SIAM J. Sci. Comput.***2012,***34*, A1110–A1125.
12. Morse, P. M.; and Feshbach, H.; Methods of Theoretical Physics. New York: McGraw-Hill Inc.; **1953,***1*.
13. John, F.; Partial differential equations. Applied Mathematical Sciences. Springer-Verlag: New York, Inc.; **1982,***1*.
14. Shen, S. Y.; A numerical study of inverse heat conduction problems. *Comp. Math. Appl.* **1999,***38*, 173–188.

CHAPTER 4

STEGANOGRAPHIC METHOD FOR COLOR IMAGES USING VARIANCE FIELD ESTIMATION AND SCALING FACTOR FOR ENERGY CONSERVATION

BLANCA E. CARVAJAL-GÁMEZ, FRANCISCO J. GALLEGOS-FUNES, and J. LÓPEZ-BONILLA

CONTENTS

4.1 INTRODUCTION

Steganography involves the secret data communications in an appropriate multimedia carrier (i.e. audio, image, and video files), under the assumption that if the secret data is visible, the point of attack is evident [1, 3]; thus, the goal here is to conceal the existence of the embedded data. In the case of image files, a steganographic method employs innocent-looking media called host or cover image to imperceptibly carry hidden data to an intended recipient [1–3]. The image embedded with the hidden data (i.e., secret data, copyright notice, and serial number) is called the stego-image and it looks as a normal image. The steganalysis techniques detect the existence of secret data in digital media, and these techniques are designed to distinguish between the cover and stego-images [4, 5].

Steganographic techniques can be classified into spatial, frequency, and adaptive methods [1]. The *spatial methods* generally use a technique to replace the direct least significant bit (LSB) substituting a redundant part of a cover image with a secret message. The *methods based in frequency domain*, such as the Fourier transform (FT), the discrete cosine transform (DCT), and the discrete wavelet transform (DWT) embed secret information in the frequency domain of a cover image. These methods hide messages in significant areas of the cover image which makes them more robust to attacks, such as compression, cropping, and some image processing, than the LSB approach [1]. Recently, there exist methods such as perceptual masking (PM) or adaptive steganography (AS), which can be applied in the spatial or frequency domain [1].

In this chapter, we present a wavelet steganographic scheme. The proposed method is capable of preventing visual degradation and providing a large embedding capacity. A wavelet domain preprocessing step is introduced before applying the proposed scheme to improve the steganography security [6, 7]. The embedding capacity for each pixel is determined by the local complexity of the cover image, allowing good visual quality as well as embedding a large amount of secret messages. These pixels are classified using a threshold based on the standard deviation of the local complexity of the cover image [7, 8]. Experimental results demonstrated that the proposed steganographic algorithm produces insignificant visual distortion because of the hidden message and provides high embedding capacity superior to that offered by the existing schemes. The proposed method is a secure steganographic algorithm due it can resist the image quality measure (IQM) steganalysis attack [4, 5, 8, 9]. Different color spaces are incorporated in the proposed scheme (i.e., RGB, YCbCr, and HSV) to ensure that the visual artifacts appeared in the stego-image are imperceptible, and the differences between the cover and the stego-image are indistinguishable by the human visual system (HVS) [10, 11].

4.2 MATERIALS AND METHODS

4.2.1 DISCRETE WAVELET TRANSFORM AND THE SCALING FACTOR FOR ENERGY ADJUSTMENT

Wavelets provide a mathematical flexible tool for practical problems in science and engineering. One of the principal properties of the wavelets is that they allow modeling better processes that depend strongly on the time and whose behavior does not have for what to be smoothing. DWT is particularly effective for extracting information from nonperiodical signals of finite life and it is closely linked to the analysis of multiresolution (MRA), that is, see the signals at different frequencies [12], which allows to have a broader knowledge of the signal and facilitates the rapid calculation when the wavelet family is orthogonal [13–16].

It can be obtained wavelets $\left\{ \psi_{j,n}(t) = \frac{1}{\sqrt{2^j}} \psi\left(\frac{t - 2^j n}{2^j} \right) \right\}_{j,n \in \mathbb{Z}^2}$ such that the family moved for j and dilated for n, it is a orthonormal basis of $L^2(\mathbb{R})$. The orthogonal wavelets transport information about the changes of the signal to the resolution 2^{-j}. Then, the MRA appears: an image is modeled with orthogonal projections on vector space of different resolution, $P_{V_j} f, V_j \subset L^2(\mathbb{R})$. The quantity of information in every projection depends on the size of Vj. For search orthogonal wavelets, it will be necessary to work with approaches of MRA [13, 14, 15, 17, 18]. For a function $f \in L^2(\mathbb{R})$, the partial sum of the coefficients wavelet $\sum_{n=-\infty}^{\infty} < f, \psi_{j,n}$ can be interpreted as the difference between two approaches of f for the resolutions 2^{-1+j} and 2^{-j}. The MRA approaches calculate the approach of signals to different resolutions with orthogonal projections in spaces $\left\{ V_j \right\}_{j \in \mathbb{Z}}$. The approach of a function of a resolution 2^{-j} is defined as an orthogonal projection in a space V_j $L^2(\mathbb{R})$. The space Vj regroups all the possible approaches to the resolution 2^{-j}. The orthogonal projection of f is the function $f_j \in V_j$ that minimizes $\|f - f_j\|$. The orthonormal wavelets carry the necessary details to increase the resolution of the approach of the signal. The approaches of f for the scales 2^j and 2^{j-1} are respectively equal for its orthogonal projections V_j and V_{j-1} with V_j and V_{j-1}. Be W_j the orthogonal complement of V_j in V_{j-1}. The orthogonal projection of f in V_{j-1} can be written as the sum of orthogonal projections P in V_j and W_j. Then, $P_{V_{j-1}} f = P_{V_j} + P_{W_j}$. The function $f(t) = A \sum_j^n \sum W_f(j,n) \psi_{j,n}(t)$ can be reconstructed from the discrete wavelets coefficients $W_f(j,n)$, where j is the scaling factor and n is the movement factor [13, 14, 15, 17, 18].

The wavelets $\psi_{j,n}(t)$ generated of the same wavelet mother function $\psi(t)$ have different scale j and place n, but they have the same form. Scale factor $j > 0$ is always used. The wavelet is dilated when the scale $j > 1$, and it is contracted when $j < 1$. This way, changing the value of j the different range from frequencies is covered. Big values of the parameter j correspond to frequencies of minor range, or a big scale of $\psi_{j,n}(t)$. Small values of j correspond to frequencies of minor range or a very small scale of $\theta_{j,n}(t)$ [13– 18]. The continuous wavelet functions with discrete factors of scale and movement are named discrete wavelets. Finally, the signal $f(t)$ can be compressed or expand in the time, this will have a few certain after effects in the plane of frequencies,

$$f(t) \text{ compression by a factor } 2^j \ (s) f_s(t) = \frac{1}{\sqrt{2^j}} f\left(\frac{t}{s}\right)$$

$$\hat{f}(w) \text{ compression by a factor } \frac{1}{2^j} \hat{f}_{2^j}(w) = \frac{1}{\sqrt{2^j}} 2^j \hat{f}(2^j w) = \sqrt{2^j} \hat{f}(2^j w) \tag{1}$$

The coefficient of the decomposition of a function f in an orthogonal base of wavelets is calculated by a subsequent algorithm of discrete convolution with h and g, and realizes a sampling of the low-pass filter (LPF) $x_{low}[k] = \sum_n x[n]h[2k-n]$ and the high-pass filter (HPF) $x_{high}[k] = \sum_n x[n]g[2k-n]$, where $g[2k-n]$ and $h[2k-n]$ are the impulse responses of HPF and LPF, respectively, subsampled by a factor of 2 [17–20]. These coefficients are calculated by cascades of discrete filters through of convolution and sampling.

DWT decomposes a discrete signal into two subsignals of half of the original length. This subsignal is known as the approaches and the other one is known as the details [19]. The first subsignal $a^1 = (a_1, a_2, \cdots, a_{m/2})$, for the signal x is obtained making the average of the signal as follows: the first value a_1 is calculated by taking the first set of values vector $x[m]: (x_1 + x_2)/2$ and multiplying it by $\sqrt{2}$, that is, $a_1 = (x_1 + x_2)/\sqrt{2}$, similarly $a_2 = (x_3 + x_4)/\sqrt{2}$, and so on. In a general form, it is given by $a_{m/2} = x_{2m-1} + x_{2m}/\sqrt{2}$, where m is the vector size [19]. The other subsignal is known as the first fluctuation of the signal x and it is denoted as: $d^1 = (d_1, d_2, \cdots, d_{m/2})$ and is calculated by taking the difference between the first pair of values of x, $(x_1 - x_2)/2$ and then is multiplied and divided by $\sqrt{2}$, and so on. The final expression can be written as $d_{m/2} = x_{2m-1} - x_{2m}/\sqrt{2}$.

After applying the DWT two vectors are obtained, which are *approximations* and *details*, with a length of half the original vector. Finally, continuing the recovery of the vector,

$$f[n] = \left\{ \frac{a_1 + d_1}{\sqrt{2}}, \frac{a_1 - d_1}{\sqrt{2}}, \cdots, \frac{a_{n/2} + d_{n/2}}{\sqrt{2}}, \frac{a_{n/2} - d_{n/2}}{\sqrt{2}} \right\} \qquad (2)$$

We note that the terms a_1 and d_1 in Eqs. (6) and (7) can be interpreted as follows $\varepsilon_{(a^1|d^1)} = a_1 + \cdots + a_{n/2} + d_1 + \cdots + d_{n/2}$,

$$a_1 + d_1 = \left[\frac{f_1 + f_2}{\sqrt{2}} \right]^2 + \left[\frac{f_1 - f_2}{\sqrt{2}} \right]^2 = \frac{f_1^2 + 2f_1 f_2 + f_2^2}{2} + \frac{f_1^2 - 2f_1 f_2 + f_2^2}{2} = f_1^2 + f_2^2 \qquad (3)$$

and similarly for each set of vectorial *approaches* and *details* [19]. So, the conservation of energy in wavelets is mentioned, the factor $1/\sqrt{2}$ is mentioned too [20, 21]. By applying the steganographic algorithm, it is necessary to use a scaling factor, but as the work is with an 8-bit RGB image, this scaling factor is closely related to energy conservation applied to wavelet theory for grayscale images as shown in most applications. However, for any space color we propose the following scaling factor [21],

$$1/\sqrt{2^j} \qquad (4)$$

where j is directly dependent on the number of bits that integrate the image [20, 21].

The most common approach of the wavelet decomposition is to decompose an image to extract energy values for all subbands as features for the subsequent classification [21]. It is suitable to select a set of subbands for sparse representation in image classification applications. For a better classification of the results, it is desired that the energy features correspond to the areas of the selected subbands independent from each other as possible [21].

4.2.2 PROPOSED STEGANOGRAPHIC METHOD

The proposed color local complexity-estimation-based steganographic (CLCES) method is described in this section. Figure (4.1) presents the block diagram of the steps used in the proposed method [8].

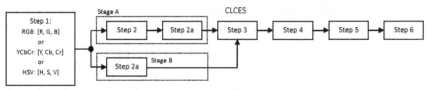

FIGURE 4.1   Block diagram of the proposed CLCES method.

Step 1: Input the cover color image We investigate the features of the red, green, blue, (RGB); hue, saturation, value, (HSV); and luminance, chromatic blue, chromatic red (YCbCr) color spaces in the proposed algorithms to ensure that the visual artifacts appeared in the stego-images are imperceptible, and the differences between the cover and the stego-images are indistinguishable by the HVS [10, 11]. Given a RGB cover color image, the HSV and YCbCr transformations are computed [22]. Then, from each color space, we separate its color components in an independent way and we apply in each component of the cover color image the next steps of the proposed methods.

Stage A: This stage improves the steganographic security and increases the embedding capacity using the Step 2 [8]. The Step 2a is used to hide data.

Step 2: Cover image preprocessing The preprocessing imposes more variation in pixel intensities of cover images compared to the original ones. It has been proved in Reference [6] that the stego-images which carried out the hiding of secret data in the cover images with more variation in their pixel intensities are less detectable by the statistical steganalysis increasing the embedding capacity [8]. Let propose a preprocessing step in the wavelet domain using the advantages of the wavelet decomposition [8]. The first-level Haar DWT and a redundancy of the approaches algorithm are used [7, 23–25]. The preprocessing step is applied in the sub-band LH of the cover image using a redundancy of the approaches algorithm. This algorithm is used because it is easy to implement, reduces the computational cost, and provides good filtering results [7, 23–25]. The sub-band LH is chosen because it provides the information of the edges and the details of the cover image which are good locations to hide the data and besides with the preprocessing step there are more variations in the pixel intensities, increasing the embedding capacity and improving the steganography security.

Step 2a: Apply second-level Daubechies db4 DWT This step is used to hide data. Let us use the subband LH obtained from the wavelet coefficients of the subband LL from the second decomposition of the resulting image of the step 2. The decomposition level and the Daubechies db4 are selected according with the extensive experimental results realized with different wavelet families under objective criteria [8, 26–29].

Stage B: This stage allows having more hiding capacity in the proposed method because it provides more decomposition levels to hide information [8].

Step 2a: Apply second-level Daubechies db4 DWT This step is the same as discussed earlier.

The next steps are applied in both outputs of the stages A and B providing more hiding capacity [8].

Step 3: Standard deviation computation The embedding capacity for each pixel is determined by the local complexity of the cover color image providing a good visual quality as well as embedding a large amount of secret messages [6]. From the wavelet decomposition, let us use the standard deviation $\sigma_k = \sqrt{\sum_{m=1}^{n}(x_m - \bar{x})^2 / n}$ of the subband LH obtained from the wavelet coefficients from the subband LL of the second decomposition of the cover color image using a 3 × 3 kernel, where x_m is an element of the current kernel k, $\bar{x} = \sum_{m=1}^{n} x_m / n$ is the mean value of current kernel, and $n = 9$ is the number of elements in the sample [8, 27, 30].

Step 4: Threshold computation The pixels are classified using a threshold based on the local complexity of the standard deviation in the cover image. The threshold $T = \sum_s (\alpha_s \cdot 2^{-s}) / \sum_s 2^{-s}$ is used to select the pixels whose values are considered as places to hide data [31, 32], where T denotes a threshold value for discriminating signal-dominant scales from the noise dominant ones, s is the level or scale used in the wavelet analysis ($s = 1$ and $s = 2$ for Haar and db4 wavelets, respectively), $\alpha_s = \sigma_k$ is the standard deviation of the current wavelet coefficient kernel in the s level, and 2^{-s} is the weighting function [8, 25, 31].

Step 5: Robust criterion to hide data The image quality of the processed images is improved using a criterion based on the median estimator. The condition $\beta_{sx} \geq T$ is applied for each kernel of the standard deviation $\alpha_s = \sigma_k$, if this condition is satisfied then this area or region is considered noisy and thus can be inserted the information to hide in the respective wavelet kernel coefficients H_k of the cover color image [8],

$$S_k = \begin{cases} D_k, & \beta_{sx} \geq T \\ H_k, & \text{otherwise} \end{cases} \tag{5}$$

where $\beta_{s1} = |\sigma_c - \text{MED}(\alpha_s)|$ and $\beta_{s2} = \text{MED}(\alpha_s)$ are the two robust criteria to hide data [26, 27], $\text{MED}(\alpha_s)$ is the median of the wavelet kernel coefficients α_s, and σ_c is the standard deviation located at the center of the kernel α_s. We propose the use of median as a robust estimation of the energy [21, 32] of the wavelet kernel coefficients given by its local standard deviation. These procedures improve the features of the proposed method to provide good invisibility, color retention, and fine detailed preservation of the processed images [8].

To recover the hidden image, the algorithm is used again but in the step 1 the input changes from the cover color image to the stego-image, and to repeat the same steps changing the conditions of the step 5 to recover the hidden data in the following way [8],

$$D_k = \begin{cases} S_k & \alpha_s < T \\ H_k & \text{otherwise} \end{cases} \tag{6}$$

$$D_k = \begin{cases} S_k, & \beta_x \geq T \\ H_k, & \text{otherwise} \end{cases} \tag{7}$$

Other versions of the CLCES algorithm are given using a threshold based on the median of the standard deviations in the current wavelet kernel coefficient in the level s changing the threshold of

$$T = \sum_s \left(\alpha_s \cdot 2^{-s} \right) \Big/ \sum_s 2^{-s} \quad \text{to} \quad T_1 = \text{MED}\{\alpha_s\} \tag{[8].}$$

Step 6: Inverse discrete wavelet transform (IDWT) computation We obtain the resulted stego-image applying the IDWT to the wavelet coefficients of the stego-image (Figure 4.1).

4.3 RESULTS AND DISCUSSION

The purpose of this research is to propose a simple steganographic algorithm implementation, with little resource consumption on mobile devices, where the results were qualitative, quantitative, and highly acceptable steganalysis. The purpose of steganography is to insert hidden information on a digital file, thus achieving high resource utilization. We present the results better PSNR, MAE, CC, and Q for a scaling factor when $j = 9$. Through analysis of steganalysis is determined the probability of detection of hidden information exceeds 95 percent, higher than results reported in classical literature.

The proposed CLCES method is evaluated [8], and its performance is compared with the LSB [33] steganographic method. We also adapt the LSB method [33] to work in the wavelet domain using the second-level Daubechies db4 DWT to compare our proposal, in here this method is named as WLSB. The image quality of various schemes is compared in terms of the peak signal-to-noise ratio (PSNR); the mean absolute error (MAE); the normalized color difference (NCD); the cross-correlation (CC); the quality index (Q); and the hiding capacity (HC) criteria [1, 4, 5, 7, 25, 33, 34, 35].

In our experiments, we use the 320 × 320 color images "Lena" and "Mandrill," and we present the results of several steganographic methods for the RGB, HSV, and YCbCr color spaces. The performance results for the stego-image "Mandrill" (the secret image "Lena") and the retrieved secret image "Lena" are shown in Tables (4.1) and (4.2), respectively.

TABLE 4.1 Performance results for the stego-image "Mandrill" with the secret image "Lena"

Algorithms	Criteria for the RGB color space					
	PSNR dB	MAE	CC	Q	NCD	HC (Kb)
LSB	34.5602	3.5758	0.9978	0.9977	7.3506e-4	1.9199e3
WLSB	28.8347	8.8469	0.9977	0.9963	0.0053	0.8352e3
CLCES (βs_1)	38.2650	1.4503	0.9983	0.9984	2.5473e-4	1.9183e3

CLCES (βs_2)	38.5287	1.4417	0.9984	0.9985	2.3584e-4	1.8698e3
C L C E S (T_1, β_{s1})	38.9540	1.3910	0.9985	0.9986	2.3017e-4	1.7980e3
C L C E S $(T_1, \beta s_2)$	38.4697	1.4478	0.9984	0.9984	2.4352e-4	1.8804e3
Criteria for the YCbCr color space						
LSB	28.0065	7.1783	0.9889	0.9886	0.0081	1.9859e3
WLSB	26.0195	7.3820	0.9885	0.9883	0.0086	0.8277e3
CLCES (βs_1)	28.2348	4.3867	0.9857	0.9866	9.5800e-4	7.1724e3
CLCES (βs_2)	28.5554	4.4563	0.9870	0.9878	0.0013	6.7308e3
C L C E S (T_1, β_{s1})	28.2612	4.4212	0.9858	0.9867	0.0013	7.1355e3
C L C E S $(T_1, \beta s_2)$	28.1469	4.3067	0.9853	0.9862	0.0012	7.2982e3
Criteria for the HSV color space						
LSB	26.0193	4.2270	0.9795	0.9801	0.0071	1.1578
WLSB	26.0155	4.2287	0.9795	0.9801	0.0073	0.7553
CLCES (βs_1)	26.5489	4.1678	0.9831	0.9830	0.0072	5.2464
CLCES (βs_2)	25.8352	4.4367	0.9803	0.9803	0.0079	5.0933
C L C E S (T_1, β_{s1})	26.6850	4.1304	0.9833	0.9833	0.0071	5.1190
C L C E S $(T_1, \beta s_2)$	26.0651	4.2298	0.9810	0.9815	0.0077	**5.2505**

TABLE 4.2 Performance results for the retrieved secret image "Lena"

Algorithms	Criteria for the RGB color space				
	PSNR dB	**MAE**	**CC**	**Q**	**NCD**
LSB	36.1233	2.7714	0.9955	0.9962	0.00200
WLSB	31.2219	5.0316	0.9954	0.9954	0.00330
CLCES (βs_1)	36.1233	2.7714	0.9955	0.9962	0.00200

TABLE 4.2 *(Continued)*

Algorithms	Criteria for the RGB color space				
	PSNR dB	**MAE**	**CC**	**Q**	**NCD**
CLCES (βs_2)	36.1233	2.7714	0.9955	0.9962	0.00200
CLCES ($T_1,\beta s_1$)	36.1233	2.7714	0.9955	0.9962	0.00200
CLCES ($T_1,\beta s_2$)	36.1233	2.7714	0.9955	0.9962	0.00200
Criteria for the YCbCr color space					
LSB	36.0827	2.7948	0.9954	0.9962	0.00200
WLSB	36.0821	2.7948	0.9954	0.9962	0.00200
CLCES (βs_1)	36.0827	2.7948	0.9954	0.9962	0.00200
CLCES (βs_2)	36.0827	2.7948	0.9954	0.9962	0.00201
CLCES ($T_1,\beta s_1$)	36.0827	2.7948	0.9954	0.9962	0.00200
CLCES ($T_1,\beta s_2$)	36.0827	2.7948	0.9954	0.9962	0.00200
Criteria for the HSV color space					
LSB	36.1222	2.7740	0.9954	0.9962	0.00200
WLSB	36.1222	2.7790	0.9954	0.9962	0.00200
CLCES (βs_1)	36.1201	2.7730	0.9951	0.9959	**7.8233e-4**
CLCES (βs_2)	36.1201	2.7730	0.9951	0.9959	**7.8233e-4**
CLCES ($T_1,\beta s_1$)	36.1201	2.7730	0.9951	0.9959	**7.8233e-4**
CLCES ($T_1,\beta s_2$)	36.1201	2.7730	0.9951	0.9959	**7.8233e-4**

From the experimental results from Tables (4.1) and (4.2), we depict in the Figure (4.2) the subjective visual results (zoom parts) using the RGB color space. We observe from the error stego-images that the proposed method provides less distortion in comparison with the LSB method. In the case of retrieved secret error images, the proposed methods provide similar subjective visual results and in some cases (see the NCD of Table 4.2) the proposed method outperforms the comparative methods. We can see that the images produced with the proposed CLCES methods appear to have a very good subjective quality [8].

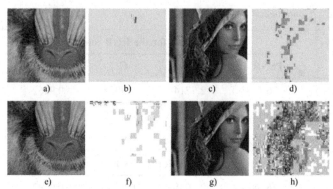

FIGURE 4.2 Subjective visual results for the stego-image "Mandrill" with the secret image "Lena" showing the stego-image, the error stego-image, the retrieved secret image, and the retrieved error secret image from the left to the right for each method. Row 1: (a)–(d) using LSB, Row 2: (e)–(h) CLCES(T_1, βs_1).

By applying the proposed scaling scheme, an improvement in visual images [21] can be seen. In the case of different j values in the scaling factor using the same images "Mandrill" [12] as cover image and "Lena" [12] as hide image, in Table (4.3), one can see when the j value increases the performance results increase too.

TABLE 4.3 Performance results for different values of j with cover image "Mandrill" and hidden image "Lena"

Proposed method		PSNR db	CC	NCD	Q	MAE
$j = 0$	Cover image	31.5084	78.52	—	0.7836	10.4878
	Recovered image	16.5327	38.80	0.4748	0.3586	4.9403
$j = 2$	Cover image	31.4999	80.46	—	0.8040	9.9490
	Recovered image	16.9537	38.89	0.4749	0.3587	4.9471
$j = 5$	Cover image	36.1233	97.81	0.0020	0.9792	3.2086
	Recovered image	27.2474	99.85	0.0020	0.9962	2.7714
$j = 9$	Cover image	36.1233	99.08	8.015e-4	0.9913	2.0309
	Recovered image	31.0781	99.80	0.0020	0.9962	2.7714
$j = 10$	Cover image	36.1233	99.34	6.0486e-4	0.9934	1.7022
	Recovered image	32.5167	99.55	0.0020	0.9962	2.7714

Figure (4.3) depicts the processed images for stego-image "Mandrill" (Figures 4.3(a), (b), and (c)) and retrieved secret image "Lena" (Figures 4.3(d), (e), and (f)) according to Table (4.3). We observe from Figures 4.3(c) and (f) that the best results are obtained when $j = 9$, where j represents the number of bits resolution of the image to hide. It is observed that when j is gradually increased, the quality image is significantly improved. From Figure 4.3(d–f), one can see that when the value of proposed scaling factor increases the subjective quality of images increases too, it is observed that Figures 4.3(a–c) have in the upper part a certain lineal distortion, which can be interpreted as external information inserted to the cover image. As j takes the value of 10 or 24 of this lineal distortion in the top of the stego-image not easily identified visually. We also present the wrong images.

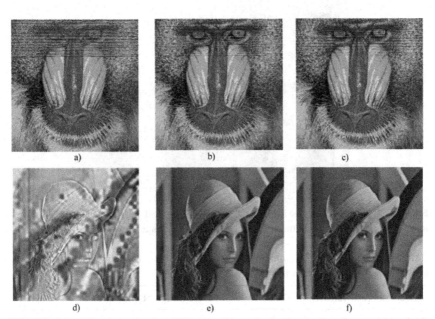

FIGURE 4.3 Visual results for different values of j in the scaling factor, (a) and (d) column with $j = 2$, (b) and (e) column with $j = 5$, and (c) and (f) $j = 9$.

More tests were performed to increase the value of j to $j = 24$, where amount is determined by the image type here manipulated. Those significant changes of stego-image and the recovered image are observed. Figure (4.4) presents the visual results for $j = 10$. The proposed scaling factor

$1/\sqrt{2^j}$ for each test presents a different result as can be seen in the previous tests, the scaling factor does not affect the steganographic algorithm and preserving the energy of images [21]. It can be seen in the Lena error image of Figure 4.4(d), the difference in values between the host image and the recovered image is approximately zero. The results shown in Table (4.4) using the scaling factor $j = 24$, we can that these are superior to those shown in Table (4.4). Being the best method LSB with PSNR equal to 34.5602 dB thing which is exceeded by the second PSNR of 36.7973 dB with $j = 24$ [21].

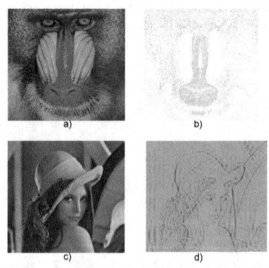

FIGURE 4.4   Visual results in the case of $j = 10$, (a) host image "Mandrill," (b) error image "Mandrill," (c) hide image "Lena", and (d) error image "Lena".

TABLE 4.4   Performance results in the case of $j = 24$ in the scaling factor with cover image "Mandrill" and hidden image "Lena".

Cover image "Mandrill"	Hide image "Lena"
$Q = 0.9968$	$Q = 0.9962$
PSNR = 36.7973 dB	PSNR = 36.1232 dB
CC = 99.67%	CC = 99.56%
NCD = 5.7204 e-4	NCD = 19.735e-4
MAE = 1.4721	MAE = 2.7714

We realize experiments of steganalysis attack to measure the robustness capabilities of several steganographic algorithms using the well-known image quality measures (IQM) steganalysis [4, 5, 8, 9]. The IQM steganalysis technique provides good results across all steganographic algorithms (i.e., spread-spectrum, quantization modulation, LSB, etc.) [4, 5, 8, 9]. In this technique, it has been observed that filtering an image without embedded data causes changes in the IQMs less than the changes brought about on embedded images [8, 13]. The IQMs used to compare different methods are the mean square error (MSE), the Czekanowski distance (CD), the angular correlation (AC), the image fidelity (IF), the normalized cross-correlation (NCC), the spectral magnitude distortion (SMD), the median of block spectral phase (MBSP), the median of weighted block spectral distortion (MWBSD), and the normalized mean square HVS error (NMSHVSE) [4, 8, 9]. We obtain the performance of different steganographic algorithms, using the condition IQMcover $\geq$ IQMstego means that the image contains the hidden data, otherwise, it does not [8].

Table (4.5) shows the total detection of the hidden data using the results of IQMs steganalysis for the cover image "Mandrill" and its filtered version and the stego-image "Mandrill" with the secret image "Lena" and its filtered version [8]. Comparing the steganalysis results with the image quality of the stego-images and the hiding capacity of the methods, we comment that the proposed CLCES methods [8] outperform other methods by balancing the image quality and the embedding capacity providing a better security against attacks of steganalyzers in comparison with the other methods [8].

TABLE 4.5 Total detection of the hidden data using the image quality measures (IQM) steganalysis

Algorithms	stego-image "Mandrill" (secret image "Lena")		
	RGB	**YCbCr**	**HSV**
LSB	4/9	2/9	4/9
WLSB	4/9	3/9	5/9
CLCES (βs_1)	3/9	3/9	2/9
CLCES (βs_2)	3/9	3/9	2/9
CLCES ($T_1, \beta s_1$)	3/9	2/9	2/9
CLCES ($T_1, \beta s_2$)	3/9	2/9	2/9

4.4 CONCLUSION

By applying the proposed scaling factor $1/\sqrt{2^j}$ in a color image, there is an adjustment factor for the energy input in each submatrix. It is also noted that when is changing the value of j, it adjusts the sharpness and image clarity, providing a visible improvement of the visual image.

The CLCES method uses thresholds based on the standard deviation of the local complexity of the cover image to provide a compromise between the embedding capacity and the image visual quality. Different color spaces are incorporated in the proposed schemes to ensure that the differences between the cover and stego-images are indistinguishable by the HVS. The proposed CLCES method is a secure steganographic method outperforming other methods by balancing the image quality and the embedding capacity providing a better security against attacks of steganalyzers in comparison with other methods. Finally, the proposed scheme is simple, efficient, and feasible for the adaptive steganographic applications.

ACKNOWLEDGMENTS

The work is supported by National Polytechnic Institute of Mexico (IPN), and National Council on Science and Technology (CONACYT) Mexico.

KEYWORDS

- **Discrete wavelet transform**
- **Scaling factor**
- **Steganographic**
- **Stegoanalysis**

REFERENCES

1. Cheddad, A.; Condell, J.; Curran, K.; and Mc Kevitt, P.; Digital image steganography: Survey and analysis of current methods. *Signal Processing*. **2010,** *90,* 727–752.
2. Petitcolas, F. A. P.; Anderson, R. J.; and Kuhn, M. G.; Information hiding—a survey. *Proc. IEEE*. **1999,** *87(7),* 1062–1078.
3. Petticolas, F.; and Katzenbeisser, S.; Information Hiding Techniques for Steganography and Digital Watermarking. Boston: Artech House; **2000.**

4. Luo, X. Y.; Wang, D. S.; Wang, P.; and Liu, F. L.; A review on blind detection for image steganography . *Signal Processing*. **2008**, *88*, 2138–2157.
5. Kharrazi, M.; Sencar, H.T.; and Memon, N.; Performance study of common image steganography and steganalysis techniques. *J. Electronic Imaging*. **2006**, *15(4)*, 1–16.
6. Sajedi, H.; and Jamzad, M.; BSS: Boosted steganography scheme with cover image preprocessing. *Expert Systems Appl*. **2010**, *37*, 7703–7710.
7. Gallegos-Funes, F. J.; Martinez–Valdés, J.; and De-la-Rosa-Vázquez, J. M.; Order statistics filters in wavelet domain for color image processing. *IEEE Sixth Mexican Int. Conf. Artif Intelligence*. **2007**, *MICAI2007*, 121–130.
8. Carvajal–Gamez, B. E.; Gallegos–Funes, F. J.; and Rosales–Silva, A. J. Color local complexity estimation based steganographic (CLCES) method. *Expert Systems Appl*. **2013**, *40*, 1132–1142.
9. Avcibas, I.; Mmon, N.; and Sankur, B.; Steganalysis using image quality metrics. *IEEE Trans. Image Process*. **2003**, *12(2)*, 221–229.
10. Cheddad, A.; Condell, J.; Curran, K.; and Mc Kevitt, P.; Biometric inspired digital image steganography. 15th IEEE Int. Conf. and Workshop on the Engineering of Computer Based Systems, ECBS2008. Belfast: Northern Ireland; **2008**, 159–168.
11. Liu, K. C.; Wavelet-based watermarking for color images through visual masking. *Int. J. Electron. Commun. (AEÜ)*. **2010**, *64*, 112–124.
12. Vetterli, M.; and Kočević, J.; Wavelets and Sub-Band Coding. 2th Edn. Prentice-Hall: New Jersey; **1995**.
13. Petrosian, A.; and Meyers, F.; Wavelets in Signal and Image Analysis. Computational Imaging and Vision. Springer: Berlin; **2002**.
14. Debnath, L.; Wavelets and Signal Processing. Birkhauser: Berlin; **2002**.
15. Sheng, Y.; The Transforms and Applications Handbook. 2th Edn. CRC Press: London; **2002**.
16. Bogges, A.; and Narcovich, F.; A First Course in Wavelets With Fourier Analysis. 2th Edn. Wiley: New York; **2009**.
17. Daubechies, I.; Orthornormal bases of compactly supported wavelets. *Commun. Pure Appl. Math*. **1988**, *41*, 909–996.
18. Mallat, S.; A theory for multiresolution signal decomposition: the wavelet representation. *IEEE Trans. Pattern Anal. Mach Int*. **1989**, *11(7)*, 674–694.
19. Walker, J.; A Primer on Wavelets and their Scientific Applications. 2th edition. London: Chapman and Hall/CRC; **2003**.
20. Carvajal–Gámez, B. E.; Gallegos–Funes, F. J.; López–Bonilla, J. L.; Computational Techniques and Algorithms for Image Processing. Ed. Berlin: Lambert Academic Publication; Chapter 13, **2010**.
21. Carvajal–Gámez, B. E.; Gallegos–Funes, F. J.; Rosales–Silva, A. J.; and López–Bonilla, J.; Adjust of energy with compactly supported orthogonal wavelet for steganographic algorithms using the scaling function. *Int. J. Phys. Sci*. **2013**, *8(4)*, 157–166.
22. Alata, O.; and Quintard, L.; Is there a best color space for color image characterization or representation based on multivariate Gaussian mixture model? *Comput Vis. Image Und*. **2009**, *113*, 867–877.
23. De Queiroz, R. L.; Reversible color-to-gray mapping using sub-band domain texturization. *Pattern Recognit. Lett*. **2010**, *31*, 269–276.

24. Ashwin, A. C.; Ramakrishnan, K. R.; and Srinivasan, S. H.; Wavelet domain residual redundancy based descriptions. *Signal Proc: Image Commun.* **2003**, *18,* 549–560.

25. Gallegos–Funes, F. J.; Carvajal–Gamez, B. E.; Lopez–Bonilla, J. L.; and Ponomaryov, V. I.; Steganographic method based on wavelets and center weighted median filter. *IEEE Int. Kharkov Symposium on Physics and Engineering of Microwaves, Millimeter, and Submillimeter Waves, MSMW2010.* Kharkov: Ukraine; **2010.**

26. Maheswaran, R.; and Khosa, R.; Comparative study of different wavelets for hydrologic forecasting. *Comput. Geosci.* doi.org/10.1016/j.cageo.2011.12.015 **2012.**

27. Huang, K.; and Aviyente, S.; Information-theoretic wavelet packet sub-band selection for texture classification. *Signal Proc.* **2006,** *86,* 1410–1420.

28. Lo, S. C. B.; Li, H.; and Freedman, M. T.; Optimization of wavelet decomposition for image compression and feature preservation. *IEEE Trans. Med. Imag.* **2003,** *22(9),* 1141–1151.

29. Nafornita, C.; and Isar, A.; On the choice of the mother wavelet for perceptual data hiding. *Int. Symp. Signals. Circuits Systems. ISSCS.* **2009,** 1–4.

30. Cheddad, A.; Condell, J.; Curran, K.; and Mc Kevitt, P.; Biometric inspired digital image steganography. *15th IEEE Int. Conf. Workshop Eng Comput Based Syst. ECBS2008.* **2008,** 159–168.

31. Gallegos–Funes, F. J.; Martinez–Valdes, J.; and De-la-Rosa-Vazquez, J. M.; Order statistics filters in wavelet domain for color image processing. *IEEE Sixth Mexican Int. Conf. Artif Int.* **2007,** *MICAI2007,* 121–130.

32. Carvajal–Gamez, B. E.; Gallegos–Funes, F. J.; and Lopez–Bonilla, J.; Energy adjustment RGB images in steganography applications. 52nd IEEE International Midwest Symposium Circuits and Systems. Mexico: Cancun; **2009,** 758–761.

33. Chan, C. K.; and Cheng, L. M.; Hiding data in images by simple LSB substitution. *Pattern Recognit.* **2004,** *37,* 469–474.

34. Gallegos–Funes, F. J.; Rosales–Silva, A. J.; and Toledo–Lopez, A.; Multichannel image processing by using the rank M-type L-filter. *J. Visual Commun. Image Representat.* **2012,** *23(2),* 323–330.

35. Yu, Y. H.; Chang, C. C.; and Lin, I. C.; A new steganographic method for color and grayscale image hiding. *Comput. Vis. Image Und.* **2007,** *107,* 183–194.

CHAPTER 5

OVERVIEW OF QUANTUM COMPUTATION

HERNANDO EFRAIN CAICEDO-ORTIZ,
and ELIZABETH SANTIAGO-CORTES

CONTENTS

5.1   INTRODUCTION

Computation and quantum information [1] are an extension of the information process concept, and they are used for the effects of quantum mechanic [2]. This new scheme provides a work scene that is not restricted to only two operations; on the contrary, this can gain multiple intermediate states as a result of these two ways of superposition. By performing this operation, the system can evaluate all possibilities in only one step by making a parallel computation; meanwhile, in the classic way, this evaluation is carried out independently of each other, and in different steps. The quantum parallelism can be defined as a reduction in time and an increase in the fast of information process. In this chapter, the fundamental elements that make possible to use the mechanical-quantum phenomena as a tool in the process information are presented.

5.2   THE QUBIT

As in the classical computational systems in which the lowest amount of information unit is the bit, in the quantum computation theory this element has its counterpart, known as quantum bit or qubit [1, 3]. Even when this entity is described as a mathematical object that has certain specific properties, it also has a physical reality, which is represented by a two-way quantum system, but in which every management is entirely abstract, giving freedom in order to generate a computation general theory and information that does not depend on the physical system needed for its performance. By considering these types of systems as minimum information units is necessary to implement the mathematical formalism of quantum mechanics in order to gain a description correct. Although many plots to describe the stages in a quantum system are available, the most adequate and brief is the "Dirac notation" [4], which has turned into a standard in modern physics [1, 3, 5–8]. In this model, a quantum stage is represented by a vector, which is named "ket" ($|\ \rangle$), and all the operations are carried out through operators that are lineal transformations that act on the ket.

The two basic possible stages for a qubit are $|0\rangle$ and $|1\rangle$ and are equal in analogy to the 0 and 1 in a classical bit. The potential of this scheme is based on that qubit can take a different value than the other two mentioned, due to the lineal combination of the stages, whereby a qubit in its most general way is represented by

$$|\psi\rangle = a_0|0\rangle + a_1|1\rangle, \tag{1}$$

where a_0 and a_1 are complex numbers that satisfy the normalization relation $|a_0|^2 + |a_1|^2 = 1$ and the kets $|0\rangle$ and $|1\rangle$ are represented by the column vectors

$$|0\rangle = \begin{pmatrix} 1 \\ 0 \end{pmatrix} \qquad |1\rangle = \begin{pmatrix} 0 \\ 1 \end{pmatrix} \tag{2}$$

The ability of a quantum system for simultaneously coexisting inside a mix of all stages is known as "Superposition Principle" [1, 3, 6–8], which is a feature absolutely quantum. Meanwhile, in a classical system, a bit has concrete information, which one can access without disturbing; the qubit always provides a probabilistic answer only for those cases when $a_0 = 0$ and $a_1 = 0$: the state of the system with no changes.

Now, considering a situation where there is more than one qubit, namely a quantum memory registration. In this case, the space of the states results in the associated spaces to every qubit. If they are represents by L_1^2 and L_2^2 with n and m dimensions, respectively, the new vector space is $L_{12}^2 = L_1^2 \; L_2^2$ with dimension nm; this at the same time is the number of elements of the base. Taking the particular case of a quantum register with two qubits (2-qubits), whose dimension of space is $2^2 = 4$; its natural base is built of two vectors. The qubit $|\psi\rangle$ is described according to the coherent superposition

$$|\psi\rangle = a_{00}|00\rangle + a_{01}|01\rangle + a_{10}|10\rangle + a_{11}|11\rangle, \tag{3}$$

where a_{ij} is a complex number. For a system with n qubits, the base is formed by 2^n elements of accessible states. In a general way, taking every one of the base's elements through ket $|x\rangle$ with $x = 0,1,2,3,...,2^n - 1$, the qubit can be represented as follows:

$$|\psi\rangle = \sum_{x=0}^{2^n-1} a_x|x\rangle. \tag{4}$$

This is how in the quantum state, which is described by Eqs. (1) and (4), not only a probabilistic combination of every state exists, but also the interference and entanglement effects are incorporated; these allow a massive processing of information that finally is traduced into an exponential increase in calculus speed regarding classical devices.

5.3 UNITARY OPERATORS

Consider the behavior of static quantum systems, namely, systems that do not change or evolve to another state with time, but do so when an external factor strikes them. Its dynamic is described by the Schrödinger equation and changes are because of external factors, expressed by lineal transformations or operators represented by a square matrix; these can be taken state by state through a way that preserves the orthogonality of unitary operators or unitary transformations [1], the only mathematical elements that fulfill these requirements. For a set of n quantum systems of 2 states, the operator acting on this is a matrix with dimension $2^n \times 2^n$. For example, for a set of two quantum systems in which an operator acts,

$$\begin{pmatrix} \alpha & \beta \\ \chi & \eta \end{pmatrix} \begin{pmatrix} a_0 \\ a_1 \end{pmatrix} = \begin{pmatrix} \alpha a_0 + \beta a_1 \\ \chi a_0 + \eta a_1 \end{pmatrix} \tag{5}$$

where $\hat{U} = \begin{pmatrix} \alpha & \beta \\ \chi & \eta \end{pmatrix}$ is the evolution operator, which is unitary. These kinds of operators play an important role in the quantum computation area, because of opening the possibility to create reversible information procedure schemes.

5.4 QUANTUM MEASUREMENTS

Unlike measurements performed on macroscopic elements whose processes give an absolute amount, in microscopic systems, the measurement process of its states generates probabilities to find it in certain settings. As soon as the measurement was performed, quantum mechanical predicts that the system evolves to a different normalized state. To organize and emphasize these ideas is necessary, remembering Eq. (4) with its natural base $|\psi\rangle = a_{00}|00\rangle + a_{01}|01\rangle + a_{10}|10\rangle + a_{11}|11\rangle$. Suppose we want to measure the system in certain state $|\phi_n^m\rangle = \hat{A}|\psi\rangle$, this could only be possible determining the probability to find the eigenvalue a_n of $\hat{A}$ associated to this state, which is given by

$$P_{a_n} = \sum_{m=1}^{g_n} \left| \langle \phi_n^m | \psi \rangle \right|^2, \tag{6}$$

where g_n is the degeneracy index of the eigenvalue a_n. When the 2-qubit given in Eq. (3) is measured regarding the base, the probability of finding a $|0\rangle$ state in the first qubit of the 2-qubit is

$$P_{1|0\rangle} = |a_{00}|^2 + |a_{01}|^2 \tag{7}$$

Analogously, the probability of finding a state $|1\rangle$ in the first qubit of the 2-qubit is

$$P_{1|1\rangle} = |a_{10}|^2 + |a_{11}|^2. \tag{8}$$

Similarly, for the second qubit, it is possible to determine the probability of finding the states $|0\rangle$ and a $|1\rangle$ in the 2-qubit and is represented by

$$P_{2|0\rangle} = |a_{00}|^2 + |a_{10}|^2 \qquad P_{2|1\rangle} = |a_{01}|^2 + |a_{11}|^2 \tag{9}$$

If the first qubit is in XX, the 2-qubit evolves to the state

$$|\psi *\rangle = \frac{a_{10} |10\rangle + a_{11} |11\rangle}{\sqrt{|a_{10}|^2 + |a_{11}|^2}} \tag{10}$$

By the other hand, if the first qubit is in $|0\rangle$, the 2-qubit evolves to a new state represented by

$$|y *\rangle = \frac{a_{00} |00\rangle + a_{01} |01\rangle}{\sqrt{|a_{00}|^2 + |a_{01}|^2}}. \tag{11}$$

Similar expressions than as above mentioned can be determined for the measure of the second bit of 2-qubit, where it is clearly represented with a probabilistic feature of the entities.

5.5   QUANTUM GATES

In quantum computation, there are circuits that make and carry out computation processes. A quantum logic gate is a function performed by a unitary operator in a set of selected qubits at a certain period of time. In a classical way, the logic gates establish an infinite set, but in quantum computation the number of possible unitary transformations is also the same, and as a consequence there are infinite quantum gates [9]. Few examples of frequently encountered quantum gates are the Hadamard gate **H**, the not gate **X**, the Pauli-**Z** gate **Z**, and the $p/8$ gate.

Is possible to prove [9–12] that in any unitary transformation, a set of n qubits can be performed by successive application of only two quantum gates: the *XOR* operation and the $\hat{R}(\theta,\phi)$ rotation.

The *XOR* operator is a particular case of any unitary transformation on only one qubit. *XOR* can be described as

$$XOR = |0\rangle\langle 0|\hat{I} + |1\rangle\langle 1|\hat{U}. \tag{12}$$

Namely, while the first qubit remains with no change, the second is applied to $\hat{I}$ or $\hat{U}$ depending on the state of the first. Specifically, the gate *XOR* turns the ordered sequence of states $|x\rangle|y\rangle$ into $|x\rangle$, where $|x \oplus y\rangle$ identifies the logic O-exclusive operation. On the other hand, the rotation operation $\hat{R}(\theta,\phi)$ can be described as

$$\hat{R}(q,f) = |0\rangle\big(\cos[q/2]\langle 0| \quad ie^{iq}\sin[q/2]\langle 1|\big) + |1\rangle\big(\quad ie^{iq}\sin[q/2]\langle 1| + \cos[q/2]\langle 0|\big). \tag{13}$$

In this case, it is necessary that θ and φ are real; this is in order to get a $\hat{R}(\theta,\phi)$ transformation through the continuous use of the same quantum gate with these values perfectly defined.

5.6   QUANTUM PARALLELISM

The feature that has turned quantum computation into one of the most promising areas is the power to support in the shortest time problems that result, and are intractable for the classical computation, by processing information in a parallel way. This idea was presented by David Deutsch [13] in 1985 and is outlined as follows: Suppose we have a quantum computer that is able to evolve any two qubits in accordance with the unitary operator $\hat{U}$ whose transformation is represented by

$$\hat{U} = |x\rangle|y\rangle \rightarrow |x\rangle|y \oplus f(x)\rangle. \qquad (14)$$

This operator changes the second $|y\rangle$ qubit to zero if f is 1 during the first $|x\rangle$ qubit; if f is 0^1 no change is seen. Considering $|y\rangle = \frac{1}{\sqrt{2}}(|0\rangle \quad |1\rangle)$

$$\hat{U} = |x\rangle|y\rangle \rightarrow |x\rangle|y \oplus f(x)\rangle. \qquad (15)$$

where the function f has been isolated in an x phase-dependent. If $|x\rangle = \frac{1}{\sqrt{2}}(|0\rangle + |1\rangle)$ and $|y\rangle = \frac{1}{\sqrt{2}}(|0\rangle \quad |1\rangle)$ is immediately checked that

$$\hat{U} : \frac{1}{\sqrt{2}}(|0\rangle - |1\rangle)\frac{1}{\sqrt{2}}(|0\rangle + |1\rangle) \rightarrow \frac{1}{\sqrt{2}}\left[(-1)^{f(0)}|0\rangle + (-1)^{f(1)}|1\rangle\right]\frac{1}{\sqrt{2}}(|0\rangle - |1\rangle). \qquad (16)$$

In this way, it is only necessary to make an orthogonal projection of the first qubit in a $\{|+\rangle, |\ \rangle\}$ base, where

$$|\pm\rangle = \frac{1}{\sqrt{2}}(|0\rangle \pm |1\rangle). \qquad (17)$$

The problem proposed in Eq. (14) has been resolved with an only one computation. This is possible because at the moment of using a quantum gadget, this has no limit to evaluate $f(0)$ or $f(1)$, but instead, acting on a superposition of the states $|0\rangle$ and $|1\rangle$ allowing to take out global information of function, namely, information that depends on combination between $f(0)$ and $f(1)$. This is the quantum parallelism.

Similarly, parallel processing can be used to identify some properties of more complex functions. Thus, if we want to calculate all the possible combinations on a set of n bits, the value of whichever function f, a classical computer will need to perform 2^n evaluations of the function. However, using a quantum computer, we only need to perform on an n given set: only one transformation given by the unitary operator $\hat{U}_r$, in which case

$$\hat{U}_r : |x\rangle|0\rangle \rightarrow |x\rangle|f(x)\rangle. \qquad (18)$$

The operation $\oplus$ denotes the binary addition or module 2, which is defined by $0 \oplus 0 = 0, 0 \oplus 1 = 1, 1 \oplus 0 = 1$ and $1 \oplus 1 = 0$.

If we choose every input register to remain in the $\frac{1}{\sqrt{2}}(|0\rangle+|1\rangle)$ state, the state of the set will be

$$\left[\frac{1}{\sqrt{2}}(|0\rangle+|1\rangle)\right]\otimes\cdots\otimes\left[\frac{1}{\sqrt{2}}(|0\rangle+|1\rangle)\right]=\frac{1}{2^{n/2}}\sum_{x=0}^{2^n-1}|x\rangle,\qquad(19)$$

which represents the tensor product of the n input states. Applying in Eq. (19), the operator $\hat{U}_r$

$$\frac{1}{2^{n/2}}\sum_{x=0}^{2^n-1}|x\rangle|f(x)\rangle,\qquad(20)$$

And this state finally gathers all global properties of function f.

5.7 ENTANGLEMENT

Entanglement probably is the key, which defines the difference between both quantum and classic theories of information; at the same time, this property is the base for 2-qubits quantum gates. Considering a quantum system made of two identical subsystems A and B, whose state spaces, L_1^2 and L_2^2 respectively, are considered two-dimensional and f, it is supposed that bases of L_1^2 and L_2^2 are formed by kets $|0\rangle$ and $|1\rangle$; the state space of set system $L_{12}^2=L_1^2\otimes L_2^2$ will have as natural base the set $\{|00\rangle,|01\rangle,|10\rangle,|11\rangle\}$.

Though not all states belonging to L_{12}^2 have a understandable physical interpretation; thus, while, for example, in $|01\rangle$ is plainly that A is in $|0\rangle$ and B is in $|1\rangle$, in other cases such as superposition $1/2(|00\rangle+|10\rangle)$, this is harder to construe, although in this case, the state of A is $|0\rangle$ and B is a $|0\rangle$ and $|1\rangle$ superposition. Finally, we can consider other examples, where it is not possible relate a quantum state to any of two subsystems independently: such a circumstance appears, for example, in $|\psi\rangle 1/\sqrt{2}(|00\rangle+|11\rangle)$. This last type of state, which is not possible to make a factorization with the form $|\psi_A\rangle\otimes|\psi_B\rangle$, is called Entanglement.

Such a state has the attribute of "no get information" if a "local" average is made in any of the subsystems: to be specific the result is entirely random (the state is called completely mixed). The instantaneous consequence of this is the impossibility to make these states through transformation done by unitary operators like $U_A \otimes U_B$; the one way to interlace two systems is allowing interaction between them.

Albert Einstein, Boris Podolsky and Nathan Rosen [14] were the first to note the consequences of existence of these two states; but when they consider such a "no locality" nature as incomplete, they propose a local hidden variable theory. Three decades later, John Bell [15–17] was able to prove through schemes involving a local behavior of both subsystems. Experiments obtained by Alan Aspect and his group [18–20] confirmed Quantum Theory predictions and established that natural behavior is "no local."

5.8 DECOHERENCE

Decoherence is the physical process in which the state that describes quantum evolution of a system, loses its phase coherence [21, 22]. The physical origin of this process is the interaction between the considered system and its environment (i.e., the external or internal degrees of freedom that are not handy for spectator). That is why such an interaction causes that system (S) and environment (A) variables correlates (separately) through evolution, causing irreversible slack of interference effects of the quantum system [21]. This happens even when the initial state of the system has no correlations between both variables and it is a consequence of unitary character of dynamic.

5.9 PHYSICAL IMPLEMENTATION: DIVINCENZO CRITERIA

At the moment of building any quantum algorithm that does a specific task, a question arises: What physical resource is necessary to implement this task in a real machine? The answer for this question was presented by David DiVicenzo [23] in five criteria that must be carried out for any propose of physical implementation of a quantum computer.

1. A physical system is scalable when qubits are well characterized.
2. It is necessary to have the ability to initialize the qubits in a basic quantum state on a physical system.
3. Decoherence times of qubits must be much longer than the operation time of quantum gate.
4. If it is possible, set up a set of universal quantum gates.
5. If it is possible, have the aptitude to measure a specific qubit.

5.10   CONCLUSIONS

The rising tide in miniaturization processes of electrical systems as well as information processes is causing apparition of problems related to limitations at the time of working at an atomic scale in which the quantum effects have a significant relevance. Applying models of quantum mechanical in the creation of a new information model, results that exceeded the predicted by information classical theory are obtained, incorporating them and these last being a particular case presented by the quantum model.

Quantum computation is a new and emerging development field that has the potential of changing dramatically the way of thinking about computers, programmers, and complexity. The challenges range from developing new suitable programming techniques for these devices, to the experimental implementation in a scalable system.

The theoretical models of quantum computation have managed to develop successfully, and at the present time, the fundaments of subatomic interactions are broadly defined, as well as qubit schemes, quantum gates, quantum parallelism, quantum transport and encryption; nevertheless at the moment, the implementation of a fully functional quantum computer with a relevant information storage capacity has not been achieved. A limitation in this information process scheme is presented in the implementation of the device itself, in which it is difficult management of multiple qubits systems where interactions affect mutually their states. Another requirement is interactions between measurement system and measured particle, because these cannot be read without producing changes on system; for this cause, it is necessary to implement complex mechanics of error correction.

At the present time, small prototypes of these computers have been implemented; with this has been allowed to demonstrate the functionality of some quantum algorithms predicting a near future full of new and promising devices with high performance in potentiality and fast in processing information mechanisms.

KEYWORDS

- **Quantum computer**
- **Quantum information**
- **Quantum mechanics**

ACKNOWLEDGMENT

The work is supported by Corporación Universitaria Autónoma del Cauca, Colombia.

REFERENCES

1. Nielsen, M.; and Chuang, I.; Quantum Computation and Quantum Information. 1st edition; United Kingdom: Cambridge University Press; **2000**.
2. Feynman, R.; Simulating Physics with Computer. *Int. J. Theor. Phys.* **1982**, *21(6/7)*, 467–488.
3. Williams, C.; Explorations in Quantum Computing. 2nd edition. London: Springer-Verlag; **2011**.
4. Feynman, R.; Hibbs, A; and Styer, D. F.; Quantum Mechanics and Path Integrals. Emended Ed. New York: McGraw-Hill; **1995**.
5. Dirac, P.; The Principles of Quantum Mechanics. 4th edition. New York: Oxford University Press; **1958**.
6. Steeb, W.; Hilbert Spaces, Wavelets, Generalized Functions and Modern Quantum Mechanics, Mathematics and its Applications. 1st edition. The Netherlands: Klumer Academics Publishers; **1998**.
7. Feynman, R.; Leighton R. B.; and Sands, M.; The Feynman Lectures on Physics Vol III, The New Millennium Edition. New York: Perseus Book Group; **2010**.
8. Cohen–Tannoudji, Claude; Diu, B.; and Laloe, F.; Quantum Mechanics. 1st edition. France: John Wiley & Sons; **1977**, *I*.
9. Barenco, A.; et al. Elementary gates for quantum computation. *Phys. Rev. A* **1995**, *52*, 3457–3467.
10. DiVincenzo, D. P.; Two-bit gates are Universal for quantum computation. *Phys. Rev. A* **1995**, *51*, 1015–1022.
11. Deutsch, D.; Barenco, A.; and Ekert, A.; Universality in quantum computation. *Proc. R. Soc. Lond. A* **1995**, *449*, 669–677.
12. Lloyd, S.; Almost any quantum logic gate is Universal. *Phys. Rev. Lett.* **1995**, *75*, 346–349.
13. Deutsch, D.; Quantum theory, the Church-turing principle and the Universal quantum computer. *Proc. R. Soc. Lond. A* **1985**, *400*, 97–117.
14. Einstein, A.; Podolsky, B.; and Rosen, N.; Can quantum mechanical description of physical reality be considered complete? *Phys. Rev.* **1935**, *47*, 777–780.
15. Bell, J. S.; On the Einstein-Podolsky-Rosen paradox. *Phys.* **1964**, *1*, 195–200.
16. Bell, J. S.; On the problem of hidden variables in quantum mechanics. *Rev. Mod. Phys.* **1966**, *38*, 447–452.
17. Jack, C.; Sherlock holmes investigates the EPR paradox. *Phys. World.* **1995**, *8*, 39–42.
18. Aspect, A.; Dalibard, J.; and Roger, G.; Experimental test of Bells` inequalities using timevarying analyzers. *Phys. Rev. Lett.* **1982**, *49*, 1804–1807.
19. Aspect, A.; Grangier, P.; and Roger, G.; "Experimental tests of realistic local theories via Bell's theorem." *Phys. Rev. Lett.* **1981**, *47*, 460–463.
20. Aspect, A.; Testing Bell's inequalities. *Europhys. News.* **1991**, *22*, 73–75.

21. Zurek, W. H.; Decoherence, einselection, and the quantum origin of the classical'. *Rev. Mod. Phys.* **2003,** *75,* 715–775.
22. Schlosshauer, M.; Decoherence, the measurement problem, and interpretations of quantum mechanics. *Rev. Mod. Phys.* **2005,** *76,* 1267–1305.
23. DiVincenzo, David P.; The physical interpretation of quantum computation. *Fortschr. Phys.* **2000,** *48,* 771–783.

CHAPTER 6

CLASSICAL CHARGED PARTICLES IN ARBITRARY MOTION

J. H. CALTENCO, J. LÓPEZ–BONILLA,
and LAURIAN IOAN PISCORAN

CONTENTS

6.1 INTRODUCTION

The Liénard–Wiechert field is the field generated by a charge with arbitrary motion in Minkowski space; the four-potential A_r and its corresponding Faraday tensor F_{rs} have fundamental importance in the electrodynamics of classical charged particles. Thus, the Section 6.1 studies the scalar and vectorial quantities associated with the path of particle, with special attention on retarded distance and the light cone: the world line's kinematics forms a powerful base for analysis of the electromagnetic field. Besides, the important Fermi's triad is considered.

In Section 6.2, we study general features about the four-potential and Faraday matrix, in accordance with the Synge's classification [1] and an interesting result of Stachel [2]. Section 6.3 is dedicated to Liénard–Wiechert field and the Teitelboim [3, 4]—Miglietta [5] splittings for A_r and F_{cb}, respectively. We also show the Plebañski's attractive theorem [6]: F_{ij} is the exterior product of two gradients. Section 6.4 deals with retarded Maxwell energy-momentum tensor; its analysis is channeled through the algebraic differential properties of its T_{ic} $_B$ and radiative T_{ab} $_R$ parts. A thoughtful study of algebraic and differential structure of the Weert potential is made for T_{rs} $_B$, and the nonlocal superpotential is exhibited for T_{ij} $_R$. In our work, the Synge's paper [7] is fundamental for the mathematical aspects of point particle electrodynamics.

6.2 MATERIALS AND METHODS AND DISCUSSION

6.2.1 KINEMATICS OF RELATIVISTIC PARTICLES

In special relativity, a "particle" means a time like world line, see Figure (6.1), whose unitary tangent vector is the four-velocity.

$$v^r = dx^r / d\tau \qquad (1a)$$

where the proper time τ is defined by

$$d\tau^2 = g_{ab} dx^a dx^b = -dx^2 - dy^2 - dz^2 + dt^2 \qquad (1b)$$

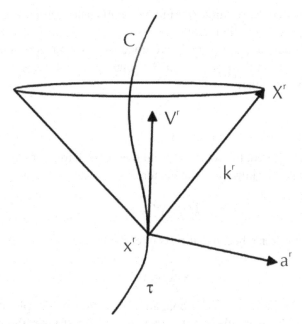

FIGURE 6.1 Time-like trajectory.

which means that the metric is Diag (−1, −1, −1, 1) and c = light's speed in vacuum = 1, then

$$(v^r) = (\gamma \vec{v}, \gamma)$$ – with $\vec{v} = (dx/dt, dy/dt, dz/dt)$ and $\gamma = (1 - \vec{v}^2)^{\frac{1}{2}}$ (1c)

Therefore, out of Eqs. (1a) and (b) we have

$$v^r v_r = -1, \; v^r a_r = 0$$ with $a^r = dv^r / d\tau = \text{4-acceleration}$,   (1d)

this implies the time-like and space-like nature of v^r and a^r, respectively; in consequence:

$$a^2 \equiv a_r a^r \geq 0$$ (1e)

From Eq. (1d), we obtain:

$$s^r v_r + a^2 = 0$$, where $s^r = da^r / d\tau = \text{superacceleration}$ (1f)

In Figure (6.1), we have not indicated this last vector since it might be outside or inside the light cone.

From an event X^t outside C, we trace its null cone's past sheet which intersects to C in the point x^r called "retarded event associated with X^{t}", therefore we say that

$$x^r = x^r \left(X^i \right) \tag{2a}$$

Thus with X^i given, the retarded point over C is automatically determined. This allows us to introduce the vector:

$$k^r = X^r - x^r \tag{2b}$$

of magnitude zero, because it rests over the cone:

$$k^r k_r = 0, \tag{2c}$$

Therefore, k^r indicates the propagation direction of the photons emitted by the particle. The null or light-type vector Eq. (2b) is truly important in electrodynamics: we could say that studying the Maxwell field is almost equivalent to an analysis of the null cone and its relation to the world line.

From X^t, we can build two distances widely used in the study of charges in Minkowski space:

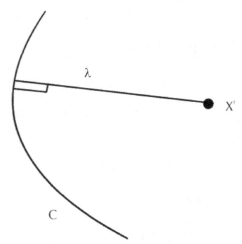

FIGURE 6.2(A)   Instantaneous distance from X^t to C.

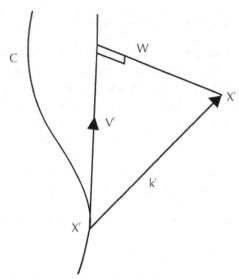

FIGURE 6.2(B) Retarded distance from X^τ to C.

The instantaneous distance (see Figure 6.2(a)) introduced by Dirac [8] is geometrically simpler than retarded distance w, (see Figure 6.2(b)) proposed by Bhabha [9] and furthered by Synge [7]; nevertheless, λ has the big disadvantage of not involving retarded effects (light cone); for this reason, w has more physical meaning and leads to simpler calculations because it intrinsically takes in account the finite velocity of interaction. Here, we will work only with w, whose expression is given by the following equation:

$$w = -k^r v_r \geq 0 \tag{3a}$$

Bearing in mind that a null vector cannot be orthogonal to a time-like one, Eq. (3a) points out that

$$w = 0 \text{ if and only if } k^r = 0 \tag{3b}$$

In other words, the retarded distance is zero only when X^τ is over C.

When making calculations, we need to know how diverse quantities change over C when an external event X^τ varies; for this, it is enough with having Change's law for τ because x^r, v^r, a^r, etc., are functions of this parameter:

$$\tau_{,r} = -w^{-1}k_r \text{ where } r = \partial / \partial X^r, \tag{4}$$

therefore we have that τ, r is a null vector because it is antiparallel to k_r. Every event X^t over the same cone has an associated unique value of τ, that is, the light cone is the τ = constant surface; therefore, τ, r is the vector normal to the cone even though our Euclidian eyes do not see it like that. Due to Eq. (4) it makes no sense to look for a unitary normal to the cone.

Thanks to Eq. (4), it is easy to obtain these useful relationships:

$$x^r_{,j} = -w^{-1}v^r k_j, \ v^r_{,j} = -w^{-1}a^r k_l, \ a^r_{,b} = -w^{-1}s^r k_b, \ k^r_{,c} = \delta^r_C + w^{-1}v^r k_C,$$

$$w_{,C} = -v_C + Bk_c, \ B = w^{-1}(1-W), \ W = -k^r a_r, \ W_{,b} = W_b = -a_b + w^{-1}k^r s_r k_b,$$

$$B_{,C} = w^{-1}\left[U_C - \left(B^2 + w^{-1}k^r s_r\right)k_c\right], U_C = Bv_C + a_C, U^C k_c = -1 \ U^C v_C = -B \tag{5}$$

$$U^C a_C = a^2, \ U^C U_C = a^2 - B^2, \ U^c w_{,c} = 0, \ U^C_{,C} = 0.$$

In relativity, a spatial triad of vectors is also important at each point of the curve because this triad is a local frame of reference for an observer mounted on the particle (see Figure 6.3):

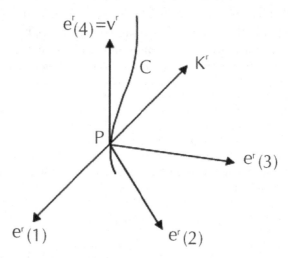

FIGURE 6.3 Orthonormal tetrad.

$$\left(e_{(a)}{}^r e_{(b)r}\right) = Diag\left(1,1,1,-1\right) \tag{6a}$$

This tetrad forms a base for each vector associated to the world line, in particular for null vector Eq. (2b):

$$k^r = b^\sigma e_{(\sigma)}{}^r + b^4 e_{(4)}{}^r ; \qquad (6b)$$

From now on the Greek indexes shall only take values 1, 2, and 3. Equation (6b) can be written as follows:

$$k^r = M^r + b^4 v^r \text{ with } M^r = b^\sigma e_{(\sigma)}{}^r , \ M^r v_r = 0, \qquad (6c)$$

M^r is space-like type because it is a lineal combination of the three space-like vectors of the tetrad (see Figure 6.4):

If $M = \left(M^r M_r\right)^{\frac{1}{2}}$ is the magnitude of M^r, then

$$M^r = M p^r \text{ with } p^r p_r = 1 \qquad (6d)$$

and by Eq. (6c):

$$p_r v^r = 0, \qquad (6e)$$

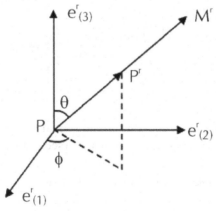

FIGURE 6.4   Spatial triad.

Therefore, p^r is a space-like unitary vector. From Eqs. (2c) and (3a), it is apparent that $M = b^4 = w$; and as a consequence, Eqs. (6b) through (6e) imply the important Synge [7]–Teitelboim [4] decomposition for k^r:

$$k^r = w\left(p^r + v^r\right), \ p^r v_r = 0 \text{ and } p_r k^r = w \tag{7}$$

which is shown in Figures 6.5(a) and (b):

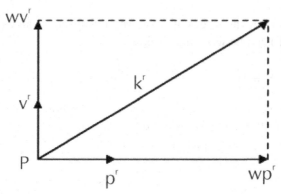

FIGURE 6.5(A) Spatial and time-like components of k^r.

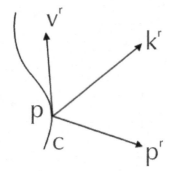

FIGURE 6.5(B)   Null vector k^r splitting.

The unitary vector p^r only depends on the spatial triad; therefore, it can be written with common spherical coordinates (see Figure 6.4):

$$p^r = \sin\theta\cos\phi e_{(1)}{}^r + \sin\theta\sin\phi e_{(2)}{}^r + \cos\theta e_{(3)}{}^r = p^{(\sigma)}e_{(\sigma)}{}^r \tag{8a}$$

$$\therefore \ p^{(\gamma)} = e^{(\gamma)}{}_r p^r$$

where we have employed the dual base $e_{(\gamma)}{}^r$, defined by the following equation:

$$e^{(\gamma)r}e_{(\sigma)r} = \delta_\sigma^\gamma \tag{8b}$$

Vector p^r does not necessarily have to be orthogonal to four-acceleration a^r.

The triad $e_{(\sigma)}{}^r$ is arbitrary except for the orthonormality conditions Eq. (6a); nevertheless, some triads may be more convenient than others in some set calculations. For our theoretical purposes, the Fermi triad [10] is very important; it satisfies over C the transport law (which we use in this work):

$$de_{(\sigma)}{}^r/d\tau = e_{(\sigma)}{}^b a_b v^r = a_{(\sigma)} v^r \tag{9a}$$

This type of transport has been very fundamental in gravitation, for example, Pirani [11] and Synge [12]; but in electrodynamics, we shall show its participation in the deduction of superpotential for the radiative part of the Maxwell tensor (see Section (6.4). In Eq. (9a)) we have used the notation:

$$a_{(\sigma)} = a^r e_{(\sigma)r} \tag{9b}$$

because a^r is space-like type; remember that the triad is only defined over C.

To end this section, we give some useful expressions:

$$w_{,b}k^b = w, \; w_{,b}v^b = W, \; w_{,b}a^b = -WB, \; w^b w_{,b} = 1-2W,$$

$$W = -wp^r a_r = -wp^{(\sigma)}a_{(\sigma)}, \; W_{,c}k^c = W, \; W_{,c}w^c = WB + k^r s_r, \; k^r{}_{,a}v^a = 0,$$

$$B_{,c}k^c = -w^{-1}, \; w_{,c}p^c = wB, \; w^{-1,a}{}_{,a} = 0, \; w^a{}_{,a} = 2w^{-1}(1-2W), \; k^r{}_{,a}p_r = p_a, \tag{10}$$

$$U^r p_r = -w^{-1}W, \; p^r{}_{,a} = w^{-1}\left[\delta_a^r + w^{-1}v_a k^r + (a^r + w^{-1}v^r - w^{-1}Bk^r)k_a\right],$$

$$p^r{}_{,a}k^r = -w^{-1}Wk_a$$

$$p^r{}_{,a}w_r = w^{-2}W^2 k_a, \; p_{(\sigma),r}k^r = 0, \; p^r{}_{,a}k^a = 0, \; p^r{}_{,r} = w^{-1}(2-W),$$

$$p_{(\sigma),r} = p_{a,r}e_{(\sigma)}{}^a$$

Relations Eqs. (5) and (10) are the basic formulary for any calculation in the electrodynamics of classical charged particles.

6.2.2 POTENTIAL AND FARADAY TENSOR

In this section, we consider the algebraical and differential properties satisfied by the electromagnetic field in vacuum. The Faraday tensor is given by the following equation:

$$F_{rc} = -F_{cr} = A_{c,r} - A_{r,c} \qquad (11a)$$

In terms of four-potential A^b—from Eq. (11a) the fulfillment of the cyclic relationship is clear:

$$F_{br,c} + F_{rc,b} + F_{cb,r} = 0 \text{, in other words } {}^*F^{rc}{}_{,c} = 0 \qquad (11b)$$

where we have employed the dual tensor:

$${}^*F^{rc} = -{}^*F^{cr} = \frac{1}{2}\varepsilon^{rcab}F_{ab} \qquad (11c)$$

such that ε^{ijkr} are the Levi–Civita antisymmetric symbols—in free space, we have the remaining Maxwell equation:

$$F^{rc}{}_{,c} = 0 \qquad (11d)$$

Which, in turn, leads to a differential equation for four-potential:

$$A^{r,c}{}_{,c} - \left(A^c{}_{,c}\right)^{,r} = 0 \qquad (11e)$$

In Eq. (11a), we have full freedom to add an arbitrary gradient to A^r without modifying the Faraday tensor; then without lack of generality, we can always demand:

$$A^c{}_{,c} = 0 \text{ Lorenz–Riemann condition} \qquad (11f)$$

Simplifying Eq. (11e),

$$A^{r,c}{}_{,c} = 0 \text{ wave equation} \qquad (11g)$$

Therefore, from the mathematical viewpoint, the problem consists of solving Eq. (11g) with the restriction Eq. (11f), which matches solving Eqs. (11b) and (11d); in other words,

$$\nabla \cdot \vec{B} = 0, \ \nabla \times \vec{E} = -\partial \vec{B} / \partial t, \ \nabla \cdot \vec{E} = 0 \ \text{and} \ \nabla \times \vec{B} = \partial \vec{E} / \partial t \qquad (12)$$

in the MKS system; remembering that $c = (\varepsilon_0 \mu_0)^{-\frac{1}{2}} = 1$.

The Faraday matrix representation becomes

$$\left[F^{ab} \right] = \begin{bmatrix} 0 & B_z & -B_y & -E_x \\ -B_z & 0 & B_x & -E_y \\ B_y & -B_x & 0 & -E_z \\ E_x & E_y & E_z & 0 \end{bmatrix} \begin{matrix} a : \text{rows} \\ \\ \\ b : \text{columns} \end{matrix} \qquad (13a)$$

And with Eq. (11c), an associated matrix for the dual tensor can be constructed:

$$\left[{}^* F^{ab} \right] = \begin{bmatrix} 0 & E_z & -E_y & B_x \\ -E_z & 0 & E_x & B_y \\ E_y & -E_x & 0 & B_z \\ -B_x & -B_y & -B_z & 0 \end{bmatrix} \qquad (13b)$$

Note that Eq. (13b) is obtained if we make the following changes to Eq. (13a):

$$\vec{B} \rightarrow \vec{E}, \ \vec{E} \rightarrow -\vec{B} \qquad (13c)$$

Therefore, it may come to mind that * executes operation Eq. (13c); then, it is clear that $^{**} F^{ar} = -F^{ar}$. Comparing Eqs. (11a) and (13a), we obtain the relationship of the electric and magnetic fields with four-potential:

$$\vec{E} = -\nabla \phi - \partial \vec{A} / \partial t, \ \vec{B} = \nabla \times \vec{A} \qquad (14)$$

because $(A^r) = (\vec{A}, \phi)$, where $\vec{A}$ and ϕ are the magnetic and electric potentials, respectively.

We are placing emphasis on ϕ as a scalar, but not as an invariant; the electromagnetic field only possesses two Lorentz invariants, namely

$$F_1 \equiv F_{ab}F^{ab} = 2\left(\tilde{B}^2 - E^2\right),\ F_2 \equiv {}^*F_{ab}F^{ab} = 4\vec{E}\cdot\vec{B} \qquad (15)$$

With $E = |\vec{E}|$ and $\tilde{B} = |\vec{B}|$,

Just like Weyl tensor invariants allow to establish the Petrov classification [13] for the gravitational field, the quantities Eq. (15) lead to the Synge [1]–Piña [14] classification for the Faraday tensor:

Type A: $F_2 \neq 0$

Type B: $F_1 < 0$ and $F_2 = 0$ (16)

Type C: $F_1 = 0$ and $F_2 = 0$ null field

Type D: $F_1 > 0$ and $F_2 = 0$

A point with a null field means that in such an event, $\vec{E} \perp \vec{B}$ and $E = \tilde{B}$. A nonnull field implies a different type of C. Classification Eq. (16) is algebraic, but the type of electromagnetic field may change from one point to another.

Further, we will see that the field that produces a relativistic charge is B type, which tends to type C (plane wave) toward infinity.

There are very important identities for the Maxwell field:

$$F^{ar}F_{br} - {}^*F^{ar}\,{}^*F_{br} = \left(F_1/2\right)\delta_b^a \qquad (17a)$$

$${}^*F^{ar}F_{br} = \left(F_2/4\right)\delta_b^a \qquad (17b)$$

which do not have a specific name, are well known and can be found in Rainich [15], Plebañski [16], Wheeler [17] pp. 239, Penney [18], and Piña [14]—Expressions (17) correspond to Lanczos identities [18] between the Riemann tensor and its double dual. If Eq. (17a) is multiplied by F_{ia} or ${}^*F_{ia}$ and Eq. (17b) is employed, valuable identities result in the calculation of an antisymmetric matrix's exponential function [14, 20]:

$$F_{ia}F^{ar}F_{rb} = (F_1/2)F_{bi} + (F_2/2)^* F_{bi} \qquad (18)$$

$$^* F_{ia}{}^* F^{ar}{}^* F_{rb} = (F_2/4)F_{bi} - (F_1/4)^* F_{bi}$$

From Eq. (13a), it is simple to show that

$$\det(F^{ab}) = (1/16)(F_2)^2 = (\vec{E} \cdot \vec{B})^2, \qquad (19a)$$

which is a particular case of the following theorem, see Drazin [21]:

"The expression $\det \underset{\sim}{F}$, with antisymmetric $\underset{\sim}{F}_{n \times n}$ and even n, is the square of a rational polynomial in F^{ij} " $\qquad (19b)$

Now, we mention the interesting and useful Stachel theorem [2] page 1261:

"If $\underset{\sim}{F}$ satisfies

$$F_{ar} = -F_{ra} - F_{ar,c} + F_{rc,a} + F_{ca,r} = 0, \ \det(F_{ab}) = 0, \qquad (20a)$$

then there exist functions β and ψ such that

$$F_{ar} = \beta_{,a}\psi_{,r} - \beta_{,r}\psi_{,a} \qquad (20b)$$

That is, the conditions (20a) reduce $\underset{\sim}{F}$ to an antisymmetric product of gradients. If we extend the Stachel result to the Maxwell field, then the first two conditions Eq. (20a) will be immediately verified, thereby

"If the Faraday tensor fulfills $F_2 = 0$, then it has the form Eq. (20b)." (20c)

The Liénard–Wiechert solution satisfies Eq. (20c), and thus permits us to write $\underset{\sim}{F}$ in the form of Plebański [6]. In general, an electromagnetic field with a different type of A has the structure Eq. (20b). Results Eq. (20) are valid in the presence of curvature because its differential expressions remain undisturbed if covariant derivatives are used instead of partial ones:

$$^* F^{ar}_{,r} = {}^* F^{ar}_{;r} = 0, \ \beta_{,r} = \beta_{;r}$$

In the following section, we shall employ the material explained in Eqs. (11–20) to analyze the field produced by a point charge with a relativistic trajectory.

6.2.3 THE LIÉNARD–WIECHERT FIELD

The solution of Eqs. (11f) and (11g) for a particle in arbitrary motion in Minkowski space was obtained by Liénard and Wiechert; the corresponding potential carries their names and is given by

$$A^r \left(X^b \right) = q w^{-1} v^r, \quad q = \text{charge} / 4\pi\varepsilon_0 \text{ (retarded potential),} \qquad (21a)$$

which is fundamental in everything that follows; by the use of Eq. (11a), it is simple to calculate the associated Faraday tensor :

$$F_{rb} = q w^{-2} \left(U_r k_b - U_b k_r \right) = q w^{-2} U_r \times k_b \qquad (21b)$$

where $\times$ means the antisymmetric product. This notation is due to Lowry [22] and will cause such expressions to be very compact. From Eqs. (11c) and (21b), it is clear that

$$^{*}F_{mn} = -q w^{-2} \varepsilon_{mnab} U^a k^b, \qquad (21c)$$

therefore

$$F_1 = -2q^2 w^{-4} < 0, \quad F_2 = 0 \qquad (21d)$$

In other words, the electric and magnetic fields generated by the charge satisfy

$$\tilde{B} < E, \quad \vec{E} \cdot \vec{B} = 0 \qquad (21e)$$

In consequence $\underset{\sim}{F}$ is type B. Note that in the asymptotic region ($w \to \infty$), the invariant F_1 tends to zero, which means that $\underset{\sim}{F}$ is close to the null case (type C) far away from the charge.

    With Eqs. (21d) and (20c) is valid; therefore, the Stachel theorem [2] implies that Eq. (21b) can be reduced to Eq. (20b). This is easy to do because from Eqs. (4) and (5), the following relationships are available:

$$k_r = -w\tau_{,r}, \ U_r = wB_{,r} + \left(B^2 + w^{-1}k^c s_c\right)k_r$$

which substituted in Eq. (21b) implies that

$$F_{rc} = -qB_{,r}x\tau_{,c} = q\left(\tau_{,r}B_{,c} - \tau_{,c}B_{,r}\right) \tag{22}$$

with the form Eq. (21b), meaning that τ and B correspond to functions β and ψ. Expression (22) was first obtained by Plebañski [6].

Now we shall consider the eigenvalue problem of $\underline{F}$. For this purpose, we stem from Eq. (21b), and due to this

$$U_r k^r = -1, \ k_r k^r = 0$$

Then, we immediately have one of the two null proper vectors of a nonnull field (different type from C) [23]:

$$F_{rm}k^m = qw^{-2}k_r, \ \text{proper value} = qw^{-2} \tag{23a}$$

This suggests that U_r may be an eigenvector, but it is not:

$$F_{rb}U^b = -qw^{-2}U_r - qw^{-2}\left(a^2 - B^2\right)k_r, \tag{23b}$$

Nevertheless, if we multiply Eq. (23a) by $\frac{1}{2}\left(a^2 - B^2\right)$ and add the resulting equation to Eq. (23b), we obtain the other null proper vector [24, 25]:

$$F_{rm}\eta^m = -qw^{-2}\eta_r, \ \text{proper value} = -qw^{-2} \ \text{with} \tag{23c}$$

$$\eta^r = U^r + \frac{1}{2}\left(a^2 - B^2\right)k^r, \ \eta^r\eta_r = 0; \tag{23d}$$

It is not usual to find η^r explicitly in the literature. It is clear that these two proper vectors are independent because:

$$k^r\eta_r = 1 \tag{23d}$$

Remember that two null vectors ξ^r and γ^r are proportional if and only if $\xi^r\gamma_r = 0$, therefore Eq. (23d) implies the nonparallelism of such proper vectors.

With Eqs. (10) and (21b), it is possible to prove that

$$F_r^b p_{c,b} = qw^{-4} W v_c k_r - F_r^b p_{(\sigma),b} = 0,$$ (24)

of great importance in the next section on the deduction of the radiative superpotential.

Teitelboim started an era in electrodynamics by employing only re-tarded fields and studying Faraday and Maxwell tensors near to and away from a point charge. This type of analysis is generated by substituting Eqs. (5) and (7) in Eq. (21b) to obtain the following decomposition:

$$F_{rb} = F_{(-1)^{rb}} + F_{(-2)^{rb}},$$ (25a)

where

$$F_{(-1)^{rb}} = qw^{-2}\left(w^{-1}W v_r + a_r\right) \times k_b$$ (25b)

$$= qw^{-1}\left(a_c p^c v_r \times p_b + a_r \times v_b + a_r \times p_b\right)$$ (25c)

$$F_{(-2)^{rb}} = qw^{-3} v_r \times k_b = qw^{-2}\left(v_r \times p_b\right)$$ (25d)

Meaning that $F_{(-i)^{rb}}, i = 1, 2$ varies like w^{-i}; the dependence on w^{-i} is clear be-cause the parenthesis in Eqs. (25c) and (25d) are independent of the re-tarded distance; their terms are functions of x^r, which remains stationary when we move away over the light cone. Thus, $F_{(-1)^{rb}}$ and $F_{(-2)^{rb}}$ are dominant away from ($w >> 1$) and near to ($w << 1$), respectively, then $F_{(-1)^{rb}}$ being re-sponsible for the Larmor formula that provides the radiation speed toward infinitum. Note that Eqs. (25b) and (25c) depend on the particle accelera-tion, which is an expected result because of the Schild theorem [26]:

"Radiation exists if and only if $a^r \neq 0$" (26)

Schild was the first author to give a covariant definition of radiation even though some of his ideas were already implicit in Synge [27], Appendix A, whose first edition was made in 1955. We call $F_{(-1)^{g}}$ the radiative part of F_{ab} because it is a null field in classification Eq. (16):

$$F_{(-1)^{ra}} F^{ra}_{(-1)} = {}^*F_{(-1)^{ra}} F^{ra}_{(-1)} = 0,$$ (27a)

This does not happens with $F_{(-2)^{ij}}$

$$F_{(-2)^{ra}} F^{ra}_{(-2)} = 2q^2 w^{-4} < 0, \quad {}^*F_{(-2)^{ra}} F^{ra}_{(-2)} = 0,$$ (27b)

which belongs to type B—this portion will be designated as the bounded part of F_{mni}, besides:

$$F_{(-1)^{ab}} F^{ab}_{(-2)} = 0, \quad {}^*F_{(-1)^{ab}} F^{ab}_{(-2)} = F_{(-1)^{ab}} {}^*F^{ab}_{(-2)} = 0$$ (27c)

These Eq. (27) relations can be found in Weert [28], page 465.

It is possible to write Eq. (25a) in the following form:

$$F_{ab} = w^{-1} N_{ab} + w^{-2} M_{ab} \text{ so that } N_{ab} = w F_{(-1)^{ab}}, \quad M_{ab} = w^2 F_{(-2)^{ab}}$$ (28)

with the following properties:

$$N_{ab} \xi^b = 0, \quad M_{ab} \xi^b = q \xi_a, \quad \xi_r \xi^r = 0, \quad \xi_r = w^{-1} k_r = -\tau_{,r}$$

Therefore, we see that Eq. (28) is coherent with Eqs. (1), (2), and (3) of the Goldberg–Kerr theorem [29] for the asymptotic behavior of electromagnetic fields.

Teitelboim's decomposition Eq. (25a) is fundamental in everything that follows, and it is interesting that Eq. (7) generates such splitting in a natural manner:

$$v^r = w^{-1} k^r - p^r$$

which substituting in Eq. (21a) gives

$$A^r = A^r_1 + A^r_2 \text{ with } A^r_1 = -qw^{-1} p^r, \quad A^r_2 = qw^{-2} k^r$$ (29a)

This partition of the Liénard–Wiechert four-potential is found in the Teitelboim [4] well-known article; however, it was also published by Migglietta [5] not-knowing Ref. [4]. Expressions (29b) are simpler than Migglietta's

Eqs. (2.3) and (3.2). Substituting Eq. (29a) into Eq. (11a), we obtain the matching Faraday's tensor decomposition Eq. (25a) with

$$F_{(-i)^{bc}} = A_{i^{e,b}} - A_{i^{b,c}}, \ i = 1, 2 \tag{29b}$$

which means that each part of F_{mn} has its own four-potential. Finally, it can be verified that Eq. (29a) does not satisfy the Lorenz–Riemann condition (11f):

$$A_{1 \ \ ,r}^r = -A_{2 \ \ ,r}^r = -qw^{-2} \neq 0 \tag{29c}$$

6.2.4   ENERGY-MOMENTUM TENSOR

Now we shall consider the Maxwell tensor T_{rb} through which an electromagnetic field's content of energy momentum is quantified:

$$T_{ab} = \tfrac{1}{2}\left(F_{ac} F_b^c + {}^*F_{ac} {}^*F_b^c \right), \tag{30a}$$

This satisfies

$$T_{ab} = T_{ba} \ \text{Symmetry} \tag{30b}$$

$$T_r^r = 0 \ \text{Null trace} \tag{30c}$$

$$T_{ac} T_b^c = \tfrac{1}{4}\left(T_{mn} T^{mn} \right) g_{ab} \ \text{Rainich identity} \tag{30d}$$

Symmetry Eq. (30b) is a property of every energy tensor, Eq. (30c) tells us that the field is made of particles with null mass at rest, photons in this case; Eq. (30d) was obtained by Rainich [15].

   If we employ Eq. (17a) in the second term of Eq. (30a), we obtain an alternative expression for the Maxwell tensor:

$$T_{ab} = F_{ac} F_b^c - \left(F_1 / 4 \right) g_{ab} ; \tag{30e}$$

Substitution of Eqs. (21d) and (25) in Eq. (30e) results in the important Teitelboim splitting [3]:

$$T_{ab} = \underset{(-2)^{ab}}{T} + \underset{(-3)^{ab}}{T} + \underset{(-4)^{ab}}{T} \tag{31a}$$

where

$$\underset{(-2)^{rn}}{T} = \underset{(-1)^{rc}}{F} \underset{(-1)^{n}}{F^c} = q^2 w^{-4} \left(a^2 - w^{-2} W^2 \right) k_r k_n \tag{31b}$$

$$\underset{(-3)^{rn}}{T} = \underset{(-1)^{rc}(-2)^{n}}{F} \underset{(-1)^{nc}(-2)^{r}}{F^c} = q^2 w^{-4} \left[k_r a_n + k_n a_r + 2w^{-2} W k_r k_n - w^{-1} W \left(k_r v_n + k_n v_r \right) \right] \tag{31c}$$

$$\underset{(-4)^{rn}}{T} = \underset{(-2)^{rc}(-2)^{n}}{F} \underset{(-2)^{n}}{F^c} - \left(F_1 / 4 \right) g_{rn} = q^2 w^{-4} \left[\tfrac{1}{2} g_{rn} + w^{-1} \left(v_r k_n + v_n k_r \right) - w^{-2} k_r k_n \right] \tag{31d}$$

with the following properties:

$$\underset{(-2)^{rn}}{T} k^n = 0 \quad - \quad \underset{(-3)^{rn}}{T} k^n = 0 \quad - \quad \underset{(-4)^{rn}}{T} k^n = -\left(q^2 / 2 \right) w^{-4} k_r \tag{31e}$$

From Eqs. (31a) and (31e), it is clear that k^r is a null proper vector of the Maxwell tensor:

$$T_{rn} k^n = \left(q^2 / 2 \right) w^{-4} k_r, \tag{32}$$

which was to be expected due to Eqs. (21d), (23a), and (30e):
$T_{rn} k^n = -qw^{-2} F_{rn} k^n + \left(q^2 / 2 \right) w^{-4} k_r = -\tfrac{1}{2} q^2 w^{-4} k_r$ - identical to Eq. (32)

The notation $\underset{(-i)^{rn}}{T}, i = 2,3,4$ evokes that Eqs. (31b), (31c), and (31d) vary like w^{-i}, in consequence:

$\underset{(-2)^{ab}}{T}$ dominates when $w \to \infty$ (away from the charge)

$$\tag{33}$$

$\underset{(-3)^{ab}}{T}$ & $\underset{(-4)^{ab}}{T}$ dominates when $w \to 0$ (close from q)

Therefore, the Larmor formula comes from $\underset{(-2)^{ab}}{T}$. This and $\underset{(-i)^{ab}}{T}, i = 3,4$ are responsible for the singularities in the point charge's position, therefore Teitelboim wrote Eq. (31a) in the following form:

$$T_{rn} = \underset{R^{rn}}{T} + \underset{B^{rn}}{T}, \tag{34a}$$

where

$$\underset{R^{rn}}{T} = \text{radiative part} = \underset{(-2)^{rn}}{T} = q^2 w^{-4}\left(a^2 - w^{-2}W^2\right)k_r k_n \qquad (34b)$$

$$\underset{B^{rn}}{T} = \text{bounded part}$$

$$= \underset{(-3)^{rn}}{T} + \underset{(-4)^{rn}}{T}$$

$$= q^2 w^{-4}\left[\tfrac{1}{2}g_{rn} + \left(k_r a_n + k_n a_r\right) + B\left(k_r v_n + k_n v_r\right)w^{-2}\left(1-2W\right)k_r k_n\right]$$

This proves that such parts are dynamically independent, which means that they verify separately (outside the world line):

$$\underset{R^{r,n}}{T^n} = 0, \qquad (35a)$$

$$\underset{B^{r,n}}{T^n} = 0 \qquad (35b$$

It is simple to obtain the relations:

$$T_{rn}U^n = \lambda U_r,\ T_{rn}B^n = \lambda B_{,r},\ T_{rn}\eta^n = \lambda \eta_r,\ \lambda = -\left(q^2/2\right)w^{-4} \qquad (36)$$

Therefore, we have that F_{aj} and T_{rc} have the same null proper vectors, which is a general result (see Synge [27], p. 337). Plebañski [6], p. 41, was the first one to observe that B_r is a proper vector of T_{ij}. If we substitute Eqs. (34b) and (34c) in Eq. (34a), we obtain the Synge [7] compact expression for the energy tensor associated to the Liénard–Wiechert retarded potential:

$$T_{rn} = q^2 w^{-4}\left[k_r U_n + k_n U_r + \left(a^2 - B^2\right)k_r k_n + \tfrac{1}{2}g_{rn}\right] \qquad (37)$$

Weert's [30, 31] attention was driven forward to the fact that Eq. (35) are valid *identically*, and he therefore suggested the existence of superpotentials for the bounded and radiative parts. However, he only obtained successfully the explicit form of the superpotential (which now carries his name) $\underset{B^{sur}}{K}$ which generates the bounded part [32–35]:

$$\underset{B^{rn}}{T} = \underset{B^{nr}}{T} = \underset{B^{nr,a}}{K^{a}}, \tag{38a}$$

$$\underset{B^{sar}}{K} = -\left(q^{2}/4\right)w^{-4}\left[w^{-1}\left(3-4W\right)\left(v_{s}\times k_{a}\right)k_{r} + 4\left(a_{s}\times k_{a}\right)k_{r} + g_{rs}k_{a} - g_{ra}k_{s}\right], \tag{38b}$$

which means that $\underset{B^{ij}}{T}$ is the divergence of $\underset{B^{sar}}{K}$. This idea of the superpotential is not Weert's original; it is actually quite old and was introduced by Freud [36] constructing the superpotential for the canonical energy-momentum pseudotensor of Einstein [37, 38].

Weert did not study deeply the algebraic and differential properties of $\underset{B^{sar}}{K}$, which was remedied in [33, 39–41] obtaining a better comprehension of such superpotential structures:

$$\underset{B^{sar}}{K} = -\underset{B^{sar}}{K} \quad \text{Antisymmetry}$$

$$\underset{B^{sr}}{K^{r}} = 0 \quad \text{Null trace} \tag{39}$$

$$\underset{B^{sa,r}}{K^{r}} = 0 \quad \text{Null divergence}$$

$$\underset{B^{sar}}{K} + \underset{B^{ars}}{K} + \underset{B^{rsa}}{K} = 0 \quad \text{Cyclic}$$

Surprisingly, Eq. (39) is also satisfied in curved spaces (replacing partial derivatives with covariant ones) for the Lanczos spintensor K_{sar} [42], which generates the Weyl conformal tensor in four-dimensions [43–49]:

$$C_{jrim} = K_{jri;m} - K_{jrm;i} + K_{imj;r} - K_{imr;j} + g_{jm}K_{ir} - g_{ij}K_{mr} + g_{ri}K_{mj} - g_{rm}K_{ij} \tag{40a}$$

so that $K_{rj} = K_{jr} = K^{a}_{rj;a}$

This fact suggests at least two things:
1. The introduction in electrodynamics of the definition:
    "A Minkowski spintensor is that which satisfies Eq. (39)," (40b)
    therefore, the Weert superpotential is a Minkowskian spintensor.

2. To construct an "electromagnetic Weyl tensor" through prescription Eq. (40a) (in this case $\underset{B^{rj}}{K} = \underset{B^{rj}}{T}$):

$$\underset{B^{jrim}}{C} = \underset{B^{jri,m}}{K} - \underset{B^{jrm,j}}{K} + \underset{B^{imj,r}}{K} - \underset{B^{imr,j}}{K} + g_{jm}\underset{B^{ir}}{T} - g_{ij}\underset{B^{mr}}{T} + g_{ri}\underset{B^{mj}}{T} - g_{rm}\underset{B^{ij}}{T} \qquad (40c)$$

The Petrov classification [13] can be applied to $\underset{B^{jrim}}{C}$, see Refs. [39, 41], resulting in Type II in the Penrose diagram, which is:

"The Liénard–Wiechert field is type II";   (40d)

This strengthens the analogies found by Newman [50] between Robin-sonTrautman metrics (Einstein's equations solution type II) [51], and the electromagnetic field of a point charge. The physical meaning of the Weert superpotential was elucidated in [40].

The idea Eq. (40b) motivates the following question:

Can $\underset{B^{sar}}{K}$ be written as the sum of two or more Minkowskian spintensors?

The answer is affirmative because the terms in Eq. (38b) can be grouped in form [33]:

$$\underset{B^{sar}}{K} = \underset{B^{sar}}{\tilde{K}} + \underset{B^{sar}}{\bar{K}} \qquad (41a)$$

with

$$\underset{B^{scr}}{\tilde{K}} = qw^{-2}\left[qw^{-3}\left(v_s \times k_c\right) - F_{sc}\right]k_r, \qquad (41b)$$

$$\underset{B^{sar}}{\bar{K}} = \left(q^2/4\right)w^{-4}\left[3w^{-1}\left(v_a \times k_s\right)k_r + g_{ra}k_s - g_{rs}k_a\right] \qquad (41c)$$

Both parts of $\underset{B^{sar}}{K}$ satisfy Eq. (39); therefore, they are spintensors. By substituting Eq. (41a) in Eq. (38a), we obtain in a natural manner the splitting of López [52]:

$$\underset{B^{ra}}{T} = \underset{B^{ra}}{\tilde{T}} + \underset{B^{ra}}{\bar{T}} \qquad (42a)$$

where
$$\underset{B^{rs}}{\tilde{T}} = \underset{B^{sr,a}}{\tilde{K}^a}, \quad \underset{B^{rs}}{\bar{T}} = \underset{B^{sr,a}}{\bar{K}^a} \qquad (42b)$$

therefore,
$$\tilde{T}^s_{B^r,s} = \bar{T}^s_{B^r,s} = 0 \tag{42c}$$

Decomposition Eq. (42a) is valuable in the study of electromagnetic angular momentum; here, it came out as a consequence of the spintensor concept Eq. (40b).

It can be proven that

$$\bar{K}_{B^{sar}} = \left(\tfrac{q^2}{4} w^{-4} D^b_{sar}\right)_{,b} = (41.c), \tag{43a}$$

where D_{ijrm} is a tensor employed by Synge [7] in another context:

$$D_{sarb} = g_{rs}k_ak_b - g_{ab}k_rk_s - g_{ar}k_sk_b - g_{sb}k_ak_r \tag{43b}$$

Identity Eq. (43a) was obtained by Rowe [53].

Weert did not study Eq. (35a); this analysis was considered in [54–61] to determine a nonlocal superpotential (it depends on integrals over the world line) for the radiative part:

$$T_{R^{rs}} = K^a_{R^{sr},a} \tag{44a}$$

with

$$K_{R^{scr}}(X^i) = qF_{sc}[P_{(\sigma)}P_{(\theta)}\left(\int_0^\tau a^{(\sigma)}a^{(\theta)}v_r d\gamma + P_{(\beta)}\int_0^\tau a^{(\sigma)}a^{(\theta)}e_r^{(\beta)}d\gamma\right) - \tag{44b}$$

$$-\int_0^\tau a^2 v_r d\gamma - P_{(\sigma)}\int_0^\tau a^2 e_r^{(\sigma)}d\gamma], \qquad \sigma,\theta,\beta = 1,2,3$$

where $e^{(\sigma)}_r$ is the Fermi triad and τ is the proper time in the retarded point associated to X^i. Trying out Eq. (44a) brings into relevance the identities Eq. (24); the integrals in Eq. (44b) indicate the nonlocal character of radiative superpotential; besides, if the four-acceleration a^r is annulated, then $K_{R^{ijc}} = 0$ which was to be expected due to Eq. (26). When obtaining Eq. (44), transport Eq. (9a) is basic; never before had the great value of the Fermi triad been shown in electrodynamics.

6.3   RESULTS

It was possible to deduce nonlocal superpotential for the radiative part of the Maxwell tensor associated to the Liénard–Wiechert field. A Petrov classification was introduced of the electromagnetic field produced by a charged particle in arbitrary motion, and it was proved that it has Type II. In our analysis, the Minkowskian spintensor concept was relevant because it enabled us to establish a connection between the Weert superpotential and the gravitational Lanczos potential for the Weyl tensor in general relativity. The participation of the Fermi triad was original and fundamental over the point charge trajectory.

6.4   CONCLUSION

In our study, the relationship between the electromagnetic superpotentials in the Minkowski space and the Lanczos spin tensor in curved space times is clear; it is then necessary to investigate this important connection. For example, the physical meaning of Lanczos potential is an open problem, whose solution can be useful to understand the corresponding meaning of nonlocal superpotential for the radiative part.

KEYWORDS

- Faraday tensor
- Liénard–Wiechert field
- Super potentials for the bounded and radiative parts of Maxwell tensor

REFERENCE

1. Synge, J. L.; Time-like helices in flat space-time. *Proc. Roy. Irish Acad.* **1967,** *A65,* 27–42.
2. Stachel, J.; Specifying sources in general relativity. *Phys. Rev.* **1969,** *180,* 1256–1261.
3. Teitelboim, C.; Splitting of the Maxwell tensor: radiation reaction without advanced fields. *Phys. Rev.* **1970,** *D1,* 1572–1582.
4. Teitelboim, C.; Splitting of the Maxwell tensor. II. Sources. *Phys. Rev.* **1971,** *D3,* 297–298.
5. Miglietta, F.; Electromagnetic quadripotential for the pure radiation field generated by a classical charged point particle. *J. Math. Phys.* **1979,** *20,* 868–870.

6. Plebañski, J.; The Structure of the Field of a Point Charge. Internal Report. Mexico City: Cinvestav-IPN; **1972**.

7. Synge, J. L.; Point-particles and energy tensors in special relativity. *Ann. Mat. Pura Appl.* **1970**, *84*, 33–59.

8. Dirac, P. A. M.; Classical theory of radiating electrons. *Proc. Roy. Soc. London.* **1938**, *A167*, 148–169.

9. Bhabha, H. J.; Classical theory of mesons. *Proc. Roy. Soc. London.* **1939**, *A172*, 384–409.

10. Fermi, E.; Sopra I fenomeni che avvengono in vicinanza di una linea oraria. *Atti. R. Accad. Lincei Rend.* **1922**, *31*, 21–33.

11. Pirani, F. A. E.; On the physical significance of the Riemann tensor. *Acta Phys. Polon. Sci. Cl.* **1956**, *15*, 389–405.

12. Synge, J. L.; Relativity: the General Theory. Amsterdam: North-Holland; **1976**.

13. Acevedo, M.; and López–Bonilla, J.; Algebraic classification of the gravitational field. *Gen. Rel. Grav.* **2005**, *37*, 627–628.

14. Piña, E.; La transformación de Lorentz y el movimiento de una carga en el campo electromagnético constante. *Rev. Mex. Fís.* **1967**, *16*, 233–236.

15. Rainich, G. Y.; Electrodynamics in the general relativity theory. *Trans. Amer. Math. Soc.* **1925**, *27*, 106–136.

16. Plebañski, J.; On algebraical properties of skew tensors. *Bull. Acad. Polon. Sci. Cl.* **1961**, *9*, 587–593.

17. Wheeler, J. A.; Geometrodynamics. New York: Academic Press; **1962**.

18. Penney, R.; Duality invariance and Riemannian geometry. *J. Math. Phys*. **1964**, *5*, 1431–1437.

19. Lanczos, C.; A remarkable property of the Riemann–Christoffel tensor in four dimensions. *Ann. Math.* **1938**, *39*, 842–850.

20. Caltenco, J. H.; López–Bonilla, J.; Martínez, M. A.; and Xeque, A.; On the exponential function of a matrix. *Aligarh Bull.Math.* **2001**, *20*, 61–73.

21. Drazin, M. P.; A note on skew-symmetric matrices. *Math. Gaz.* **1952**, *36*, 253–255.

22. Lowry, E. S.; Geometrical representation of the Maxwell field in Minkowski space. *Phys. Rev.* **1960**, *117*, 616–618.

23. Gaftoi, V.; López–Bonilla, J.; and Ovando, G.; Eigenvectors of the Faraday tensor for the Liénard–Wiechert field. *Aligarh Bull. Math.* **1997–1998**, *17*, 59–62.

24. Gaftoi, V.; López–Bonilla, J.; and Ovando, G.; Eigenvectors of the Faraday tensor of a point charge in arbitrary motion. *Canad. J. Phys.* **2001**, *79*, 75–80.

25. López–Bonilla, J.; Morales, J.; and Ovando, G.; On the homogeneous Lorentz transformation. *Bull. Allahabad Math. Soc.* **2002**, *17*, 53–58.

26. Schild, A.; On the radiation emitted by an accelerated point charge. *J. Math. Anal. Appl.* **1960**, *1*, 127–131.

27. Synge, J. L.; Relativity: the special theory. Amsterdam: North-Holland; **1965**.

28. Van Weert, Ch. G.; Relativistic treatment of multipole radiation from an extended charge-current distribution. I. Asymptotic properties of the electromagnetic field. *Physica.* **1973**, *65*, 452–468.

29. Goldberg, J. N.; and Kerr, R.; Asymptotic properties of the electromagnetic field. *J. Math. Phys.* **1964**, *5*, 172–176.

30. Van Weert, Ch. G.; Direct method for calculating the bound four-momentum of a classical charge. *Phys. Rev.* **1974**, *D9*, 339–341.
31. Van Weert, Ch. G.; On the covariant equations of motion with explicit radiation damping. *Physica.* **1974**, *76*, 345–363.
32. Gaftoi, V.; López–Bonilla, J.; and Ovando, G.; A generator for the Weert superpotential. *Int. J. Theor. Phys.* **1999**, *38*, 939–943.
33. López–Bonilla, J.; Morales, J.; and Ovando, G.; A splitting of the Weert superpotential. *Indian J. Phys.* **2000**, *B74*, 167–169.
34. López–Bonilla, J.; Ovando, G.; and Rivera, J.; Generators for 4-potential and the Faraday's tensor of the Liénard-Wiechert field. *Indian J. Pure Appl. Math.* **1997**, *28*, 1355–1360.
35. Gaftoi, V.; López–Bonilla, J.; and Ovando, G.; A double generator for the Maxwell tensor of the Liénard–Wiechert field. *Nuovo Cim.* **1999**, *B114*, 423–426.
36. Von Freud, Ph.; Über die ausdrücke der gesamtenergie und des gesamtimpulses eins materiellen systems in der allgemeinen relativitätstheorie. *Ann. Math.* **1939**, *40*, 417–419.
37. Caltenco, J.; López–Bonilla, J.; and Ovando, G.; A new energy-momentum pseudotensor in general relativity. *Indian J. Theor. Phys.* **2003**, *51*, 273–274.
38. Caltenco, J. H.; López–Bonilla, J.; Peña, R.; and Rivera, J.; Landau–Lifshitz energy-momentum pseudotensor for metrics with spherical symmetry. *Proc. Pakistan Acad. Sci.* **2005**, *42*, 261–264.
39. Aquino, N.; López–Bonilla, J.; Núñez–Yépez, H.; and Salas-Brito, A. L.; Conformal tensor and Petrov classification for the bounded part of the Liénard–Wiechert field. *J. Phys. A*: *Math. Gen.* **1995**, *28*, L375–L379.
40. López–Bonilla, J.; Ovando, G.; Rivera, J., On the physical meaning of the Weert potential. *Nuovo Cim.* **1997**, *B112*, 1433–1436.
41. Caltenco, J. H.; López–Bonilla, J.; and Peña, R.; Electromagnetic Weyl tensor for the Liénard-Wiechert field. *Indian J. Theor. Phys.* **2002**, *50*, 1–3.
42. Lanczos, C.; The splitting of the Riemann tensor. *Rev. Mod. Phys.* **1962**, *34*, 379–389.
43. Gaftoi, V.; López–Bonilla, J.; and Ovando, G.; The Lanczos invariants as ordinary divergences. *Nuovo Cim.* **1998**, *B113*, 1489–1492.
44. López–Bonilla, J.; Morales, J.; and Ovando, G.; A potential for the Lanczos spintensor in Kerr geometry. *Gen. Rel. Grav.* **1999**, *31*, 413–415.
45. López–Bonilla, J.; Ovando, G.; and Peña, J.; A Lanczos potential for plane gravitational waves. *Found. Phys. Lett.* **1999**, *12*, 401–405.
46. López-Bonilla, J.; Morales, J.; Ovando, G.; and Rivera, J.; Lanczos spintensor. *Indian J. Theor. Phys.* **2000**, *48*, 289–298.
47. Caltenco, J. H.; López–Bonilla, J.; Morales, J.; and Ovando, G.; Lanczos potential for the Kerr metric. *Chinese J. Phys.* **2001**, *39*, 397–400.
48. Acevedo, M.; López–Bonilla, J.; Vidal, S.; A note on the Lanczos potential for the Kerr metric. *Grav. Cosm.* **2004**, *10*, 328–328.
49. Caltenco, J. H.; Linares, R.; and López–Bonilla, J.; A note on the Lanczos potential for the Gödel solution. *Proc. Pakistan Acad. Sci.* **2005**, *42*, 153–154.
50. Newman, E.; Liénard–Wiechert field and general relativity. *J. Math. Phys.* **1974**, *15*, 44–44.

51. López–Bonilla, J.; and Rivera, J.; Robinson–Trautman spacetimes and Lanczos spin-tensor. *Indian J. Math.* **1998,** *40,* 159–167.
52. López, C. A.; Splitting in energy and splitting in angular momentum of the classical field of a radiating point charge. *Phys. Rev.* **1978,** *D17,* 2004–2009.
53. Rowe, E. G. P.; Structure of the energy tensor in the classical electrodymanics of point particles. *Phys. Rev.* **1978,** *D18,* 3639–3654.
54. Aquino, N.; Chavoya, O.; López–Bonilla, J.; and Navarrete, D.; Superpotential for the Liénard–Wiechert field. *Nuovo Cim.* **1993,** *B108,* 1081–1085.
55. López–Bonilla, J.; Morales, J.; and Rosales, M.; The Maxwell tensor for the Liénard–Wiechert field as an exact divergence. *Pramana J. Phys.* **1994,** *42,* 89–95.
56. López–Bonilla, J.; Núñez–Yépez, H.; Salas–Brito, A. L.; On the radiative part of the Maxwell tensor for a Liénard–Wiechert field. *J. Phys. A: Math. Gen.* **1997,** *30,* 3663–3669.
57. López–Bonilla, J.; and Ovando, G.; A potential for the radiative part of Liénard–Wiechert field. *Gen. Rel. Grav.* **1999,** *31,* 1931–1934.
58. López–Bonilla, J.; and Ovando, G.; A splitting of the radiative part of Liénard–Wiechert field. *Indian J. Theor. Phys.* **2001,** *49,* 139–142.
59. Caltenco, J. H.; López–Bonilla, J.; Morales, J.; and Ovando, G.; Generators for the Liénard–Wiechert electromagnetic field. *Chinese J. Phys.* **2002,** *40,* 214–222.
60. Acevedo, M.; López–Bonilla, J.; and Sosa, P.; Inactive part of the radiative part of the Liénard-Wiechert field. *Apeiron.* **2002,** *9,* 43–48.
61. Barrera, V.; López–Bonilla, J.; and Sosa, J.; Electromagnetic superpotentials for the Liénard–Wiechert field. *Comm. Phys.* (Viet Nam) **2009,** *19,* 229–234.

CHAPTER 7

SECOND-ORDER LINEAR DIFFERENTIAL EQUATION IN ITS EXACT FORM

A. HERNÁNDEZ–GALEANA and J.M. RIVERA-REBOLLEDO

CONTENTS

7.1   INTRODUCTION

The following nonhomogeneous equation,

$$p(x)\, y'' + q(x)\, y' + r(x)\, y = \Phi(x) \tag{1}$$

can be established as follows:

$$\hat{L}\, y = \Phi, \quad \hat{L} = p\,\frac{d^2}{d\,x^2} + q\,\frac{d}{d\,x} + r \tag{2}$$

It is known [1] that $x(x)\,\hat{L}$ is an exact operator:

$$\frac{d}{d\,x}\left(a\, y' + b\right) = x\,\Phi \tag{3}$$

if ξ satisfies the differential equation

$$p\,\hat{\imath}'' + \left(2\,p' - q\right)\hat{\imath}' + \left(p'' - q' + r\right)\hat{\imath} = 0 \tag{4}$$

and in this case,

$$\alpha = \xi\, p \quad , \qquad \beta = \xi\, q - \alpha' \tag{5}$$

In several situations, the following property is true:

$$p'' - q' + r = 0 \tag{6}$$

Therefore, it is evident that Eq. (4) is fulfilled for $\xi = 1$, which means that $\hat{L}$ is already exact, with $\alpha = p$ and $\beta = q - p'$. On the contrary, it is straightforward to show the identity:

$$\frac{\beta}{\alpha} = -\frac{(w\, p)'}{w\, p} \quad , \qquad w = \exp\left(-\int^{x} \frac{q}{p}\, d\,\xi\right) \quad , \qquad \frac{w'}{w} = -\frac{q}{p} \tag{7}$$

such that Eq. (3) adopts the structure:

$$\frac{d}{dx}\left[w\,p^2\,\frac{d}{dx}\left(\frac{y}{w\,p}\right)\right]=\Phi \tag{8}$$

thus giving $y(x)$ after integrating twice.

7.2   METHOD

Although Eq. (6) is not verified in general, it is possible to write Eq. (1) in exact way. To do that, let us multiply this equation by

$$\xi=\frac{\tau}{w\,p} \tag{9}$$

Therefore, Eq. (4) reduces to

$$p\,\tau''+q\,\tau'+r\,\tau=0 \tag{10}$$

which is precisely the homogeneous equation associated to Eq. (1); therefore, if $\tau = y_1(x)$ is one of the two independent solutions:

$$p\,y_1''+q\,y_1'+r\,y_1=0, \tag{11}$$

Eqs. (5) and (9) give:

$$\alpha=\frac{y_1}{w}, \quad \beta=-\frac{y_1'}{w}, \quad \xi=\frac{y_1}{w\,\Phi} \tag{12}$$

As a consequence, Eq. (3) takes its exact version:

$$\frac{d}{dx}\left[\frac{y_1^2}{w}\frac{d}{dx}\left(\frac{y}{y_1}\right)\right]=\frac{y_1}{w\,p}\,\Phi, \tag{13}$$

and $y(x)$ can be obtained after two integrations.

   Equations (8) and (13) give the general solution of Eq. (1), in complete harmony with the variation of parameters method developed by Lagrange [2–4].

7.3 CONCLUSION

In this work, we have found a compact form for a second-order linear differential equation such that its solution can be derived after two consecutive integrations. This form follows directly by just renaming their coefficients, and is independent of any requirement on such coefficients. That is, the expression posses all generality.

KEYWORDS

Second-order linear differential equation
Variation of parameters method

REFERENCES

1. Greenberg, M.; Application of Green's function in Science and Engineering. New Jersey: Prentice-Hall; **1971**.
2. Spiegel, M.; Ecuaciones Diferenciales Aplicadas. Mexico: Prentice-Hall; **1983**.
3. Lanczos, C.; Linear Differential Operators. New York: Dover; **1997**.
4. López–Bonilla, J.; Yaljá Montiel, J.; and Zaldívar, A.; Factor integrante para una arbitraria ecuación diferencial lineal de 2do. orden. *Bol. Soc. Cub. Mat. Comp.* **2010**, *8(1)*, 35–39.

CHAPTER 8

ON THE OPERATOR EXP (2 Λ (P + Q))

J. MORALES, G. OVANDO, R. CRUZ-SANTIAGO,
and J. LÓPEZ-BONILLA

CONTENTS

8.1   INTRODUCTION

In general, if P and Q are arbitrary operators, then it is not possible to give a nontrivial splitting for exp $(2\lambda(P + Q))$, λ being a parameter. Here, we study the realization of a factorization of the type:

$$\exp(2\lambda(P + Q)) = \exp(f(\lambda)Q)\exp(g(\lambda)P)\exp(h(\lambda)Q), \qquad (1)$$

where f, g, and h are functions that determine whether P and Q verify the following relations between commutators:

$$[[P, Q], P] = -2P, \qquad [[P, Q], Q] = 2Q \qquad (2)$$

which are present in the analysis of the time evolution operator for the harmonic oscillator in one dimension.

In Section 8.2, without restrictions on P and Q, it is proved that $f = h$, $f(-\lambda) = -f(\lambda)$ and $g(-\lambda) = -g(\lambda)$, that is, into Eq. (1) f and g are odd functions. In Section 8.3, we accept the conditions (Eq. 2) to obtain the useful expressions:

$$[\exp(g\,P), Q] = (g^2 P + g[P, Q])\exp(g\,P),$$
$$[\exp(f\,Q), P] = (f^2 Q - f[P, Q])\exp(f\,Q), \qquad (3)$$
$$[\exp(f\,Q), [P, Q]] = -2f\,Q\exp(f\,Q).$$

Section 8.4 is dedicated to the construction of f and g; therefore,

$$f(\lambda) = \tan\lambda, \qquad g(\lambda) = \sin(2\lambda), \qquad (4)$$

Then for Eq. (2), it is valid the splitting:

$$\exp(2\lambda(P + Q)) = \exp(Q\tan\lambda)\exp(P\sin(2\lambda))\exp(Q\tan\lambda), \qquad (5)$$

And also it is shown its application to time evolution operator $U = \exp(-itH/\hbar)$ for the one-dimensional harmonic oscillator.

8.2 METHOD

8.2.1 *P* AND *Q* ARE ARBITRARY

If Eq. (1) is modified as $\lambda \to -\lambda$, $P \to -P$, $Q \to -Q$, we obtain the following equation:

$$\exp(2\,\lambda(P + Q)) = \exp(-f(-\lambda)Q)\ \exp(-g(-\lambda)P)\ \exp(-h(-\lambda)Q), \quad (6)$$

as *P* and *Q* are arbitrary, Eq. (6) coincides with Eq. (1) if the functions involved are odd:

$$f(\lambda) = -f(-\lambda),\ g(\lambda) = -g(-\lambda),\ h(\lambda) = -h(-\lambda) \tag{7}$$

The properties $(ABC)^{-1} = C^{-1}B^{-1}A^{-1}$ and $(\exp A)^{-1} = \exp(-A)$ permit to deduce the inverse operator of Eq. (1):

$$\exp(-2\,\lambda(\underline{p} + Q)) = \exp(-h(\lambda)\,Q)\exp(-g(\lambda)\,\underline{p})\ \exp(-f(\lambda)Q), \quad (8)$$

And if in Eq. (1) only we realize the change $\lambda \to -\lambda$ in accordance with Eq. (7):

$$\exp(-2\,\lambda(\underline{p} + Q)) = \exp(-h(\lambda)\,Q)\exp(-g(\lambda)\,\underline{p})\ \exp(-f(\lambda)Q), \quad (9)$$

Again, as *P* and *Q* are arbitrary, we obtain the total compatibility between Eqs. (8) and (9) if $f = h$; therefore, the factorization of Eq. (1) is equivalent to

$$T(\lambda)\ ^{\circ} \exp(2\,\lambda(P + Q)) = \exp(f\,Q)\exp(g\,P)\ \exp(f\,Q), \quad (10)$$

where *f* and *g* are odd functions of the parameter λ.

8.2.2 *P* AND *Q* VERIFY

$$\big[\,[\,P\,,Q\,]\,,P\,\big] = -2\,P \text{ and } \big[\,[\,P\,,Q\,]\,,Q\big] = 2\,Q$$

Expression (3) is correct if *P* and *Q* satisfy Eq. (2); then, we shall consider the operator:

$$M(g) = \exp(g\,P)\,Q\,\exp(-g\,P) - Q, \qquad (11)$$

with the function g as a parameter; it is clear that

$$M(0) = 0. \qquad (12)$$

From the double derivative of Eq. (11) with respect to g, we obtain

$$M'(g) = \exp(g\,P)\,[\,P,Q]\,\exp(-g\,P)$$
$$\therefore \qquad M'(0) = [P,Q]\,, \qquad (13.a)$$

$$M''(g) = -\exp(g\,P)\,\big[\,[\,P,Q],P\,\big]\,\exp(-g\,P), \qquad (13.b)$$

Then Eq. (2) can be substituted in Eq. (13.b) to derive:

$$M''(g) = 2\,P, \qquad (14)$$

because the operators $\exp(\pm\,g\,P)$ commute with P. Now the integration of Eq. (14) gives:

$$M'(g) = 2\,g\,P + N(P,Q), \qquad (15)$$

Therefore, $M'(0) = N(P,Q)\ \overset{(13.a)}{=}\ [P,Q]$; thus, Eq. (15) adopts the form $M'(g) = 2\,g\,P + [P,Q]$, whose integration implies that

$$M(g) = g^2\,P + g\,[P,Q] + R(P,Q), \qquad (16)$$

But $R(P,Q) = 0$ due to Eq. (12). Then, Eqs. (11) and (16) give

$$\exp(g\,P)\,Q\,\exp(-g\,P) - Q \;=\; g^2\,P + g\,[P,Q]\,,$$

which is equivalent to first expression (3); in a similar manner, it is possible to show the corresponding relations for $[\exp(f\,Q),P]$ and $[\exp(f\,Q)\,,[P,Q]\,]$. It can be noted that the formula (8.105) given in the reference [1] permit to give an alternative proof for Eq. (3).

8.2.3   CONSTRUCTION OF F AND G

From the derivative of Eq. (10) with respect to λ,

$$2\,(P+Q)T = f'QT + f'e^{fQ}\left(\left[e^{gP},Q\right]+Q\,e^{gP}\right)e^{fQ}+g'\left(\left[e^{fQ},P\right]+P\,e^{fQ}\right)e^{gP}\,e^{fQ},$$

$$\underline{(3)}\left(2f'Q+g'P+g'\left(f'^2Q-f\left[P,Q\right]\right)\right)T+\left(f'g^2\left(\left[e^{fQ},P\right]+P\,e^{fQ}\right)+f'g\left(\left[e^{fQ},\left[P,Q\right]\right]+\left[P,Q\right]e^{fQ}\right)\right)e^{gP}\,e^{fQ}$$

$$\underline{(3)}\ \ \left(\left(g'+f'g^2\right)P+\left(2f'+g'f^2-2f'f'g+f'g^2f^2\right)Q+\left(f'g-g'f-f'g^2f\right)\left[P,Q\right]\right)T$$

Then, from the compatibility of the coefficients of P, Q, and $[P, Q]$ in both members, we obtain differential equations for f and g:

$$g'+f'g^2 = 2,\tag{17.a}$$

$$f'g-f\left(g'+f'g^2\right)=0,\tag{17.b}$$

$$f^2\left(g'+f'g^2\right)+2f'\left(1-fg\right)=2\tag{17.c}$$

By Substituting Eq. (17.a) in Eqs. (17.b) and (17.c) implies

$$g=\frac{2f}{f'},\tag{18.a}$$

$$f^2+f'\left(1-fg\right)=1\tag{18.b}$$

And substituting Eq. (18.a) in Eq. (18.b) leads to the equation $f'=1+f^2$ whose integration gives $f(\lambda)=\tan(\lambda+c)$, but $c=0$ because f is an odd function; thus, $f(\lambda)=\tan\lambda$ and due to Eq. (18.a) $f(\lambda)=\tan\lambda$. Therefore, it is a complete proof of Eqs. (4) and (5), in accordance with Eq. (10).

The time evolution operator for the harmonic oscillator in one-dimension is given by the following equation:

$$U=\exp(-it\,H/\hbar)\quad,\quad H=-\frac{\hbar^2}{2m}\frac{d^2}{dx^2}+\frac{1}{2}mw^2x^2\ ,\tag{19}$$

Then, U has the structure exp $(2\lambda\,(P+Q))$ with

$$\lambda = \frac{1}{2}\,wt, \qquad P = \frac{i\,h}{2\,m\,w}\frac{d^2}{d\,x^2}\,, \qquad Q = -\frac{i\,m\,w}{2\,h}x^2, \tag{20}$$

verifying Eq. (2). Therefore, Eq. (5) permits to factorize this evolution operator:

$$U = \exp\left(-\frac{i\,m\,w}{2\,\hbar}x^2\tan\left(\frac{wt}{2}\right)\right)\exp\left(\frac{i\,\hbar}{2\,m\,w}\sin(w\,t)\frac{d^2}{d\,x^2}\right)\exp\left(-\frac{i\,m\,w}{2\,\hbar}x^2\tan\left(\frac{wt}{2}\right)\right), \tag{21}$$

which can be useful in the calculation of the propagator (Green function) for the harmonic oscillator.

8.3   CONCLUSION

In this work, we have showed that if the operators P and Q satisfy the conditions $\big[\,[\,P\,,Q\,]\,,P\,\big] = -2\,P$ and $\big[\,[\,P\,,Q\,]\,,Q\,\big] = 2\,Q$, then it is valid the relation $\exp(\,2\,\lambda\,(P+Q)\,) = \exp(Q\tan\lambda)\,\exp(P\sin(2\,\lambda))\,\exp(Q\tan\lambda)$. This result is important in the study of the time evolution operator for the one-dimensional harmonic oscillator.

KEYWORDS

- **Arbitrary operators**
- **Harmonic oscillator**
- **Time evolution operator**

REFERENCE

1. Merzbacher, E.; Quantum Mechanics. New York: John Wiley & Sons; Chapter 8, **1970,** 167 p.

CHAPTER 9

QUANTUM COMPUTATIONAL STUDIES ON PORPHYCENE

NAZMUL ISLAM

CONTENTS

9.1 INTRODUCTION

Porphycene is a constitutional isomer of porphyrin that has attracted strong interest because of its versatile medicinal use such as its use in the photodynamic therapy, which is a promising treatment for cancer. The chemistry of porphycene is interesting because of its biological significance. The aromatic macromolecule porphycene has been the object of physicochemical research for years. Porphycene exhibits high fluorescence yields, which can be used for tumor detection [1]. The compound possesses strong intramolecular hydrogen bonds and it undergoes rapid tautomerization. The compound and its derivatives show strong absorptions in the red region of the UV–vis spectrum. These unique physical and optical properties of the compounds have made them suitable for use in biomedical applications and in the design of new materials. They are mainly used for photodynamic therapy, which is a promising treatment for cancer. This theoretical study was designed to provide more detailed information on the various binding sites of the porphycene.

From the early days of modern science, the explanation of the molecular interactions has been a great challenge from the experimental as well as theoretical point of view. A lot of endeavors have been made to explain the nature of bonding and reactivity of molecular systems based on some insightful ideas and pragmatic rules [2].

Porphyrins are a group of organic compounds having four pyrrol rings in their structure. The interesting structures of naturally occurring porphyrins, its isomer, and substituted analogs have been perfected by nature to give functional dyes par excellence [3]. The important roles these tetrapyrrolic macrocycles play in vital biological processes, in particular, chlorophyll (Mg–porphyrin) plays an important role in the photosynthesis, in bloodoxygen transport occurs by hemoglobin (Fe–porphyrin), and in the electron transport process, cytochromes (Fe–porphyrin) play a vital role. These compounds are clinically effective and because ofthisbiological importance, the porphyrins are called the "Pigments of Life" [3, 4]. The porphyrins are highly stable and thus also they are useful in material science as components in organic metals, molecular wires, and other devicesattributed to the presence of the conjugated π-electrons. Moreover, because of the advent of photodynamic therapy, porphyrins are now very essential in the treatment of cancer and dermatological diseases [5]. The porphyrias constitute a heterogeneous group of diseases, all of which exhibit increased excretion of porphyrin or porphyrin precursors. Some forms of porphyrias are inherited, whereas others are acquired. Recently, the anti-cancer drugs are synthesized using several gold–porphyrin complexes [5]. The porphyrins are biologically handy compounds. Their functions can be varied by changing the metal, its oxidation state, or the nature of the organic substituents on the porphyrin structure. It is a general principle that the evaluation tends to proceed by modification structures and functions that are already present on the organism rather than producing new ones de novo [6]. As evidenced by the host of expanded, reshuffled, inverted, contracted, and otherwise modified porphyrins brought to light in recent years, the quest for this concept has proven to be highly successful.

The interdisciplinary interests on the porphyrins induced scientists to introduce a new research line relating to the development of novel porphyrin-like molecules. The molecules are designed by the structural variation of the tetrapyrrolic macrocycle while maintaining a $(4n+2)\pi$ main conjugation pathway anticipated to exhibit special properties. During the development of the quantum-chemical method, many of the empirical chemical concepts were derived rigorously and it has provided a method for the calculation of the properties of chemical systems and the bonding that is involved in the formation of molecular systems. Computational theoretical chemistry is a branch of chemistry that uses theoretical studies to assist in solving chemical problems. It uses the results of theoretical chemistry, incorporated into efficient computer programs, to calculate the structures and properties of molecules and solids. While its results normally complement the information obtained by chemical experiments, it can in some cases predict hitherto unobserved chemical phenomena. Quantum-chemical (QC) calculations are a key element in biological research. When constantly tested for their range of validity QC methods, provide a description of how molecules interact and form their three-dimensional shape, which in turn determines molecular function. They can aid the formulation of hypotheses that provide the connecting link between experimentally determined structures and biological function. QC calculations can be used to understand enzyme mechanisms, hydrogen bonding, polarization effects, spectra, ligand binding, and other fundamental processes both in normal and aberrant biological contexts. The power of parallel computing and progress in computer algorithms are enlarging the domain of QC applications to ever more realistic models of biological macromolecules.

The key insight of chemistry is the relationship between molecular structure and molecular function. We use the details of molecular structure to predict the properties of molecules. Medicinal chemistry is a particularly glaring example of our use of structure-function relationships. There is a tremendous need to be able to quickly design new drugs for curing human disease. The rapid prediction of the activities of compounds for use as drugs and the discovery of new compounds is an important goal.

Since porphyrins and porphyrin metal complexes play a fundamental role in many biochemical processes, we believe that it is important to make use of quantum chemical methods to calculate the global and local reactivity parameters for porphyrin and substituted porphyrin system in order to carry out a more detailed analysis of the different effects that have an influence on the chemical reactivity at the carbon atom and at the N atom in terms of the local version of the Hard Soft Acid Base (HSAB) principle [7]. The failure of HSAB principle [8] in case of biological environments of metal ions is reported [9]. Although there are a good number of literatures [10, 11] discussing the study of the global quantum chemical reactivity parameter of porphyrins, but the study of the local quantum chemical reactivity parameters of porphyrins are limited [12]. Thus we feel it necessary to study of the local reactivity parameters for better understanding of the preferred sites for coordination with the metal ion (electron acceptor) of the porphyrins [13, 14]. We also venture to study the global reactivity parameters for them for the better understanding of the stability of these systems. We have invoked some semiempirical methods to realize the charge distribution on the different atomic sites of porphyrins to analyze the use of different reactivity descriptors for the prediction of the coordination sites for them.

In a recent work, we have established the fact that the largest and smallest value of the Fukui function and local softness do not necessarily correspond to the softness and hardness regions of the molecule porphyrin [13, 14].

In a previous work [14], we have adopted semiempirical AM-1 calculation [15, 16] for this venture. Our finding was "neither the Fukui functions nor the local softnesses can predict the preferred donor sites of porphyrins toward metal ions". The Local version of the HSAB is found to be very difficult to apply to study the preferred site for coordination at least through AM-1 method. However, when we look at the atomic charges, computed using both methods, we see that the results show a good correlation between the chemical observations and the mathematical formulae.

This investigation was undertaken to determine whether the Fukui functions, the local softnesses, or the local charges can predict the preferred donor sites of porphycenes toward metal ions.

In this work[14],we have adopted two very popular calculation procedures[15–18] for the calculation of the global and local reactivity descriptors of porphycene to find whether the Fukui functions, the local softnesses or the local charges can predict the preferred donor sites of porphycenes toward metal ions.

This analysis was performed using fully optimized AM1 geometries and the Hückel method. With the help of AM1 and Hückel molecular orbital (HMO) calculation procedures, we study the local reactivity parameters for better understanding of the preferred sites for coordination with the metal ion (electron acceptor) of porphycene. We also venture to study the global reactivity parameters for them for the better understanding of the stability of porphycene. The semiempirical method is invoked to study the charge distribution on the different atomic sites of porphycene and hence to analyze the use of different reactivity descriptors for the prediction of the coordination sites for them.

9.1.1 THE GLOBAL REACTIVITY PARAMETERS

9.1.1.1 IONIZATION POTENTIAL

The ionization energy, or ionization potential, is the energy required to completely remove an electron from a gaseous atom or ion. The closer and more tightly bound an electron is to the nucleus, the more difficult it will be to remove, and the higher its ionization energy will be. The first ionization energy is the energy required to remove one electron from the parent atom. The second ionization energy is the energy required to remove a second valence electron from the univalent ion to form the divalent ion, and so on. Successive ionization energies increase. The second ionization energy is always greater than the first ionization energy. Ionization energies increase moving from left to right across a period (decreasing atomic radius). Ionization energy decreases moving down a group (increasing atomic radius). Group I elements have low ionization energies because the loss of an electron forms a stable octet.

9.1.1.2   ELECTRON AFFINITY

Electron affinity reflects the ability of an atom to accept an electron. It is the energy change that occurs when an electron is added to a gaseous atom. Atoms with stronger effective nuclear charge have greater electron affinity. Some generalizations can be made about the electron affinities of certain groups in the periodic table. The Group IIA elements, the alkaline earths, have low electron affinity values. These elements are relatively stable because they have filled s subshells. Group VIIA elements, which are the halogens, have high electron affinities because the addition of an electron to an atom results in a completely filled shell. Group VIII elements, which are noble gases, have electron affinities near zero, as each atom possesses a stable octet and will not accept an electron readily. Elements of other groups have low electron affinities.

9.1.1.3   ELECTRONEGATIVITY AND HARDNESS

Electronegativity is a measure of the attraction of an atom for the electrons in a chemical bond. Parr et al. [19] discovered a new fundamental quantity as a new index of chemical reactivity known as the electronic chemical potential (μ). The chemical potential (μ) is a characteristic property of atoms, molecules, ions and radicals and is the first derivative of energy with respect to the number of electrons. Within the DFT formalism, Parr et al. [19] showed that the slope, $[\partial E(r)/\partial N]_v$ of the energy $e(r)$ versus the number of electrons (N) curve at a constant external potential (v), is the chemical potential, μ, and this property, like thermodynamic chemical potential[20]measures the escaping tendency of electrons in the species. Then, following Iczkowski and Margrave [21], Parr et al. [19] defined the electronegativity as the additive inverse of the chemical potential

$$\chi = -\mu \tag{1}$$

or
$$\chi = -[\partial E/\partial N]_v \tag{2}$$

Parr and Pearson [22] using the DFT as a basis have rigorously defined the term hardness as the second-order derivative of energy with respect to the number of electrons, that is,

$$\eta = \frac{1}{2}[(\delta^2 E/\delta N^2)_V] \tag{3}$$

The softness (S) is the reciprocal of the hardness; $S = 1/\eta$ (4)

Invoking finite difference approximation, Parr and Pearson [22] gave approximate and operational formulae for electronegativity and hardness as under

$$\chi = \frac{1}{2}(I + A) \tag{5}$$

$$\eta = \frac{1}{2}(I - A) \tag{6}$$

where I and A are the first ionization potential and electron affinity of the chemical species.

According to Koopmans' theorem, the orbital energies of the frontier orbitals can be written as

$$-\varepsilon_{HOMO} = I \tag{7}$$

and

$$-\varepsilon_{LUMO} = A \tag{8}$$

In 1986, within the limitations of Koopmans' theorem, Pearson [23] substituted electronegativity and hardness into a MO framework as follows:

$$\chi = (\partial E/\partial N)v = (I + A)/2$$

or

$$\chi = -(\varepsilon_{LUMO} + \varepsilon_{HOMO})/2 \tag{9}$$

and

$$\eta = (\partial^2 E/\partial N^2)v = (I - A)/2$$

or,

$$\eta = (\varepsilon_{LUMO} - \varepsilon_{HOMO})/2 \tag{10}$$

He again pointed out that a hard species has a large HOMO–LUMO gap and a soft species has a small HOMO–LUMO gap [23].

9.1.1.4 ELECTROPHILICITY INDEX

The electrophilicity, ω is a descriptor of reactivity that allows a quantitative classification of the global electrophilic nature of a molecule within a relative scale. Parr et al. [24] suggested that electronegativity squared divided by hardness measures the electrophilic power of a ligand its prosperity to "soak up" electrons.

Thus,

$$\omega = \mu^2/2\eta = \chi^2/2\eta \tag{11}$$

It is further anticipated that electrophilicity, ω should be related to electron affinity, because both ω and electron affinity measure the capacity of an agent to accept electrons. Electron affinity reflects the capability of an agent to accept only one electron from the environment, whereas electrophilicity index measures the energy lowering of a ligand because of maximal electron flow between the donor and acceptor. The electron flows may be either less or more than 1. Thus, the electrophilicity index provides direct relationship between the rates of reaction and the electrophilic power of the inhibitors [25].

9.2 THE LOCAL REACTIVITY PARAMETERS

9.2.1 FUKUI FUNCTION

Fukui functions play a prominent role in the field known as conceptual density functional theory (DFT). Parr and Yang [26] based on the original ideas of Fukui [9], introduced Fukui function that reflects the response of a molecular system toward a change in the number of electrons (N_e) of the molecular system under consideration .The Fukui functions is a measure of local reactivity and defined as

$$f(r) = (\partial \rho(r)/\partial N)_v \tag{12}$$

where $\rho(r)$ is the electron density.

As is clear from previous equation, Fukui functions measured the response of the electron density at every point r, in front of a change in the number of electrons, N under the constant external potential, v. The sites with the largest value for the Fukui functions are those with the largest response, and as such the most reactive sites within a molecule. In chemistry, often chemical reactivity and molecular properties, in general, are preferably interpreted in terms of the atoms composing molecular structure. It is then logical to introduce the so-called atom-condensed Fukui functions. This means that some way of calculating the change in the total atomic electron density of an atom α with respect to N is needed. As the nuclear change of an atom is a constant, one of the easiest ways is to use the concept of atomic charges, which introduces the following expression for atom-condensed Fukui function:

$$f_\alpha = -(\partial q_\alpha / \partial N)_v \qquad (13)$$

Yang and Mortier [27] were the first to use such atom-condensed Fukui functions, and used Mulliken charges to obtain values for the above-defined atom-condensed Fukui functions.

Now, let us discuss the operational definitions of Fukui functions.

Modern chemical reactivity theory is based on the concept of Frontier orbitals .The lowest unoccupied molecular orbital (LUMO) and the highest occupied molecular orbital (HOMO) or the frontier orbitals are of great theoretical interest. Parr and Young [26, 28] demonstrated that the most of the frontier electronic theory of chemical reactivity can be rationalized from the DFT of electronic structure. In spite of the great success in chemistry, frontier orbital theoretical background was not simple to determine because the molecular orbitals are not quantum mechanical observable.

Parr and Yang [26, 28]considered a species S with N electrons, having ground-state electronic energy E $[N, v]$ and chemical potential μ $[N, v]$. The energy as a function of N has a discontinuity of slope at each integral N, and so there are three distinct chemical potentials for each integral N, $\mu^- = (dE/dN)_v^-$. $\mu^+ = (dE/dN)_v^+$ and $\mu^0 = (dE/dN)_v^0 = \frac{1}{2}(\mu^+ + \mu^-)$.

Fundamental equation for changes in energy and chemical potential are

$$dE = \mu dN + \int \rho(r) dv(r) dr \qquad (14)$$

and

$$d\mu = 2\eta dN + \int f(r) dv(r) dr \qquad (15)$$

The function $f(r)$ is defined by

$$f(r) = [\delta\mu/\delta v(r)]_N \qquad (16)$$

Assuming that the total energy E as a function of N and functional of $v(r)$ is an exact differential, the Maxwell relations between derivatives may be applied to write the Fukui function or the frontier function as $f(r) = [\partial\rho(r)]/\partial N]_v$.

A very important condition can be found for the Fukui function is that it must be normalized to 1.

$$\int f(r)dr = 1 \qquad (17)$$

Owing to the discontinuity of the chemical potential at integer N, the derivative of $\mu = (dE/dN)$ will be different if taken from the right or the left-hand side. One has μ when the derivative is taken from above ($N + \delta$, $\delta \rightarrow 0$), μ when the derivative is taken from below ($N - \delta$, $\delta \rightarrow 0$), and for the cases where is not a net charge exchange a good approximation is to use the average $\mu = \frac{1}{2}(\mu + \mu)$. Therefore, one has three different functions $f(r) = [\partial\rho(r)/\partial N]$, where the subscript $\alpha = \pm$ indicate whether the derivative is evaluated at ($N \pm \delta$, $\delta \rightarrow 0$), and $f(r)$, which is the average of the other two. Now, to answer the question "If a reagent (R) approaches to substrate (S), what direction will be preferred?" one can assume that in the usual cases the preferred direction is the one for which the initial $d\mu$ for the species S is a maximum. The first term from the RHS of the Eq. (17) involved only the global quantity and at the large distant is ordinary less direction sensitive than second. Parr et al. [26, 28], therefore, opinioned that "*the preferred direction is the one with largest f(r) at the direction side*" and gave us the firm prediction –

Governing electrophilic attack $f^-(r) = [\partial\rho(r)/\partial N]^-_v$ (18)
Governing nucleophilic attack $f^+(r) = [\partial\rho(r)/\partial N]^+_v$ (19)
Governing neutral attack $f^0(r) = [\partial\rho(r)/\partial N]^0_v$ (20)

These three cases have $\mu_s > \mu_r$, $\mu_s < \mu_r$ and $\mu_s \sim \mu_r$.

Computation of the local reactivity indices like the Fukui function in the real molecular space is a very demanding task but difficult to evaluate without further approximation. A "frozen core" approximation now gives $d\rho = d\rho_{value}$ in each case and therefore governs electrophilic attack,

$$f^-(r) \approx \rho_{(HOMO)}(r) \qquad (21)$$

Governing nucleophilic attack, $\quad f^+(r) \approx \rho_{(LUMO)}(r)$ (22)

Governing neutral attack $\quad f^0(r) \approx \frac{1}{2}[\rho_{(HOMO)}(r) + \rho_{(LUMO)}(r)]$ (23)

The Fukui function has been used in several works as a natural descriptor of site selectivity. Within the Li and Evans reactivity and selectivity rules [29], *"for soft–soft interactions, the preferred reactive site in a molecule should have the highest value of the Fukui function, whereas the hard–hard interactions are supposed to be described through the minimum value of this local index"* often the reactivity in molecules with only one reactive site can be correctly characterized.

However, for polyfunctional systems where more than one site can be attacked, the Fukui function seems to fail, predicting the selectivity of hard–hard interactions as hard–hard interactions are charge controlled and soft–soft interactions are frontier controlled, the Fukui function is not expected to describe well the hard–hard interactions. Using the properties of Fukui function, more powerful descriptor of chemical reactivity and site selectivity have been proposed by Chattaraj et al. [30].

9.2.2 LOCAL HARDNESS AND LOCAL SOFTNESS

In addition to the knowledge of global softness (S), different local softnesses were used to describe the reactivity of atoms in molecule. The local softness is generally defined [28] as

$$S_k^\alpha = S f_k^\alpha$$ (24)

where $\alpha = +, -$ and 0 represent the local softness quantities which describe the nucleophilic, electrophilic, and radical attacks, respectively.

$$S^+ = S f^+ \text{ for nucleophilic attack}$$ (25)

$$S^- = S f^- \text{ for electrophilic attack}$$ (26)

$$S^0 = S f^0 \text{ for radical attack}$$ (27)

where S is the total softness of the molecule.

The purpose of mathematical definitions of a local softness is to provide a quantitative representation of qualitative concepts.

9.2.3 LOCAL CHARGES

9.2.3.1 MULLIKEN CHARGE

Mulliken charges [31–33] provide a means of estimating partial atomic charges from calculations carried out by the methods of computational chemistry, particularly those based on the linear combination of atomic orbital molecular orbital method. The charge thus arises from the Mulliken population analysis.

Let us consider $C_{\mu i}$ is the coefficients of the basis functions in the molecular orbital for the μ'th basis function in the i'th molecular orbital. Then, the density matrix terms are given by

$$D_{\mu v} = 2 \sum_i c\mu i\, C^*_{vi} \qquad (28)$$

For a closed-shell system, where each molecular orbital is doubly occupied, the population matrix P has terms:

$$P_{\mu v} = D_{\mu v} S_{\mu v} \qquad (29)$$

where S is the overlap matrix of the basis functions and the sum of all terms of $P_{\mu v}$ is N, which is the total number of electrons.

The Mulliken population analysis aims first to divide N among all the basis functions. This is done by taking the diagonal element of $P_{\mu v}$ and then dividing the off-diagonal elements equally between the two appropriate basis functions. As the off-diagonal terms include $P_{\mu v}$ and $P_{\mu v}$, this simplifies to just the sum of a row. This defines the gross orbital population (GOP) as

$$(GOP)_\mu = \sum_v P\mu v \qquad (30)$$

The $(GOP)_\mu$ terms sum to N and thus divide the total number of electrons between the basis functions. It remains to sum these terms over all basis functions on a given atom A to give the gross atom population (GAP). The sum of $(GAP)_A$ terms is also N. The charge, Q_A, is then defined as the difference between the number of electrons on the isolated free atom, which is the atomic number Z_A, and the GAP:

$$Q_A = Z_A - (GAP)_A \qquad (31)$$

The problem with this approach is the equal division of the off-diagonal terms between the two basis functions. This leads to charge separations in molecules that are exaggerated. In a modified [33] population analysis, this problem can be reduced by dividing the overlap populations $P_{\mu v}$ between the corresponding orbital populations $P_{\mu\mu}$ and P_{vv} in the ratio between the latter. This choice, although still arbitrary, relates the partitioning in some way to the electronegativity difference between the corresponding atoms.

9.2.3.2 ZERO DIFFERENTIAL OVERLAP CHARGE

Numerous approximations were being tried out for getting around the problem of computing the more difficult integrals. In the zero differential overlap (ZDO), approximation the product of two different atomic orbitals is set to zero. The integral which survived the ZDO approximation was partly computed using the uniformly charged sphere approximation and the rest parameterized. The result procedure was a quantitative theory, which went well beyond Hückel theory by explicitly taking into account electron repulsions. Pariser and Parr [34] used the method for the prediction of the spectral procedure of conjugate systems. Pople [35] independently used the ZDO approximation to work out the same computational strategy.

Now, let us have a look on the ZDO approximation [36] to pound over the subject.

It is well known in quantum chemistry that for two different atomic functions χ_μ and χ_v, the overlap integral is

$$S_{\mu v} = \int \chi_\mu \chi_v d\tau \; (\mu \neq v) \tag{32}$$

The differential overlap between these two function which is simply the product $\chi_\mu(i) \chi_v(ii)$ gives the probability of finding an electron i in a common volume element to them. It can be expressed as

$$\chi_\mu(i) \chi_v(ii) = \delta_{\mu v} \tag{33}$$

If χ_μ and χ_v are centered on two atoms distant from each other or their spatial orientations are quite different their differential overlap is nearly zero. All approximate LCAO–MO–SCF schemes have made use of this feature by neglecting all or most of the integrals containing the product $\chi_\mu(i) \chi_v$ (ii) unless μ is equal to v. If all such integrals are neglected, we come at the so-called zero differential overlap (ZDO) approximation in which $\delta_{\mu v}$ is set equal to zero unless μ and v are equal. Actually orbitals, which are centered on the same or even on two directly bonded atoms, have a rather larger differential overlap. Setting such differential overlap equal zero is far from being a correct approximation. As mentioned earlier, the essential advantage of applying the ZDO approximation is the considerable simplification, it introduces in the computation. The capability of the ZDO methods to describe the different molecular properties is an important measure of the appropriateness of the ZDO approximation. Practical experience with different ZDO methods has proved that they can be brought about to reasonably represent chemical properties [37–41]. However, it is not expected that ZDO methods may provide calculated values, which are in good agreement with rigorous *ab initio* calculations.

9.3   METHOD OF COMPUTATION

The hardness, softness, electronegativity, electrophilicity index, local softnesses, and Fukui functions, and so on were calculated on the basis of a new panorama in chemistry called "conceptual density functional theory (CDFT)" [42], which has ramified research in theoretical chemistry in the present time.

The AcuraHuckel Version 1.2 software [43] was used to generate the Hückel determinant for the molecules pyrrol and porphycene. Solving this determinant, eigenvalues are obtained for the molecular orbitals in terms of α and β.

The eigen values for the HOMO and the LUMO are taken as the orbital energy of HOMO and LUMO. The global reactivity descriptors for the molecules were evaluated considering $I = -\varepsilon_{HOMO}$ and $A = -\varepsilon_{LUMO}$ (Koopmans' theorem) and using the density functional definitions [22, 23] [Eqs. (1), (7), (8), (4), and (13)] of the corresponding reactivity descriptors.

In addition, we have used the eigen functions for the HOMO and the LUMO to compute the local reactivity parameters, the Fukui functions, and the local softnesses for the corresponding molecule. The Fukui functions and local softnesses for each site of the molecules are computed using the Eqs. (23–25) and (27–29).

In order to evaluate the value of α and β for the molecule studied in this work, we have compared the HOMO and LUMO orbital energies obtained on the basis of HMO calculations with those obtained from Austin model 1(AM1) method [15, 16] of the corresponding compound.

The bond orders, bond lengths, and π charge densities of the corresponding molecules are calculated on the basis of Huckel molecular orbital theory [17, 18] and using AcuraHuckel Version 1.2 software [43].

We have also applied the best semiempirical calculation procedure Austin Model 1(AM1) [15, 16] for the study of the electronic structure and chemical reactivity of the chemical systems, pyrrol and porphycene. The AM1 calculations are carried out using ArgusLab4.0 software [44].

All the structures considered in this study were initially taken as planar, and the geometry optimizations were done using Hartree–Fock self-consistence field (HF-SCF) method and a minimal STO-3G basis set is used. The optimized structure and the HOMO and LUMO charge densities are used in the figure to understand the most stable (less repulsion) configuration and electronic distribution of the molecules.

9.3.1 HMO CALCULATIONS

In the pioneering days of quantum chemistry, Erich Hückel put forward an approximate method for solving the Schrödinger equation of benzene, which was equally suitable for other molecules containing conjugated π-electrons. This approach is nowadays known under the name HMO theory. The HMO model was originally introduced to permit qualitative study of the π-electron systems in planar, conjugated hydrocarbon molecules. It is thus most appropriate for molecules such as benzene or butadiene, but the approach and concepts have wider applicability. Solving the HMO secular equation for complex molecules can become very difficult by hand.

However, we enlist the help of the computer program AcuraHuckel Version 1.2 [43] to solve the secular equation of pyrrol and porphycene.

For pyrrol, the determinant is

	1	2	3	4	5
1	x	1	0	0	1
2	1	x	1	0	0
3	0	1	x	1	0
4	0	0	1	x	1
5	1	0	0	1	x

For porphycene, the determinant is

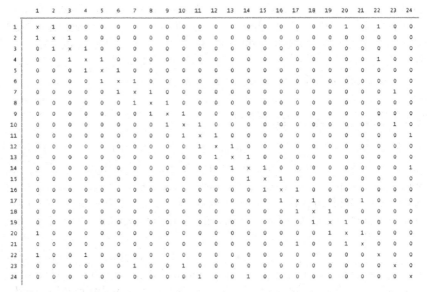

where $x = (\alpha - E)/\beta$

By solving these determinants, eigen values are obtained for the molecular orbitals in terms of α and β. The calculated α's and β's for the molecules are given as follows:

Molecule	α(au)	β(au)
Pyrrol	−0.178601	−0.227117
Porphycene	1.056	2.67686

The density functional global reactivity parameters μ, χ, η, S, and ω for the above-mentioned four molecules are calculated using the Eqs. (1), (7), (8), (4), and (13), respectively.

9.3.2 AM1 CALCULATIONS

AM1 studies are carried out on pyrrol and porphycene. The eigen values are for the HOMO, and the LUMO of the molecules studied in this work is taken as the HOMO and LUMO orbital energies. Using these orbital energies, we have computed the global reactivity descriptors such as μ, χ, η, S,ω for pyrrol and porphycene following Eqs. (1), (7), (8), (4), and (13), respectively.

The Fukui functions and local softnesses for each site of the pyrrol and porphycene are computed using the ansatz Eqs. (23–25) and (27–29), considering the LCAO coefficient of each carbon atom. Physical properties of pyrrol and porphycene (on the basis of AM1 calculation) are also tabulated. The ZDO atomic charges and Mulliken charges, obtained in this method for each molecule are also tabulated.

9.4 RESULT AND DISCUSSION

In Table9.1, we have tabulated the computed (on the basis of AM1 calculation) physical properties of pyrrol andporphycene.

TABLE 9.1   Physical properties of pyrrol and porphycene (on the basis of AM1 calculation)

System	Energy (SCF) (au)	Energy (geometrical) (au)	Heat of formation (kcal/mol)	Total dipole moment (Debye)
Pyrrol	−28.9101022	−28.911379	40.5046	1.94334174
Porphycene	−131.07762072	−131.3313443	257.2120	3.58039015

The computed (on the basis of HMO theory)π charge density, bond order, and bond length of pyrrol are presented in Tables 9.2(A–C), respectively.

TABLE 9.2 (A)   Computed πcharge density of pyrrol on the basis of HMO theory

Atom	Pi charge density
P(1,1)	1.03462
P(2,2)	1.10556
P(3,3)	1.10556
P(4,4)	1.03462
P(5,5)	1.71965

TABLE 9.2(B) Computed bond order of pyrrol on the basis of HMO theory

Atom	Pi bond order
P(1,2)	0.79029
P(2,3)	0.55277
P(3,4)	0.79029
P(4,5)	0.4395
P(1,5)	0.4395

TABLE 9.2(C) Computed bond length of pyrrol on the basis of HMO theory

Atom	Pi bond length (Å)
P(1,2)	1.37355
P(2,3)	1.41156
P(3,4)	1.37355

(Estimated C–C bond lengths based on the equation $R = 1.5 - 0.16P$ (in Angstroms))

The computed (on the basis of HMO theory) π charge density, bond order, and bond length of porphycene are presented in Tables 9.3(A–C), respectively.

TABLE 9.3(A) Computed Pi- charge density on the basis of HMO theory of porphycene

Atom	π charge density	Atom	π charge density
P(1,1)	0.90411	P(13,13)	0.99716
P(2,2)	1.02575	P(14,14)	0.92993
P(3,3)	0.99716	P(15,15)	0.7853
P(4,4)	0.92993	P(16,16)	0.7853
P(5,5)	0.7853	P(17,17)	0.92993
P(6,6)	0.7853	P(18,18)	0.99716
P(7,7)	0.92993	P(19,19)	1.02575
P(8,8)	0.99716	P(20,20)	0.90411
P(9,9)	1.02575	P(21,21)	1.35775
P(10,10)	0.90411	P(22,22)	1.35775
P(11,11)	0.90411	P(23,23)	1.35775
P(12,12)	1.02575	P(24,24)	1.35775

TABLE 9.3(B) Computed bond order on the basis of HMO theory of porphycene

Linkage	Pi bond order	Linkage	Pi bond order
P(1,2)	0.50055	P(15,16)	0.52104
P(2,3)	0.76436	P(16,17)	0.65902
P(3,4)	0.48262	P(17,18)	0.48262
P(4,5)	0.65902	P(18,19)	0.76436
P(5,6)	0.52104	P(19,20)	0.50055
P(6,7)	0.65902	P(20,21)	0.62714
P(7,8)	0.48262	P(1,20)	0.44143
P(8,9)	0.76436	P(1,22)	0.62714
P(9,10)	0.50055	P(4,22)	0.4152
P(1) 0,11	0.44143	P(7,23)	0.4152
P(11,12)	0.50055	P(10,23)	0.62714
P(12,13)	0.76436	P(11,24)	0.62714
P(13,14)	0.48262	P(14,24)	0.4152
P(14,15)	0.65902	P(17,21)	0.4152

TABLE 9.3(C) Computed bond length of on the basis of HMO theory of porphycene

Linkage	Bond length	Linkage	Bond length
R(1,2)	1.41991 Å	R(11,12)	1.41991 Å
R(2,3)	1.3777 Å	R(12,13)	1.3777 Å
R(3,4)	1.42278 Å	R(13,14)	1.42278 Å
R(4,5)	1.39456 Å	R(14,15)	1.39456 Å
R(5,6)	1.41663 Å	R(15,16)	1.41663 Å
R(6,7)	1.39456 Å	R(16,17)	1.39456 Å
R(7,8)	1.42278 Å	R(17,18)	1.42278 Å
R(8,9)	1.3777 Å	R(18,19)	1.3777 Å
R(9,10)	1.41991 Å	R(19,20)	1.41991 Å
R(10,11)	1.42937 Å	R(1,20)	1.42937 Å

(Estimated C–C bond lengths based on the equation $R = 1.5 - 0.16P$ (in Angstroms))

In Tables 9.4(A) and (B), we have tabulated the computed (on the basis of HMO method) total energy (E), ε_{HOMO}, ε_{LUMO}, ionization energy (I),electron affinity (A), delocalization energy (D), and the global reactivity parameters (chemical potential, electronegativity, hardness, softness, and electrophilicity index) of pyrrol and porphycene.

TABLE 9.4(A)   Computed total energy (E), ε_{HOMO}, ε_{LUMO}, ionization energy (I), electron affinity (A), and delocalization energy (D) on the basis of HMO method

System	E(au)	ε_{HOMO}(au)	ε_{LUMO}(au)	I(au)	A(au)	D(au)
Pyrrol	$6\alpha + 8.25258\beta$ $=-2.9459$	$A + 0.618034$ $\beta =-0.318967$	$\alpha - 1.008258\ \beta$ $=0.05039$	0.318967	0.05039	8.25258β $=-1.8743$
Porphycene	$24\alpha + 32.48875$ $\beta = -61.624485$	$A+0.5\beta =-$ 0.28243	$\alpha + 0.425734$ $\beta= -0.0836303$	0.28243	0.0836303	32.48875β $=-86.968$

TABLE 9.4(B)   Computed global reactivity parameters on the basis of HMO method

System	μ(au)	χ(au)	η(au)	S(au)	ω(au)
Pyrrol	$\alpha - 0.195112$ $\beta =$ -0.1342877	$-\alpha +$ $0.19511\beta=-0.1342877$	$-0.813146\ \beta =$ 0.184679	5.4148008	0.048823
Porphycene	$\alpha +$ $0.462867\ \beta =$ -0.183032	$-\alpha-0.462867\ \beta =$ 0.183032	$-0.037133\ \beta =$ 0.0993998	10.0636	0.168515

In Table9.5, we have tabulated the computed (on the basis of AM1 method) ε_{HOMO}, ε_{LUMO}, global reactivity parameters (chemical potential, electronegativity, hardness, softness, and electrophilicity index) of pyrrol and porphycene.

TABLE 9.5   Computed global reactivity parameters from AM-1 calculation

System	εHOMO	εLUMO	μ(au)	χ(au)	η(au)	S(au)	ω(au)
Pyrrol	−0.3189670	0.050388	−0.134288	0.134288	0.184679	5.4148008	0.001665
Porphycene	−0.279314	0.08085	−0.1798995	0.1798995	0.0994	10.0636	0.001608

The calculated Fukui functions (au) and local softnesses (au) of pyrrol using HMO theory is presented in Table 9.6.

TABLE 9.6 Calculated Fukui functions (au) and local softnesses (au) of pyrrol using HMO theory

Atom no.	$f^+(r)$	$f^-(r)$	$f^0(r)$	S^+	S^-	S^0
1	0.68890322	0.7236045	0.70625386	3.730274	3.918174	3.824224
2	0.17087858	0.27632178	0.22360018	0.925273	1.496227	1.21075
3	0.17087858	0.27632178	0.22360018	0.925273	1.496227	1.21075
4	0.68890322	0.7236045	0.70625386	3.730274	3.918174	3.824224
5	0.28035072	0	0.14017536	1.518043	0	0.759022

In Table 9.7, we have summarized the HMO Fukui functions (au) and local softnesses (au) of porphycene.

TABLE 9.7 Calculated HMO Fukui functions (au) and local softnesses (au) of porphycene

Atom no.	$f^+(r)$	$f^-(r)$	$f^0(r)$	S^+	S^-	S^0
1	0.0725805	0.11319282	0.09288666	0.730421	1.139127	0.934774
2	0.02138312	0.05030792	0.03584552	0.215191	0.506279	0.360735
3	0.04286592	0.05030792	0.04658692	0.431385	0.506279	0.468832
4	0.05497928	0.11319282	0.08408605	0.553289	1.139127	0.846208
5	0.16669538	0.05030792	0.10850165	1.677556	0.506279	1.091917
6	0.16669538	0.05030792	0.10850165	1.677556	0.506279	1.091917
7	0.05497928	0.11319282	0.08408605	0.553289	1.139127	0.846208
8	0.04286592	0.05030792	0.04658692	0.431385	0.506279	0.468832
9	0.02138312	0.05030792	0.03584552	0.215191	0.506279	0.360735
10	0.0725805	0.11319282	0.09288666	0.730421	1.139127	0.934774
11	0.0725805	0.11319282	0.09288666	0.730421	1.139127	0.934774
12	0.02138312	0.05030792	0.03584552	0.215191	0.506279	0.360735
13	0.04286592	0.05030792	0.04658692	0.431385	0.506279	0.468832
14	0.05497928	0.11319282	0.08408605	0.553289	1.139127	0.846208
15	0.16669538	0.05030792	0.10850165	1.677556	0.506279	1.091917
16	0.16669538	0.05030792	0.10850165	1.677556	0.506279	1.091917

TABLE 9.7   *(Continued)*

Atom no.	$f^+(r)$	$f^-(r)$	$f^0(r)$	S^+	S^-	S^0
17	0.05497928	0.11319282	0.08408605	0.553289	1.139127	0.846208
18	0.04286592	0.05030792	0.04658692	0.431385	0.506279	0.468832
19	0.02138312	0.05030792	0.03584552	0.215191	0.506279	0.360735
20	0.0725805	0.11319282	0.09288666	0.730421	1.139127	0.934774
21	0.141512	0.12280968	0.13216084	1.42412	1.235907	1.330014
22	0.141512	0.12280968	0.13216084	1.42412	1.235907	1.330014
23	0.141512	0.122880968	0.13216084	1.42412	1.236625	1.330014
24	0.141512	0.12280968	0.13216084	1.42412	1.235907	1.330014

In Table 9.8, the computed AM1 Fukuifunctions (au) and local softnesses(au) of various sites of Pyrrol are tabulated.

TABLE 9.8   Calculated AM1 Fukui functions (au) and local softnesses (au) of Pyrrol

Atom no	Total $f^+(r)$	Total $f^-(r)$	f^0	S^+	S^-	S^0
1 C	0.170630296	0.26346256	0.217046428	0.923929063	1.426597281	1.175263
2 C	0.62453288	0.736538605	0.680535743	3.381721138	3.988209828	3.684965
3 N	0.409693666	3.58×10^{-10}	0.2048468	2.21840959	1.9384986×10^{-9}	1.1092046
4C	0.6245209	0.73653198	0.68052644	3.381656269	3.988173955	3.684915
5 C	0.170622453	0.263453495	0.217037974	0.923886595	1.426548195	1.175217

We have tabulated the calculated AM1 Fukui functions (au) and local softnesses (au) of various sites of porphycene in Table 9.9.

TABLE 9.9   Calculated AM1 Fukui functions (au) and local softnesses (au) of porphycene

Atom no	$f^+(r)$	$f^-(r)$	f^0	S^+	S^-	S^0
1 N	0.0028379	0.0109086	0.00687325	0.02856	0.10978	0.06917
2 C	0.0168583	0.2413346	0.12909645	0.169656	2.428695	1.299175
3 C	0.016241	0.2413521	0.12879655	0.163443	2.428871	1.296157
4 N	0.0028301	0.0109081	0.0068691	0.028481	0.109775	0.069128
5 C	0.0053452	0.3120736	0.1587094	0.053792	3.140584	1.597188

TABLE 9.9 *(Continued)*

Atom no	$f^-(r)$	$f^+(r)$	f^0	S^+	S^-	S^0
6 C	0.097135402	0.0006817	0.35711095	7.180783	0.00686	3.593822
7 C	0.0001613	0.13814	0.06915065	0.001623	1.390186	0.695904
8 C	0.2217079	0.0080204	0.11486415	2.23118	0.080714	1.155947
9 C	0.2216047	0.0080254	0.11481505	2.230141	0.080764	1.155453
10 N	0.0726758	0.0393522	0.056014	0.731381	0.396025	0.563702
11 C	0.2892425	0.0135438	0.15139315	2.910821	0.136299	1.52356
12 C	0.2892615	0.0135687	0.1514151	2.911012	0.13655	1.523781
13 N	0.0726602	0.0393214	0.0559908	0.731223	0.395715	0.563469
14 C	0.0053416	0.3119116	0.1586266	0.053756	3.138954	1.596355
15 C	0.0970323	0.0006829	0.0488576	0.976494	0.006872	0.491683
16 C	0.0001601	0.1380742	0.06911715	0.001611	1.389524	0.695567
17 C	0.0096495	0.1611856	0.08541755	0.097109	1.622107	0.859608
18 C	0.0251791	0.072370221	0.374440655	0.253393	0.0728305	3.768221
19 C	0.1233896	0.0011756	0.0622826	1.241743	0.01183	0.626787
20 C	0.1365343	0.0012688	0.06890155	1.374027	0.012769	0.693398
21 C	0.1364893	0.0012636	0.06887645	1.373573	0.012716	0.693145
22 C	0.1234044	0.0011776	0.062291	1.241893	0.011851	0.626872
23 C	0.0251996	0.0723239	0.04876175	0.253599	0.727838	0.490719
24 C	0.0096572	0.1612301	0.08544365	0.097186	1.622555	0.859871

In Table 9.10, we have presented the computed Mulliken and ZDO charge of various sites of pyrrol on the basis of AM1 calculation.

TABLE 9.10 Computed Mulliken and ZDO charge of pyrrol on the basis of AM1 calculation

Atom	Mulliken atomic charge	ZDO atomic charge
1 N	−0.3358	−0.1836
2 C	−0.1783	−0.1438
3 C	−0.2539	−0.1957
4 C	−0.2539	−0.1957
5 C	−0.1783	−0.1438

TABLE 9.10 *(Continued)*

Atom	Mulliken atomic charge	ZDO atomic charge
6 H	0.2297	0.1613
7 H	0.2143	0.1495
8 H	0.2143	0.1495
9 H	0.2297	0.1613
10 H	0.3125	0.2408

The computed Mulliken and ZDO charge of various sites of porphycene on the basis of AM1 calculation is presented in Table 9.11.

TABLE 9.11 Computed Mulliken and ZDO charge of porphycene on the basis of AM1 calculation

Atom	Mulliken atomic charge	ZDO atomic charge	Atom	Mulliken atomic charge	ZDO atomic charge
1 N	−0.2885	−0.1419	20C	−0.2333	−0.1666
2 C	0.0181	−0.0031	21 C	−0.2333	−0.1666
3 C	0.018	−0.0031	22 C	−0.2083	−0.1408
4 N	−0.2884	−0.1418	23 C	−0.2085	−0.1537
5 C	−0.0744	−0.0902	24 C	−0.2296	−0.1769
6 C	−0.0518	0.0009	25 H	0.3777	0.2948
7 C	−0.2339	−0.1824	26 H	0.1932	0.1317
8 C	0.0674	0.0575	27 H	0.1929	0.1311
9 C	0.0673	0.0575	28 H	0.3776	0.2947
10 N	−0.2453	−0.2038	29 H	0.1931	0.1317
11 C	0.031	0.0188	30 H	0.193	0.1311
12 C	0.0309	0.0188	31 H	0.2222	0.1555
13 N	−0.2453	−0.2038	32 H	0.2151	0.1498
14 C	−0.0743	−0.09	33 H	0.2276	0.1594
15 C	−0.0518	0.0008	34 H	0.2284	0.1598
16 C	−0.2337	−0.1823	35 H	0.2284	0.1599
17 C	−0.2296	−0.1769	36 H	0.2276	0.1594
18 C	−0.2087	−0.1538	37H	0.2152	0.1498
19C	−0.2082	−0.1408	38 H	0.2222	0.1555

For understanding the equilibrium structures of the compounds and for the better visualization of the computed results, we have presented the optimized structures, charge densities on various sites of the two compounds invoked in this study, and the computed results in various figures.

The optimized structures of pyrrol and porphycene are presented in Figures 9.1(A) and (B), respectively.

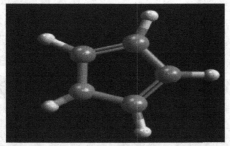

FIGURE 9.1(A)   Optimized structure of pyrrol.

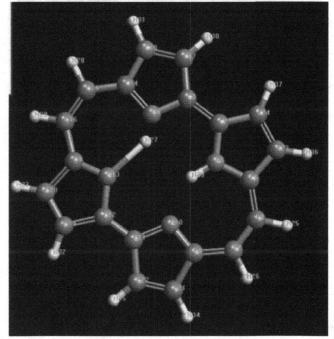

FIGURE 9.1(B)   Optimized structure of porphycene.

The analysis of the densities of HOMO and LUMO of various sites of pyrrol molecule is presented in Figures 9.2(A) and (B), respectively.

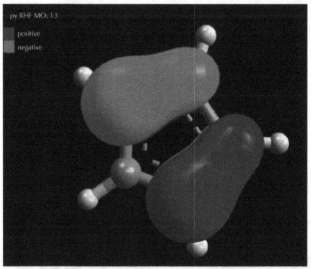

FIGURE 9.2(A)   (i) Charge density on HOMO of pyrrol molecule.

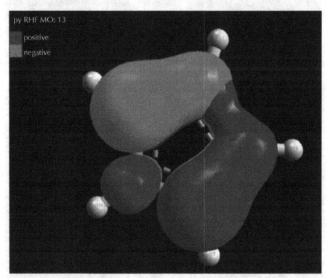

FIGURE 9.2(B) (ii) Charge density on LUMO of pyrrol molecule.

The HOMO and LUMO charge densities of various sites of porphycene molecules are presented in Figures 9.3(A) and (B), respectively.

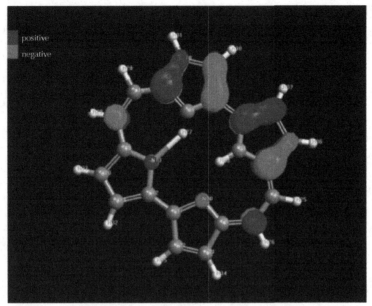

FIGURE 9.3(A)   Charge density on HOMO of porphycene molecule.

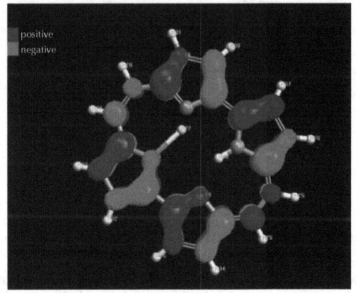

FIGURE 9.3(B)   Charge density on LUMO of porphycene molecule.

The computed (HMO method) $f^+(r)$ and $S^+(r)$ values on several atomic sites of porphycene are depicted in Figures 9.4(A) and (B), respectively.

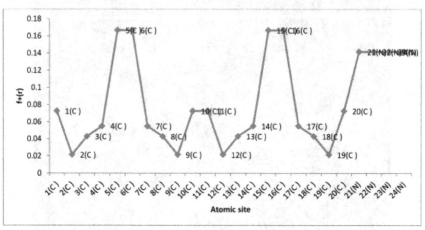

FIGURE 9.4(A) Computed $f^+(r)$ value of porphycene on the basis of HMO method.

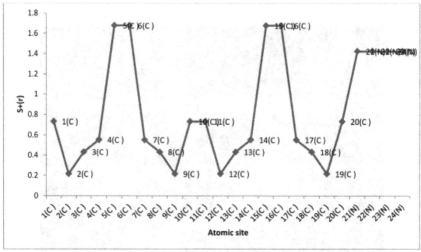

FIGURE 9.4(B)   Computed $S + (r)$ value of porphycene on the basis of HMO method.

The computed (AM1 method) $f^+(r)$ and $S^+(r)$ values on several atomic sites of porphycene are depicted in Figures 9.5(A) and (B), respectively.

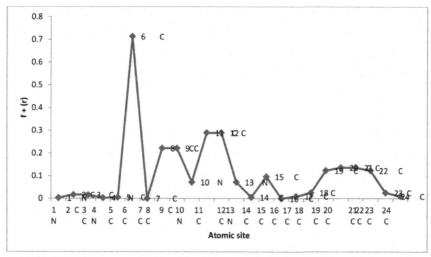

FIGURE 9.5(A)   Computed $f^+(r)$ of porphycene on the basis of AM1 method.

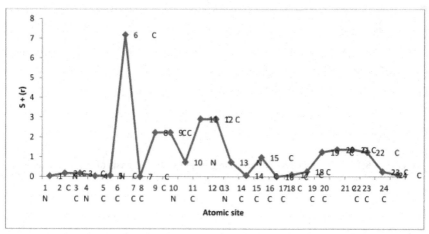

FIGURE 9.5(B)   Computed $S + (r)$ of porphycene on the basis of AM1 method.

The computed π charge densities, Mulliken charges, and ZDO charges of pyrrol on the basis of AM1 calculation are presented in Figures 9.6(A–C), respectively.

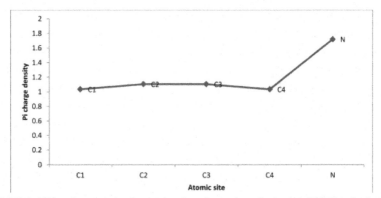

FIGURE 9.6(A)   Computed πcharge density of pyrrol on the basis of HMO calculation.

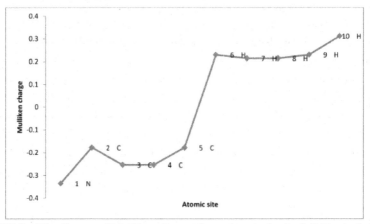

FIGURE 9.6(B)   Computed Mulliken charge of pyrrol on the basis of AM1 calculation.

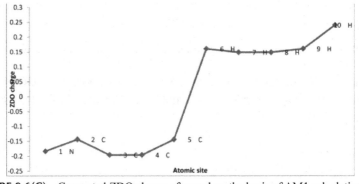

FIGURE 9.6(C)   Computed ZDO charge of pyrrol on the basis of AM1 calculation.

The computed π charge densities, Mulliken charges, and ZDO charges of porphycene on the basis of AM1 calculation are presented in Figures 9.7(A–C), respectively.

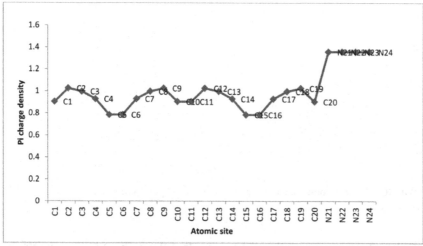

FIGURE 9.7(A) Computed π charge density of porphycene on the basis of HMO calculation.

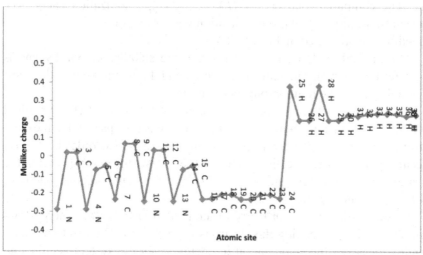

FIGURE 9.7(B) Computed Mulliken atomic charge of porphycene on the basis of AM1 calculation.

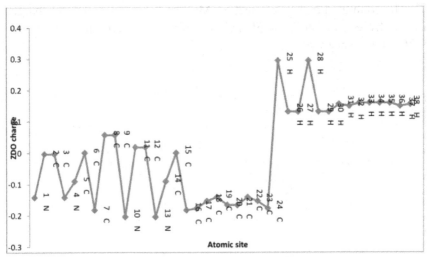

FIGURE 9.7(C)   Computed ZDO atomic charge of porphycene on the basis of AM1 calculation.

An observation on Table 9.1 reveals that the SCF and the geometrical energy of porphycene are less than those of pyrrol. Hence, porphycene is more stable. The heat of formation data also supports the observation.

The computed total energy (E), ε_{HOMO}, ε_{LUMO}, ionization energy (I), electron affinity (A), and delocalization energy (D) on the basis of HMO method are presented in Table 9.4(A).

From Table 9.4(A), it is distinct that the stability of porphycene is greater than pyrrol. The ionization energy and dipole moment of the compound follows the trendporphycene < pyrrol.

Computed global reactivity parameters on the basis of HMO method are presented in Table 9.4(B).From this table, it is transparent that the electronegativity order is pyrrol< porphycene. The hardness order is porphycene < pyrrol. Of course, the softness value follows the reverse trend of the hardness. The hardness and softness data reveal that the order of reactivity of porphycene > pyrrol.

Electrophilicity is a property of atoms that signifies the energy-lowering process on soaking the electrons from donors. The electrophilicity index measures the stabilization in energy when the system acquires an additional electronic charge from the environment. The elctrophilicity indices follow the trend porphycene > pyrrol. Thus, porphycene tend to undergo electrophilic reaction more than pyrrol.

It is worth nothing to mention that the frontier orbital energy is not the only criterion that governs the chemical characteristics of a compound.

Nevertheless, the energy criterion may be applied to deduce gross features. Compounds that have a large HOMO–LUMO gap will be stable against self-reaction, for example, dimerization, polymerization, and intramolecular rearrangements.

If the HOMO is low in an absolute sense, the compound will be chemically resistant to reaction with Lewis acids. If the LUMO is high in an absolute sense, the compound will be chemically resistant to reaction with Lewis bases:

Compounds with a high LUMO and a low HOMO will be chemically inert. Compounds with a low HOMO and LUMO tend to be stable to self-reaction but are chemically reactive as Lewis acids and electrophiles. Compounds with a high HOMO and LUMO tend to be stable to self-reaction but are chemically reactive as Lewis bases and nucleophiles. Compounds with a narrow HOMO–LUMO gap are kinetically reactive and subject to dimerization or reaction with Lewisacids or bases.

Larger the HOMO–LUMO energy gap more hard is the species and thus is less reactive. A big advantage of using hardness as the function is that the quantities concerned are physical. Larger η means larger I and smaller A, which implies that the system is more stable than its competitor.

From Table 9.5, we have surprisingly noted that the calculated results of the AM1 study are numerically same with those values calculated on the basis of HMO theoretical procedure. Thus, the AM1 studies also reveal the same result.

Now let us analyze the various atomic sites on the molecule on the basis of some very important local reactivity descriptors.

9.4.1 PYRROL

We invoked simple HMO theory for the computation of π charge density on each atomic site of pyrrol. The computed results are presented in Table 9.2(A). The analysis of the densities of HOMO and LUMO shows that both the orbital are centered on the four C atoms of the ring.

It is distinct from Table 9.2(A) that the π charge density of the positions P(1,1) and P(1,4); and P(2,2) and P(3,3) is the same for pyrrol. The computed result supports the presence of two double bonds in pyrrol. The π charge density at the P(1,5) is maximum, this observation clearly indicates the presence of more electronegative element (nitrogen) in pyrrol. Table 9.2(A) further reveals that the pair C-2 and C-3 has greater electron density than other C pair.

The computed results in Tables 9.2(B) and (C) support the presence of two double bonds in pyrrol.

The computed Fukui functions and local softnesses on the basis of HMO calculation are presented in Table 9.6. An observation on the Table 9.6 reveals that the C-1 and C-4 are almost equal in their $f^+(r)$ and $f^-(r)$ values, the C-2 and C-3 centers are almost equal in their $f^+(r)$ and $f^-(r)$ value, the C-2 and C-3 have the lowest, and C-1 and C-4 have the highest $f^-(r)$ value, the N-5 has the lowest $f^-(r)$ value, and the pair C-1 and C-4 has the highest $f^-(r)$ value.

It is also distinct from Table 9.6 that the local softnesses of each atomic sites of pyrrol follow the similar trend of variation as Fukui functions.

We are in a venture to study the Fukui function in the AM1 method we have optimized in the planner structure of pyrrol in Argus lab software to generate the eigen functions for the atomic sites of the molecule. The computed results are presented in Table 9.8.

A deeper scrutiny of the Table 9.8 reveals that the $f^+(r)$ and $f^-(r)$ values at the centers C-1 and C-5, C-2 and C-4 are almost the same. The centers C-1 and C-5 have the lowest and the centers C-2 and C-4 have the highest $f^+(r)$ value, and the centers C-2 and C-4 have the highest $f^-(r)$ value. The center N-3 has the lowest $f^-(r)$ value.

It is distinct from Table 9.8 that the local softnesses of each atomic sites of pyrrol follow the similar trend of variation like Fukui function.

We have computed the ZDO and Mulliken charge of the pyrrol molecule using the AM1 procedure and the computed results are presented in Table 9.10.

An observation on Tables 9.6 and 9.8 reveals that on the basis of AM1 calculation, the Fukui function and local softness on the N atom is not the maximum but from Table 9.10 it is distinct that the charges on the N atom are maximum in both ZDO and Mulliken method. The same observations are also found (Table 9.2(a)) in case of HMO calculation where the Fukui functions and local softness are not the maximum on the N atom, but on some C atom that contradict the experimental observations. Thus, we may point out that the Fukui function fails to predict the donor site of pyrrol. However, when we look at the pi charge density, ZDO, and Mulliken charges on the atomic sites we surprisingly noted that they are maximum on the N atom of the pyrrol and hence it is the donor site of the base.

9.4.2 PORPHYCENE

The analysis of the densities of HOMO (Figure 9.3(A)) shows that both the orbitals are centered on the four C atoms of two adjacent pyrrol rings only. The analysis of the densities of LUMO (Figure 9.3(B)) shows that the distribution of electron cloud is of two types. In type-1 both the orbitals are centered on the two C atoms of two pyrrol rings, and in type orbitals are delocalized over the rings.

We have applied simple HMO theory for the computation of π charge density on each atomic site of the porphycene. The computed results are presented in Table 9.3(A). An observation on Table 9.4(A) reveals that the π charge density on atom number C-1,C-10,C-11,C-20 and C-2,C-9,C-12,C-19, and C-3,C-8,C-13,C-18,and C-4,C-7,C-14,C-17, and C-5,C-6,C15,C-16 are the same and that on the four N-atoms is the same and maximum. We can say that the decreasing order of the charge C-2,C-9,C-12,C-19> C-3,C-8,C-13,C-18> C-4, C-7,C-14,C-17 > C-1,C-10,C-11,C-20 > C-5,C-6,C-15,C-16 from this output which is in accord with our normal experiences. We have also computed the bond orders and bond lengths for porphyrin on the basis of HMO theory and presented in Tables 9.3(B) and (C), respectively

It is transpires from Table 9.7 that with respect to the f^{+} and f^{-} values the centers C-1,C-10,C-11,C-20; C-2,C-9,C-12,C-19; C-3,C-8,C-13,C-18;C-4,C-7,C-14,C-17; C-5,C-6,C-15,C-16; N-21,N-22,N-23,N-24; are identical. It can be also noted that the centers C-5,C-6,C-15,C-16 have the highest f^{+} value (0.16669538) and the centers C-2,C-9,C-12,C-19 have the lowest f^{+} value (0.02138312) and the centers N-21,N-22,N-23,N-24 have the highest f^{-} value (0.12280968) and the centers C-2,C-9,C-12,C-19,C-3,C-8,C-13,C-18,C-5,C-6,C-15,C-16 have the lowest f^{-} value (0.05030792).

It is distinct from Table 9.7 that the local softnesses of each atomic sites of porphycene follow exactly the same trend of variation of Fukui function.

The AM1 Fukui functions and local softnesses are presented in Table 9.9. Considering the $f^{+}(r)$ and $f^{-}(r)$ value we can say from the Table 9.9

that the N-1,N-4 centers, N-10,N-13 centers, C-2,C-3 centers, C-7,C-16 centers, C-5,C-14 centers C-6,C-15 centers, C-8,C-9, centers C-11,C-12 centers ,C-17,C-24 centers, C-20,C-21 centers, C-18,C-23 centers and the C-19,C-22 centers are identical.

A observation on Table 9.9 reveals that the center C-7,C-16 have the lowest and C-8,C-9 have the highest $f^{+}(r)$ value and the center C-7,C-16 has the lowest and C-5,C-14 has the highest $f^{-}(r)$ value.

It is distinct from Table 9.9 that the local softnesses of each atomic sites of porphycene follow the similar trend of variation like Fukui function.

An observation on Table 9.11 reveals that on the basis of AM1 calculation, the two sets of N-centers have high atomic charge value. The N-1 and N-4 have the maximum atomic charge and the other set N-10 and N-13 have also very high atomic charge. This observation supports the view that two trans N atoms donate two lone pairs of electrons to metal ion during donor acceptor interaction. The observation of the work is the Fukui function and local softness on the N atoms is not the maximum but the charges on the N atoms are maximum in both ZDO and Mulliken method. The same observations are also found in case of HMO calculation, where the Fukui functions and local softness are not the maximum on the N atoms, but on some C atom, which contradicts the experimental observations. Thus, we may point out that the Fukui function fails to predict the donor site of pyrrol and porphycene. But when we look on the pi charge density, ZDO and Mulliken charges on the atomic sites we surprisingly noted that they are maximum on the N atoms of the pyrrol and porphycene and hence it is the donor site of the compounds under study.

9.5 CONCLUSION

A theoretical study of the stability, reactivity, and site selectivity was carried out at the AM1 and Huckel method. Further we made an attempt to compare the local reactivity indices of the DFT (Fukui function and local softness) and atomic charges. This study provides evidence that both the Fukui functions and local softnesses fail to explain the maximum reactive or more precisely the donor site of the molecule/ligand porphycene. However, the π charge density, ZDO, and Mulliken charges show maxima on the Trans N atoms. We surprisingly noted that two sets of the trans N atoms of the molecule has the same atomic charge and higher in magnitude than all C atoms.

ACKNOWLEDGMENT

The authors would like to thank the management of Techno Global-Balurghat and Techno India Group for providing research facility.

KEYWORDS

- **AM1**
- **Atomic charges**
- **Global reactivity descriptors**
- **HMO**
- **Local reactivity descriptors**
- **Porphycene**

REFERENCES

1. Gundy, S.; Van der Putten, W.; Shearera, A.; Ryderc, A. G.; and Ball, M.; Time-resolved fluorescence studies of porphycene and tetrasulfonated phthalocyanine dyes in varying solvents. *Proc. SPIE*, Diagnostic Optical Spectroscopy in Biomedicine. **2001,** *4432,* 299–310.
2. García, D. S.; Sessler, J. L.; Porphycenes: synthesis and derivatives. *Chem. Soc. Rev.* **2008,** *37,* 215–232.
3. Smith, K. Ed.; Porphyrins and Metalloporphyrins. Elsevier, Amsterdam; **1975,** I–VII.
4. Kral, V.; Kralova, J.; Kaplanek, R.; Briza, T.; and Martasek, P.; Where is porphyrin chemistry going? *Physiol. Res.* **2006,** *55(Suppl. 2),* S3–S26.
5. Wai-Yin Sun, R.; and Ming Che, C.; The anti-cancer properties of gold(III) compounds with dianionic porphyrin and tetradentate ligands. *Coord. Chem. Rev.* **2009,** *253,* 1682–1691.
6. Huheey, J. E.; Keiter, E. A.; Keiter, R. L.; and Medhi, O. K.; Inorganic Chemistry. 4th Edn. Pearson Education, South Asia; **2008.**
7. Pearson, R. G.; Hard and soft acids and bases. *J. Am. Chem. Soc.* **1963,** *85,* 3533–3539.
8. Mendez, F.; Gazquez, J. L.; Chemical reactivity of enolate ions: the local hard and soft acids and bases principle viewpoint. *J. Am. Chem. Soc.* **1994,** *116,* 9298–9301.
9. Martin, R. B.; Metal ion stabilities correlate with electron affinity rather than hardness or softness. *Inorg. Chem. Acta.* **1998,** *283,* 30–36.
10. Ghosh, A.; and Almlof, J.; Structure and stability of cis-porphyrin. *J. Phys. Chem.* **1995,** *99,* 1073–1075.
11. Punnagai, M.; Joseph, S.; and Sastry, G. N.; A theoretical study of porphyrin isomers and their core-modified analogues: cis-transisomerism, tautomerism and relative stabilities. *J. Chem. Sci.* **2004,** *116,* 271–283.

12. Feng, X. T.; Yu, J. G.; Lei, M.; Fang, W. H.; and Liu, S.; Toward understanding metal-binding specificity of porphyrin: aconceptual density functional theory study. *J. Phys. Chem. B.* **2009,** *113,* 13381–13389.

13. Islam, N.; and Das, M.; Do the Fukui function and local softness specify the softest and hardest regions of porphyrin? *Int. J. Chem. Model.* **2013,** *5,* 67–81.

14. Islam, N.; and Das, M.; Semi empirical AM1 studies on porphyrin. *Modern Trends Chem. Chem. Eng.* Ed. Haghi, A. K.; Apple Academic Press; **2011,** 124–136.

15. Dewar, M. J. S.; Zoebisch, E. G.; Healy, E. F.; and Stewart, J. J. P.; "Development and use of quantum mechanical molecular models. 76. AM1: a new general purpose quantum mechanical molecular model." *J. Am. Chem. Soc.* **1985,** *107,* 3902–3909.

16. Dewar, M. J. S.; Jie, C.; and Yu, J.; "SAM1; the first of a new series of general purpose quantum mechanical molecular models." *Tetrahedron.* **1993,** *49,* 5003–5038.

17. Hückel, E.; Zur quantentheorie der doppelbindung. *Zeitschrift für Physik.* **1930,** *60,* 423–456.

18. Hückel, E.; "Quantentheoretische beiträge zum benzolproblem."*Zeitschrift für Physik.* **1931,** *70(3–4),* 204–286.

19. Parr, R. G.; Donnelly, R. A.; Levy, M.; and Palke, W. E.; Electronegativity: the density functional viewpoint. *J. Chem. Phys.* **1978,** *68,* 3801–3807.

20. Gyftpoulous, E. P.; and Hatsopoulos, G. N.; Quantum-thermodynamic definition of electronegativity. *Proc. Natl. Acad. Sci.* **1968,** *60,* 786–793.

21. Iczkowski, R. P.; and Margrave, J. L.; Electronegativity. *J. Am. Chem. Soc.* **1961,** *83,* 3547–3551.

22. Parr, R. G.; and Pearson, R. G.; Absolute hardness: companion parameter to absolute electronegativity. *J. Am. Chem. Soc.* **1983,** *105,* 7512–7516.

23. Pearson, R. G.; Absolute electronegativity and hardness correlated with molecular orbital theory. *Proc. Natl. Acad. Sci.* **1986,** *83,* 8440–8441.

24. Parr, R. G.; Szentpaly, L. V.; and Liu, S.; Electrophilicity index. *J. Am. Chem. Soc.* **1999,** *121,* 1922–1924.

25. Maynard, A. T.; and Covell, D. G.; Reactivity of zinc finger cores: analysis of protein packing and electrostatic screening. *J. Am. Chem. Soc.* **2001,** *123,* 1047–1058.

26. Parr, R. G.; and Yang, W.; Density functional approach to the frontier-electron theory of chemical reactivity. *J. Am. Chem. Soc.* **1984,** *106,* 4049–4050.

27. Fukui, K.; Yonezawa, T.; and Shingu, H. A.; Molecular orbital theory of reactivity in aromatic hydrocarbons. *J. Chem. Phys.* **1952,** *20,* 722–725.

28. Yang, W.; and Parr, R. G.; Hardness, softness, and the Fukui function in the electronic theory of metals and catalysis. *Proc. Natl. Acad. Sci. USA.* **1985,** *82,* 6723–6726.

29. Li, Y.; and Evans, J. N. S.; The Fukui function: Akey concept linking frontier molecular orbital theory and the hard-soft-acid-base principle. *J. Am. Chem. Soc.* **1995,** *117,* 7756–7759.

30. Chattaraj, P. K.; Maity, B.; and Sarkar, U.; Philicity: A unified treatment of chemical reactivity and selectivity. *J. Phys. Chem. A.* **2003,** *107,* 4973–4975.

31. Mulliken, R. S.; Electronic population analysis on LCAO–MO molecular wave functions. I *J. Chem. Phys.***1955,** *23,* 1833–1840.

32. Csizmadia, G.; Theory and Practice of MO Calculations on Organic Molecules. Amsterdam: Elsevier; **1976.**

33. Bickelhaupt, F. M.; Van Eikema Hommes, N. J. R.; Fonseca Guerra, C.; and Baerends, E. J.; Organometallics. *The Carbon-Lithium Electron Pair Bond in (CH3Li)n (n = 1, 2, 4)*. **1996,** *15,* 2923–2931.

34. Pariser, R.; and Parr, R. G.; A semi-empirical theory of the electronic spectra and electronic structure of complex unsaturated molecules. *J. Chem. Phys.* **1953,** *21,* 466–71.

35. Pople, J. A.; Electron interaction in unsaturated hydrocarbons. *Trans. Faraday Soc.* **1953,** *49,* 1375–85.

36. Hasanein, A. A.; and Evans, M. W.; Computational Methods in Quantum Chemistry: Quantum Chemistry. Singapore: World Scientific; **1996,** *2.*

37. McWeeny, R.; The valence-bond theory of molecular structure. III. Cyclobutadiene and benzene. *Proc. R. Soc. Lond. A.* **1955,** *227,* 288–312.

38. Lowdin, P. O.; Quantum theory of cohesive properties of solids. *Adv. Phys.* **1956,** *5,* 1–172.

39. Parr, R. G.; Quantum Theory of Molecular Electronic Structure. New York: W. A. Benjamin, Inc.; **1963.**

40. Pople, J. A.; Reply to a letter by H. F. Hameka. *J. Chem. Phys.* **1962,** *37,* 3009–3009.

41. Fischer–Hjalmars, I.; Deduction of the zero differential overlap approximation from an orthogonal atomic orbital basis. *J. Chem. Phys.* **1965,** *42,* 1962–1972.

42. Geerlings, P.; Proft, F. De; and Langenaeker, W.; Conceptual density functional theory. *Chem. Rev.* **2003,** *103,* 1793–1874.

43. AcuraHuckel; Version 1.2, Acurasoft Huckel Program. Acurasoft. **2009.** http://www.acurasoft.com

44. ArgusLab; 4.0 Mark A. Thompson Planaria Software LLC. Seattle, WA; **2010.** http://www.arguslab.com

CHAPTER 10

THE EVALUATION OF PROTONATION ENERGY OF MOLECULES IN TERMS OF QUANTUM THEORETICAL DESCRIPTORS

SANDIP KUMAR RAJAK and DULAL C. GHOSH

CONTENTS

10.1 INTRODUCTION: THE CONCEPT OF PROTON AND THE PHYSICOCHEMICAL PROCESS OF PROTONATION IN CHEMISTRY

10.1.1 PROTON IN PHYSICS

Proton is a subatomic hadron particle with the symbol p or p^+ with a positive electric charge of 1 elementary charge. One or more protons are present in the nucleus of each atom, along with neutrons.

The proton is also stable by itself. Free protons are emitted directly in some rare types of radioactive decay, and result from the decay of free neutrons from other radioactivity. They soon pick up an electron and become neutral hydrogen atom. Free protons may exist in plasmas or in cosmic rays in vacuum.

The proton particle comprises three fundamental particles: two up quarks and one down quark. It is about 1.6–1.7 fm in diameter.

10.1.2 PROTON IN CHEMISTRY

In chemistry, the number of protons in the nucleus of an atom is known as the atomic number, which determines the chemical element to which the atom belongs. In chemistry, the term *proton* refers to the hydrogen ion, H^+. The proton itself is some 1,800 times smaller than a hydrogen atom, and therefore is extremely reactive. The free proton has an extremely short lifetime in chemical systems. It reacts rapidly with any available molecule. In aqueous solution, it forms the hydronium ion, which in turn is further solvated by water molecules in clusters such as $[H_5O_2]^+$ and $[H_9O_4]^+$.

The transfer of H^+ in an acid–base reaction is usually referred to as "proton transfer." The acid is referred to as a proton donor and the base as a proton acceptor. Likewise, biochemical terms such as proton pump and proton channel refer to the movement of hydrated H^+ ions.

10.1.3 BOHR MODEL IN GENERAL AND STRUCTURE OF HYDROGEN ATOM

According to Bohr model of atomic structure, there are quantized energy levels in the atom called stationary states where the electrons are likely found and revolve round the nucleus. Therefore, atom is a multistoried building with shells/energy levels as floors.

In the hydrogen atom, the single electron revolves round the nucleus in any orbit extended up to infinity, and the path is circular in nature. This model of atom has corroboration from spectroscopic observation. However, on the demand of finer resolution spectroscopic observation, the hydrogen atomic model was modified by Sommerfeld who replaced the circular orbit by elliptical path and incorporated the relativistic correction of electron mass.

10.1.4 SHELL MODEL

In atomic physics and quantum chemistry, electron configuration is the arrangement of electrons of an atom, a molecule, or other physical structure. It concerns the way electrons can be distributed in the orbitals of the given system (atomic or molecular, for instance). The shell model or electron configuration that was developed from the classical concept of quantum numbers and Pauli exclusion principle has been manifest in the quantum mechanical model of the atoms.

Like other elementary particles, the electron is subject to the laws of quantum mechanics, and exhibits both particle-like and wave-like nature. Formally, the quantum state of a particular electron is defined by its wave function, a complex-valued function of space and time. According to the Copenhagen interpretation of quantum mechanics, the position of a particular electron is not well defined, and the concept of probability picture was invoked in atomic structure problem.

Energy is associated with each electron configuration, and the knowledge of the electron configuration of different atoms is useful in understanding the structure of the elements of the periodic table. The concept is also useful for describing the chemical bonds that hold atoms together.

The quantum mechanical study of many electron atoms is the Hartree–Fock (HF) model or its numerous variants. However, Schrodinger equation for hydrogen atom was solved and showed that electrons may occur in different quantized energy level but do not rotate in a circular path of Bohr model. Hartree–Fock model also calculates the same shell model of atomic structure. The shell structure is revealed in X-ray studies [1]. Therefore, the identical conclusion was made both by the quantum mechanics and classical mechanics that there are shells and subshells in atoms and molecules shell model and was verified by X-ray (experimental) method [1].

Now, if the electron is removed from the hydrogen atom, there will be only one proton and some quantized energy level without electron.

10.2   THE PHYSICOCHEMICAL PROCESS OF PROTONATION

When a proton dynamically approaches a molecule, in the physicochemical process of protonation, from a long distance, it is attracted by the electron cloud of the molecule equally from all the directions. Thus in the process, a proton, acting as an electrophile, starts soaking the electron density from the entire skeleton of the nucleophile [2]. As a result, the electron density of the host molecule is reorganized and redistributed. Ultimately, the proton fixes at a site of lone pair—the preferred site of protonation in the molecule. However, if there is no lone pair in the structure of the molecule, the proton remains electrostatically attached to the sphere of the charge cloud of the molecule. Thus, it is implied that the physicochemical process of protonation can be covalent as well as electrostatic interaction. During the process of protonation, the proton induces, concomitant with the charge density reorganization, a physical process of structural and energetic changes in the molecule. And the structural and energetic changes induced by the polarizing power of the proton are expected to be at its maximum at the gas phase of the molecule.

10.3   PROTON AFFINITY

The proton affinity defined as the negative of the enthalpy change of a protonation reaction at standard conditions. Brønsted [3] described basicity as the tendency of a molecule B to accept a proton in the reaction

$$B + H^+ = BH^+, \Delta H^0 = -PA \tag{1}$$

where PA is the proton affinity of the base B, and this is the enthalpy change of this reaction, and BH^+ is the base–acid (proton) adduct. This concept of basicity was generalized further and freed from reference to a specific acid (H^+) by Lewis [4].

Proton affinity can be also expressed in terms of individual heats of formation of the species involved in the adduct formation reaction [5].

10.4 EFFECT OF PROTONATION

The protonated form of the molecule is totally a new chemical species having different charge distribution of the atomic sites within the molecule, polarizability, dipole moment, bond length, and bond angle. Protonating or deprotonating a molecule or ion alters many chemical properties, in addition to the change in the charge and mass, hydrophilicity, reduction potential, optical properties, etc. are among others.

In 1972, Hehre et al. [6] studied the protonation of benzene theoretically. They [6] introduced the simple *ab initio* molecular orbital theory to study the possible geometries and energies of protonated benzene. Using the STO-3G minimal basis set, the optimum form of the ion was found to be one in which the proton was bonded to a ring carbon that was assumed approximately tetrahedral coordination. The form in which the proton bridges a carbon–carbon bond was found to less favored, and structures corresponding to the edge and face protonation were found to be poorer still. The calculated proton affinity of benzene was in good agreement with experiment, and a theoretical value was proposed for the energy required for the proton to migrate from one carbon to another through a bridge intermediate.

An experimental and theoretical investigation on the effect of protonation on the molecular structure and reactivity of a typical Merocyanine dye were investigated by Abdel-Halim et al. [7] in 1993.

The molecular reactivity of 1-methyl-2-(4-hydroxystyryl) pyridiniumbetaine (B) was affected upon protonation in both ground and excited states. In aqueous solution, the protonated *trans* form was photochemically active and isomerizes to give the *cis* form. The quantum yields Φ_{tc} and Φ_{ct} were determined. The rate constant and the thermodynamic parameters of the reverse cis-trans thermal reaction, from the unprotonated cis form, were also calculated. Due to the irreversibility of the thermal reaction, a complete molecular reaction cycle was performed in one direction. The excited molecule exhibited more acidic character than in the ground state. To correlate with the experimental work, ASED-MO (atom superposition and electron delocalization molecular orbital) [8] calculations were applied for both unprotonated and protonated forms. The photochemical isomerization and the thermal reactions were discussed in terms of changes of the geometrical structure from the quinonoid to the benzenoid form upon protonation in both ground and excited states. Upon excitation, it seemed that the molecular polarity character decreased in the case of B but increases for BH^+. Protonation was found as an exothermic, downhill reaction in the ground state and as an endothermic, uphill reaction in the excited state. It was shown that the lowest electronic transition is $\pi - \pi^*$, which was higher for BH^+ than for B.

A theoretical study of the effects of protonation and deprotonation on bond dissociation energies were introduced by Boyd et al. [9] *Ab initio* molecular orbital calculations indicated that the bond dissociation energies (BDEs) for hemolytic cleavage of CX bonds (X = C, N, O, F) were increased by protonation of the corresponding alkyl, amine, alcohol, or fluoride functional groups; the effect of deprotonation of these groups was rather small for saturated species; whereas for unsaturated ones, deprotonation leads to large increases in the CX BDEs. The effects on the CC BDEs in CCX compounds were quite systematic: protonation of X increased the CC BDE, whereas the converse holds for deprotonation. Two types of correlation between bond lengths and homolytic bond dissociation energies were observed. First, protonation and deprotonation lead to a normal correlation for the adjacent CC bonds. But the bond length decreased with the increase in BDE. Protonation, however, gave an anomalous correlation for the CX bonds that the bond length and BDE both increased in the same way. These observations were rationalized in terms of electronegativity, resonance stabilization, and competing heterolytic dissociation.

Protonation in series of aldehydes and ketones of formula R_1-CO-R_2 (with R_1, R_2=H, Me, Et, Pr, and Bu) was studied by using the theory of atoms in molecules to examine the atomic and bond properties of the carbonyl group and its relationship to the energy involved in the protonation process [10]. Based on the results, aldehydes, methyl keones, and the remainder dialkylketones studied exhibit three different behaviors. Small differences were resulted on the protonation of the C=O bond. Although the atomic charge of the carbonyl group hardly changes, the proton bonded to the oxygen exhibits high positive charge after protonation. Atomic contributions to the total energy depend on molecular size.

10.5 PROTONATION ITS IMPORTANCE IN CHEMISTRY, BIOCHEMISTRY, AND BIOLOGY

The proton affinities (PAs) of molecules have been used as the primary information of many chemicophysical processes and to characterize the reactivity surface of molecular sites. Protonation and/or deprotonation are the first step in many fundamental molecular rearrangements and in most of the enzymatic reactions [11]. Some ions and molecules can undergo protonation in more than one sites, and these are labeled as polybasics, which represent many biological macromolecules. In protein and RNA macromolecules, only a limited number of different side-chain chemical groups are available to function as catalysts. The myriad of enzyme-catalyzed reactions results from the ability of most of these groups to function either as nucleophilic, electrophilic, or general acid–base catalysts. And the key to their adapted chemical function lies in their states of protonation [12]. Protonation is also an essential step in certain analytical procedures such as electrospray mass spectrometry. The proton transfer (PT) reactions are of great importance in chemistry and in biomolecular processes of living organisms. The latter includes most enzymatically catalyzed reactions such as ATP hydrolysis/synthesis. Further, the protonation state of chemical groups, for example, the side chains of amino acids, is fundamentally related to their biomolecular function [5, 11, 13–15].

Shan et al. [16] demonstrated the importance of conformation change in many protein kinases. Many kinase inhibitors—including the cancer drug imatinib—selectively target a specific DFG conformation, but the function and mechanism of the flip remain unclear. Using long molecular dynamics simulations of the Abl kinase, Yibing et al. visualized the DFG flip in atomic-level detail and formulated an energetic model predicting that protonation of the DFG aspartate controls the flip. Shan et al. [16] also established experimentally that the kinetics of imatinib binding to Abl kinase have a pH dependence that disappears when the DFG aspartate is mutated.

Protonation reaction is also important in the study of the titration behavior of carbonmonoxy-myoglobin (MbCO) in the pH range from 3 to 7 by conventional electrostatic continuum methods with subsequent Monte Carlo (MC) sampling [17].

The knowledge of the intrinsic basicity and the site of protonation of a compound in the gas phase are central to the understanding of its reactivity and mechanism of chemical reactions involving proton. In recent years, acid–base interactions are extensively studied so that experimental techniques could be devised to permit the quantitative study of the thermochemistry of the PT reaction in the gas phase [18].

10.6 LITERATURE SURVEY ON THE METHODS OF DETERMINATION OF PROTON AFFINITIES OF MOLECULES

The survey of literature shows that is plethora of information have appeared on the determination of proton affinity both experimental and theoretical.

In 1964, Munson and Franklin [19] studied the energetics of some gaseous oxygenated organic ions, and they measured the proton affinities of some oxygenated organic compounds. The heat of formation of some simple oxygenated organic compounds were measured from sources; $\Delta H_f(CH_2OH^+) = 174$ kcal/mol and $\Delta H_f(CH_3O^+) = 202$ kcal/mol. The proton affinities of formic, acetic, and propionic acids were determined from rearrangement ions of esters as about 170–180 kcal/mol. The protonated acid ions were readily formed by ionic reactions in the gaseous aliphatic acids. The potential data for H_3O^+ and $CH_3OH_2^+$ were interpreted to give P $(H_2O) \approx P(CH_3OH) \approx 170$ kcal/mol.

In 1966, Harrison et al. [20] used the energetic of formation of some oxygenated ions and the proton affinities of carbonyl compounds to estimate more reliable values of gas-phase proton affinities of a number of carbonyl compounds.

In 1968, Beauchamp et al. [21] used the ion cyclotron single- and multiple-resonance spectroscopy technique to identify and examine the energies of ion–molecule reactions in which H_3O^+ and H_3S^+ were involved either as product or reactant. To evaluate the proton affinities of the H_2S and H_2O, they [21] used the following scheme:

The proton affinity (PA) of a molecule (B) is defined as the negative of the enthalpy change for the reaction

$$B + H^+ \longrightarrow BH^+ \qquad (2)$$

The hydrogen affinity (HA) could be similarly defined as the negative of the enthalpy change for the reaction:

$$B^+ + H \longrightarrow BH^+ \qquad (3)$$

From thermochemical considerations, the relations

$$PA(B) = \Delta H_f(B) + H_f(H^+) - H_f(BH^+), \qquad (4)$$

$$HA(B^+) = \Delta H_f(B^+) + H_f(H) - H_f(BH^+), \qquad (5)$$

$$PA(B) - HA(B^+) = IP(H) - IP(B), \qquad (6)$$

where IP(B) is the ionization potential of species B. As defined in Eq. (3), the hydrogen affinity is simply the hydrogen bond strength in the ion, $D(B^+\text{–}H)$.

With the help of the above model (Eq. 6), Beauchamp et al. [21] observed that the gas-phase proton affinities of H_2S and H_2O were 164 ± 4 kcal/mol and 178 ± 2 kcal/mol, respectively.

Thus ion–cyclotron single- and multiple-resonance techniques gave a simple means for identifying ion –molecule reactions and examining certain aspects of their energetics even in complex mixtures. This simple method by which proton affinities of water and hydrogen sulfide were determined could directly be applicable to determine the proton affinities of other molecules.

In 1969, Haney et al. [22] invoked mass spectrometric method of determination of PA and estimated the heat of a PT reaction.

Aue et al. [23] in 1971, for the first time, tried to evaluate the accurate quantitative relative gas phase basicity introducing the equilibrium techniques. They defined the gas phase basicity (GB) of B as the negative of the free energy ($\Delta G°$) for reaction 3, whereas the proton affinity (PA) is the negative of the enthalpy ($\Delta H°$) for reaction 3. The HA

$$B + H^+ \rightleftharpoons BH^+ \qquad (7)$$

$$B^+ + H \rightleftharpoons BH^+ \qquad (8)$$

$$PA(B) = -IP(B) + HA(B^+) + IP(H) \qquad (9)$$

of B^+ is the negative enthalpy for reaction 8 and is equivalent to the bond dissociation energy of BH^+. Then, the proton affinity of base B, PA(B), then can be written as Eq. (9) above.

From their PAs and from known adiabatic IPs [24], accurate relative hydrogen affinities were calculated for the first time. They [23] used this technique to evaluate the accurate quantitative relative gas-phase basicities of amines.

Long et al. [25] utilized the bracketing technique of gaseous PT reaction to evaluate the proton affinity for some acids, esters, and alcohols. They observed that the each methyl substituent on the α-carbon of the acids, esters, and alcohols increased the proton affinity by about 15 cal/mol.

Quantitative proton affinities of a series of alkylamines and related alicyclic and saturated heterocyclic amines were measured by equilibrium ion cyclotron resonance techniques by Aue et al. [26] in 1976.

An *ab initio* and ion cyclotron resonance study of the protonation of borazine was investigated by Doiron et al. [27]. The experimental proton affinity was determined from competitive PT equilibria with the standard reference bases and found to be 196.4 ± 0.2 kcal/mol. But in case of *ab initio* calculations, the proton affinity of borazine was 203.4 kcal/mol.

Core binding energies, lone pair ionization potential and proton affinities of molecules are known to have direct correlation. The electronic relaxations accompanying lone-pair ionization and proton attachment are similar in character and energy.

But Lee et al. [28] determined the phosphorus core binding energies for a wide variety of tervalent phosphorus compounds. These values are compared with literature values of the corresponding lone pair ionization potentials and proton affinities. No single correlation is found between all the core binding energies and the corresponding lone pair ionization potentials or proton affinities.

The absolute PA of ammonia was calculated invoking the *ab initio* molecular orbital theory by Eades et al. [29] in 1980. Calculations at the SCF level were carried out by invoking both Gaussian-type orbitals (GTOs) and Slater-type orbitals (STOs). The STO basis was used in CI calculations with all single and double excitations included. A correction for quadruple excitations was considered. The zero-point energy difference between NH_3 and NH_4^+ was calculated at the SCF level with the GTO basis and the value obtained in the calculation for $PA(NH_3)$ was 205.6 ± 1 kcal/mol.

A molecular orbital study of some protonated bases were carried out by Del Bene et al. [30] in 1982. HF and fourth-order Møller–Plesset (MP4) calculations with the 6–31G** basis set were employed to evaluate the proton affinities of the protonated hydrides NH_3, H_2O, and HF and the protonated closed-shell bases H_mABH_n, where the two nonhydrogen atoms might be C, N, O, or F. Inclusion of correlation generally guided to relatively small changes in computed protonation energies and did not necessarily yield better agreement between computed and experimental data. However, both HF and MP protonation energies were reasonable, and trend in protonation energies for related bases were the same at both levels of theory. The HF and MP relative stabilities of the isomers that result when protonation occurred at nonbonded electron pairs on A and B are similar, except for the C- and O-protonated forms of C≡O. However, the HF barrier to PT which separated the isomers is significantly lowered by electron correlation. Correlation also lowered the barrier to PT for ions $H_m AAH_{n+1}^+$ except for N_2H^+. Zero-point vibrational energy corrections were also evaluated and found to lead to significant decreases in computed protonation energies.

Lohr [31] conceived for the first time the protofelicity as a protonic counterpart of electronegativity. Such a new structural descriptor involving the physicochemical process of protonation depends on both number of electrons and number of protons in the molecule. The method relies on a concept of a charge-dependent electronegativity is extended to protons by the use of a polynomial representation of molecular energies as a function of the number of protons and the number of electrons. The relationships provide an organizing principle for gas-phase acidity and basicity data by expressing succinctly the interdependence of the energies of proton-transfer and electron-transfer reactions. Application is made to the energetics of strongly hydrogen-bonded systems.

In 1984, the accident in Bhopal, India, in which heavy casualties resulted from the release of a large quantity of methyl isocyanate, CH_3NCO, considerable attention focused on its chemistry. Methyl isothiocyanate, CH_3NCS, and methyl thiocyanate, CH_3SCN, which are closely related to CH_3NCO as far as their toxicity and chemical properties were concerned, had been the subject of an ICR study [32]. The gas-phase ion chemistry of CH_3NCO, CH_3NCS, and CH_3SCN was investigated by pulsed ICR techniques, and their proton affinities were determined as being 184.5 ±0.5, 193.0 ± 0.4, and 192.6 ± 0.5 kcal/mol, respectively, by Karpas et al. [33]. The main reaction of the molecular ion in the three compounds was production of the protonated molecule. The CH_2X^+ ions, where X = NCO, NCS, or SCN, were unreactive toward the parent molecule. The fragment ions CH_2Y^+, where n = 0–3 and Y = 0 or S, reacted by charge transfer or PT. Those protonated molecules reacted very slowly with their parent compounds. Although protonated dimers were observed, their production was inefficient. *Ab initio* calculations at the SCF level were used to determine the structures of the neutral and protonated molecules. The calculated proton affinities, 188.5, 188.6, and 193.7 kcal/mol for CH_3NCO, CH_3SCN, and CH_3NCS, respectively, were in good agreement with the experimental values.

With some exceptions, Dewar et al. [34] efficiently invoked the AM1 semiempirical molecular orbital model to calculate the PAs for 60 compounds and deprotonation enthalpies (DPEs) for 80 compounds. Intermolecular hydrogen bonding in protonated bifunctional bases is also effectively reproduced.

In the case of small anions with the AM1 study, some problems were encountered. Systematic errors were accompanied on the introduction of methyl or phenyl substituents at anionic centers. Systematic error was also found in the extension of alkyl chains by addition of methene groups and in substitution of amine and hydroxyl groups for methyl groups bonded to secondary or tertiary carbons in neutral molecules. The errors involved in the deprotonation of alcohols and protonation of amines were not, however, totally systematic. As a result, the relative DPEs of alcohols and PAs of amines were not accurately reproduced by AM1 study.

Dewar et al [34] also observed that AM1was able to perform well as compare to the high-level *ab initio* procedures. But the fact is that they [34] made the comparisons with few simple cases . Also *ab initio* procedure was not tested. To carry out with full geometry optimization at that level of calculation, it became very expensive for large molecules. Since the accuracy achieved by AM1 was sufficient for the results to be chemically useful and since it was used to study reactions of quite large molecules at moderate cost, AM1 was considered as an aid in interpreting PT in chemistry and biochemistry.

Ab initio molecular orbital calculations using the STO-3G, STO-3G**, 3-21G, and 6-31G** basis sets were performed for the series HCOOH, CH_3COOH, CH_3OH, and C_2H_5OH by Nagy-Felsobuki et al. [35] in 1990. Structural calculations of the neutrals and predictions of the structure of the respective cations were discussed and reported. Relative proton affinities were calculated. Only at the 6-31G**//6-31G**, HF level of theory were effective to evaluate the relative proton affinities and trend for this simple organic acid/base series were in agreement with the experimental value. The STO-3G//STO-3G model was the most effective of the other models.

Smith et al. [36] in 1993 invoked the *ab initio* molecular orbital calculations at the G2 level to obtain absolute values for the proton affinities of a variety of prototypical small molecules. A total of 31 molecules were examined in their study. The results were compared with the standard proton affinity scale of that time and with more advanced revisions of that scale.

At the lower end of the proton affinity scale, there was generally good correlation between the theoretical and various experimental proton affinities. At the upper end of the scale, the theoretical proton affinities were closer to the original values.

The temperature dependence of the PT equilibrium constants for approximately 80 pairs of bases ranging in proton affinity from N_2 to tert-butylamine has been examined by Szulejko et al. [36] in 1993. An excellent agreement was obtained with appearance energy determinations of proton affinities as well as *ab initio* calculation. An important finding of the work was that the value of ΔH_f° for the tert-butyl cation must be significantly higher than that derived from appearance energy measurements by Traeger [37], which had formed the basis for the proton affinity assignment for isobutene—an important reference point in the proton affinity scale. The obtained data suggested that the proton affinity of isobutene must be revised downward by ~4 kcal mol^{-1} with important consequence for all proton affinities in the vicinity of isobutene and above. In addition, it also indicated that the significant revisions were needed to calculate the proton affinities between those of propene and isobutene. By contrast, however, the substantial upward revision of the proton affinity scale in the basicity region above ammonia had been proposed by Mautner and Sieck [38]. But this experiment did not support the revision.

According to the Mulliken [39] definition, electronegativity is the ability to relate energy to the movement of charge within a molecule. As one of the simplest and thoroughly studied reactions, the role of charge movement associated with the proton affinity was examined by Reed [40] in 1994. Of interest has been the energy required to bring each atom to the charge it would carry in the product molecules. This was called the atomic charging energy. It was found to be a significant part of the proton affinity. Within a series of similar bases, the charging energy accounts for the difference in reactivity. In addition, it was determined that although the atomic charge of the donor atom was a poor indicator of base strength, the amount of charge transferred upon protonation was an excellent indicator of basicity.

Eekert-Maksic et al. [41] studied on the theoretical calculations of proton affinities in phenol. They invoked that a relatively simple MP2 (fc)/6-31G**//HF/6-31G* model that was capable of providing a quantitative description of protonation in phenol. The use of the 6-31G** basis set in the single-point MP2 calculation was crucial in that respect. The zero-point energy (ZPE) contribution to the PA was estimated at the HF/6-31 G* level of approximation. It appeared that the contribution of the ZPE to relative ΔPA proton affinities was negligible. They showed that in calculation, the empirical ZP energies for the protonated species the simple additivity rule could be the better option. The energetically most favorable site of the proton attack was para to the OH substitution in accordance with the experimental finding. Performance of the MP2 (fc) 6-31G** + ZPE (HF/6-31G*) model in reproducing protonation at the oxygen atom was verified in some medium-sized alcohols and ethers. The calculated PA values were in good agreement with the measured data.

A mass spectrometric and computational study of the protonation and methylation of H_2NOH was reported by Angelelli et al. [42] in 1995. The FT-ICR "bracketing" technique and by the kinetic method based on the unimolecular fragmentation of proton-bound were employed to evaluate the gas-phase PA of H_2NOH, and the PA value obtained in these experimental procedure was 193.7 ± 2 kcal mol^{-1} at 298 K, which was in excellent agreement with the 193.8 kcal mol^{-1} PA computed at the GAUSSIAN 1 level of theory for the N atom.

The computed PAs of the N atom of CH_3NHOH and H_2NOCH_3, that is, 203.9 and 201.0 kcal mol^{-1}, respectively, were also in good agreement with the values obtained from FT-ICR equilibrium measurements, 205.1 $\pm$ 2 and 202.7 $\pm$ 2 kcal mol^{-1}, respectively, whereas the PAs calculated for the O atom were much lower, 175.1 and 179.8 kcal mol^{-1}, respectively.

Smith et al. [43] introduced the G2(MP2, SVP) method to calculate the proton affinity of some molecules.

The G2(MP2, SVP) method was shown to reproduce proton affinities for a set of reference molecules to within the G2 target accuracy of 10 kJ mol^{-1} but at significantly lower computational cost.

Ab initio calculations of 12-crown-4, 15-crown-5, and 18-crown-6 and their protonated species were performed by Wasada et al. [44] (Wasada 1996) in 1996. As a reference molecule, 1-(2'-methoxy)ethoxy-2-methoxyethane (glyme-2) was also examined. Three protonated crown ethers was found to have quite similar moieties to that of glyme-2H$^+$. The ring strain due to formation of intramolecular hydrogen bonds was a measure of PA values. The computed result supports Meot-Ner's and Sharma's PA values [45, 46] of 12-crown-4. Those of 15-crown-5 and 18-crown-6 reported by Sharma [46] were very close to the theoretical values.

Cavity sizes of crown ethers correlate generally with trapped cation radii. Since the extent of ring strain due to formation of intramolecular hydrogen bond was employed to measure the PA values, the geometry of the protonated 1-(2'-methoxy)ethoxy-2-methoxyethane could be a standard for the extent. Three protonated crown ethers had the glyme-2H+ moiety. The computed PA value of their study of 12-crown-4 was in good agreement with two experimental data [45, 46]. In addition, those of 15-crown-5 and 18-crown-6 were similar to Kebarle's one [46], respectively.

Chandra et al. [47] in 1996 used the density functional theory (DFT) with different combinations of exchange and correlation functional to study the proton affinities of six organic molecules, namely H_2CO, CH_3CHO, CH_3OH, C_2H_5OH, HCOOH, and CH_3COOH. Complete geometry optimizations were carried out for both the neutral and protonated species with all combinations of functionals. The calculated proton affinity values were then compared with the corresponding experimental values. They combined Perdew's and Becke's exchanges with Proynov's correlation functional, which was the most effective in reproducing the proton affinity.

The absolute proton affinities of some carbenes were calculated using *ab initio* methods by Josefredo et al. [48] in 1997. The studied species have a range of absolute proton affinities from 177.4 to 275.0 kcal mol^{-1}. The more basic carbenes (CPh and fluorenylidene) should react in protic solvents by PT, whereas the less basic ones (CF_2, FCOH) should not. The intermediate species CH_2, CCl_2, $C(OH)_2$ could abstract a proton in neutral and acidic solutions.

Simple *ab initio* model for calculating the absolute PA of aromatics was invoked by Maksic et al. [49] in 1997. In their method, they [49] showed that a simple scaled HF (ScHF) model was able to describe very well the ring PA of a vast variety of polysubstituted benzenes, naphthalenes, and biphenylenes. Its utility in predicting PAs of large alternant aromatics was illustrated on pyrene and monofluoropyrenes. The calculated PAs were in well agreement with the available experimental. Finally, they [49] found that PAs in polyfluoropyrenes followed the same simple additivity rule, based on the independent substituent approximation (ISA), which was observed earlier in smaller alternant aromatic systems.

Maksic et al. [49] in 1997 have shown that the ScHF model was able to describe very well the ring PA of a wide variety of polysubstituted benzenes, naphthalenes, and biphenylenes. The average absolute deviation from the full MP2 calculations, which in turn were very close to the best available experimental results, was on the order of 1 kcal/mol. The calculated PAs were in well agreement with available experimental evidence. Finally, their study showed that multiple fluorinated pyrenes follow a simple ISA additivity rule observed earlier in benzenes, naphthalenes, and biphenylenes [41, 42, 49–53]. The origin of this additivity was found in the remarkable similarity of the intramolecular interference energies in initial bases and their conjugate acids.

Howard et al. [54] in 1997 were the first to calculate the PA of arylphosphines. At the MP2 [FC] level, with moderately-sized basis sets, arylphosphine PAs were overestimated by 15 kJ mol^{-1} (after the application of basis set superposition corrections).

Both experimental and theoretical PAs of limonene were studied by Fernandez et al. [55]. Gas-phase basicity (GB) and PA of limonene were derived from measurements of PT equilibria carried out by high-pressure pulsed electron beam source mass spectrometry. Experimental GB and PA were 842.5 kJ mol^{-1} and 875.5 kJ mol^{-1}, respectively. The proton affinity of $C_{10}H_{16}$ was compared with *ab initio* (HF and MP2) and density-functional predictions for the protonation energy. Theoretical calculations based on DFT were in very good agreement with experimental results.

PAs and intrinsic basicities for nitrogen and oxygen protonation in the gas phase of the amino acids glycine and alanine were calculated using DFT (Dm) and *ab initio* methods at different levels of theory from HF to G2 approximations by Topola et al. [56] in 1998. All methods gave good agreement for proton affinities for nitrogen protonation for both amino acids. However, dramatic differences were found between DFT, MP4//MP2, and G2 results on the one hand, and MP4//HF results on the other hand to the calculation of structural and energetic characteristics of oxygen protonation in glycine and alanine.

Using Dunning's basis set saturation approach, electronic energies for proton affinities for both ammonia and water were evaluated with hybrid DFT methods by Jursic [57, 58]. It was demonstrated that the zero-point vibrational correction for both of these PAs computed at the B3LYP/6-311G(2d,2p) theory level was identical to the values obtained from excellent agreement with values obtained by G2 and CBSQ *ab initio* computational studies. The final PA values were 201.8 kcal/mol for ammonia and 162.4 kcal/mol for water.

A simple model to analyze charge redistribution associated with PT reaction was derived from a classical ion transport model by Pérez et al.

[59]. The model was applied to the gas-phase acid–base equilibria of alkyl alcohols. PT was simulated as the motion of a charged particle in an applied external potential defined by the chemical environment of the proton, and represented by the difference in PA of the conjugated bases RO– and CH3O–; the latter was taken as reference. The electronic chemical potential of transfer accounted for both the amount and direction of charge transfer (CT). The relative acidity for a short series of alkyl alcohols was determined by the difference in proton affinity $(\Delta PA) = PA(RO^-)$ $- PA(CH3O^-))$ of the conjugated bases.

PAs of the four smallest cyclic amines—aziridine (C_2H_5N), azetidine (C_3H_7N), pyrrolidine (C_4H_9N), and piperidine $(C_5H_{11}N)$, were calculated by Vayner et al. [60] using ab $initio$ methods and density functional calculations. The methods varied in their ability to calculate accurate $\Delta_f H$'s, with MP2 calculations being the most accurate and HF calculations the least. Most methods were able to predict the proton affinities well, typically to within 30 kJ/mol (or about 5%).

The relative gas-phase acidity of halosubstituted acetic acids CH_2X-CO_2H, CHX_2CO_2H, and CX_3CO_2H (X)F, Cl, and Br) was analyzed in terms of global and local descriptors of reactivity by Pérez et al. [61]. The model was based on the analysis of proton-transfer equilibria with reference to acetic acid CH_3CO_2H. The relative acidity pattern displayed by the series was rationalized in terms of the hard and soft acids and bases principle. The relative stability between the neutral species and the corresponding anions is in agreement with the maximum hardness principle. Charge transfer between the conjugated bases present in the proton-transfer equilibria was correctly accounted for by using a classical ion-transport model that introduces the electronic chemical potential of transfer. The local reactivity analysis based on regional Fukui functions and local softness was able to display a good correlation with the experimental gas-phase acidity within the series.

Silva et al. [62] in 2000 used the thermodynamical cycle to calculate the absolute pKa values for Brønsted acids in aqueous solution. The polarizable continuum model (PCM) was used to describe the solvent, and absolute pKa values were computed for different classes of organic compounds: aliphatic alcohols, thiols, and halogenated derivatives of carboxylic aliphatic acids. The model was competent to furnish pKa values in good agreement with the experimental results for some classes of compounds.

Correlation of proton affinity and HOMO energy of neutral and negatively charged bases were given by Cerofolini et al. [63] in 2002. High-level quantum mechanical calculations were performed to verify the extent to which the proton affinities of closed-shell molecules or anions were related to the energy E_{HOMO} of the highest occupied molecular orbital. The accuracy of calculations was verified comparing the calculated PAs with the experimental ones (when available). The data in their analysis corroborated that the PA was a decreasing function of $|E_{HOMO}|$ modulated by the atomic number of the proton-hosting atom.

A quadratic configuration interaction methods were invoked by Miller et al. [64] to obtain the optimize geometry and harmonic vibrational frequencies of neutral and protonated acetic acid. The proton affinity of acetic acid was calculated at the QCISD(T)/6-311++G(3df,3pd)//QCISD/6-311+G(2d,2p) level of theory. The value obtained in the calculation was 187.9±0.7 kcal/mol, which was in excellent agreement with the experimental value of 187.3 kcal/mol. Thermochemical calculations using the CBS-Q, CBS-QB3, CBS-APNO, G2, and G2(MP2) model chemistries also displayed excellent agreement with the experimental PA, which suggested that these model chemistries would provide accurate PAs for the carboxylic acids that were too large to treat with high-level *ab initio* method.

The experimental PA of diborane (B2H6), based on an unstable species, $B_2H^+_7$, which is observed only at low temperatures. Invoking the Gaussian-3 method and other high-level compound *ab initio* methods, Betowski et al. [65] calculated the PA of diborane to check its experimental value. The calculated value of the PA of diborane in their study was thus reported at 147.7 kcal/mol, compared with the experimental value of 147.4 kcal/mol. However, the experimental value was found to be based on two values, each of which were found to be held in error by 12 kcal/mol, but in opposite directions.

Beelen et al. [66] studied on the PAs of furan, the methylphenols, and the related anisoles both experimentally and theoretically. The study showed that the average literature value for the proton affinity of furan of 803 kJ mol^{-1} was too low. It was recommended to alter the value to 812 kJ mol^{-1} in keeping with the experimental results obtained in the study and the outcome of the G3(MP2) calculations.

Rao et al. [67] employed *ab initio* quantum chemical calculations, G3B3, second-order MP (MP2), and the hybrid density functional method

B3LYP to compute the PAs of 24 heterocyclic amines. A range of basis sets starting from double-polarization quality to triple-quality basis set with augmented diffuse and polarization function were employed in their calculation. Experimental values were used to calibrate the performance of various theoretical models. For the given series of compounds, the performance of B3LYP/6-31++G** and G3B3 levels of theory were in excellent agreement with the experimental results and the deviations were found to be minimum i.e., like the experimental error.

Dinadayalane et al. [68] tried more to compute the accurate PAs of naturally occurring amino acids. Systematic quantum chemical studies of HF and MP2 methods, and B3LYP functional, with a range of basis sets were employed to evaluate PA values of all naturally occurring amino acids. The B3LYP and MP2 in conjunction with 6-311 + G (d,p) basis set calculated the PA values. The computed values were in very good agreement with the experimental results, with an average deviation of ~1 kcal/mol.

High-level calculations of PA and electron affinity (EA) of CH_2X^- and $H2CHCHX^-$ (with X = F, Cl, Br, and I) systems were obtained by Morgon [69] in 2006. The methodology employed in the calculation of PA and EA based on (completely renormalized-coupled cluster with single and double and perturbative triple excitation) CR-CCSD[T]/B1// MP2/B0 and CCSD(T)/B1//MP2/B0 levels, respectively. The differences between calculated results of PA and EA and the experimental values were in the range of 0.2– 4.5 kJ mol^{-1} and 0.01 to 0.10 eV, respectively.

Gas-phase PAs of a series of 25 small, aliphatic carbanions were computed using different Gaussian-3 methods: G3, G3(B3LYP), G3(MP2), and G3(MP2, B3LYP) and complete basis set extrapolation methods: CBS-4M,CBS-Q,CBS-QB3, and CBS-APNO by Danikiewiczin [70] in 2009. The results were compared with critically selected experimental data. The analysis of the result showed that for the majority of the studied molecules, all compound methods (Gaussian-3 and CBS), except for CBS-4M, gave comparable results, which differed no more than ±2 kcal mol^{-1} from the experimental data. As an additional proof, the result obtained by these two methods a compared with the values obtained using CCSD(T) *ab initio* method with large basis set. It was also found that some of the published experimental data were erroneous and should be corrected. The results described in this work show that for the majority of the studied compounds PA values calculated using compound methods could be used with the same or even higher confidence as the experimental ones because even the largest differences between Gaussian-3 and CBS methods mentioned earlier were still comparable with the accuracy of the typical PA measurement.

The PA scale of small aminal cages was investigated by Rivera et al[71] using the experimental (FT-IR) and theoretical (DFT) methodologies. The formation constant (K_f) was determined for 1:1 hydrogen-bonded complexes between p-fluorophenol (PEP) and some aminal cage type (B) in CCl_4 at 298K using FT-IR spectrometry. Then, the total interaction energy ($E_{PFF...B}$), the energy of protonation (E_{HB+}), the HOMO–LUMO gap values and Fukui index were calculated using the DFT/B3LYP/6-31G(d,p) level of theory as theoretical scales was observed, evidence for the existence of a relationship between the total energy of interaction calculated by structural parameters and proton affinity in this series.

We may summarize the above survey in the following way. The primary experimental methods used for measurement of gaseous PA was ion cyclotron resonance (ICR) spectroscopy for measurement of the proton transfer to another base, or chemical ionization (CI) measurements to "bracket" the compound between two bases of known PA. These measurements are experimentally difficult to perform and interpret [72]. Their accuracy depends on the presence of chemical equilibrium between the species, a certainty in the local temperature in the measurement cell, and the assumption that the rotational and vibrational components of ΔST are zero or known. In addition, there may be uncertainty as to the site of protonation on the molecule. Despite these difficulties, there exists a scale of relative proton affinities, which is well-established and well-accepted [18]. The relative values of PA's are most often determined by mass spectroscopic measurement of the equilibrium constant for the proton-exchange gas phase reactions [4,18,73–75], and the absolute proton affinities can be obtained from ionization thresholds [18]. However, these "acid–base" adducts are not stable and/or does not exist in all cases. In addition, experimental determination of the PAs of molecules is not easy [75].

An alternative to the measurement of PAs of small molecules is their determination through the measure of the probability of a chemical group to be protonated/unprotonated. The probability of a chemical group to be protonated/unprotonated is given by the legend pKa which is defined by pKa = –log[A$^-$][H$^+$]/[AH]. The pKa of a protonable group strongly depends on its molecular environment. It is possible to measure the pKa experimentally, but this is generally not an easy task.

For this reason, in recent years, much attention has been given to the possibility of calculating proton affinities through some quantum mechanical as well as DFT models [43,57,76–78]. Modern computational chemical methods can yield very accurate values for the proton affinity of molecules composed of first-row elements [43]. Fontaine et al. [79] performed HF calculations for a number of small molecules.

From the study of the vast literature on the determination of PAs and effect of protonation on molecules, it reveals that the physicochemical process of protonation is a complex phenomenon and the determination of PA is not a simple procedure—both experimentally and theoretically. Therefore, there is enough scope of exploring some other methods—namely modeling and simulation—an well-known procedure for scientific study.

In this study, we have resorted to modeling and simulation in the study of physicochemical process of protonation. We have introduced modeling to calculate PA.

10.7 METHOD OF COMPUTATION

MULTILINEAR REGRESSION (MLR) IN MODELING TO SUGGEST ALGORITHM FOR THE EVALUATION OF PROTONATION ENERGY.

As we have mentioned earlier in Section 10.6 that still there is some difficulties in both the theoretical and experimental procedures of evaluating the protonation energy. In this backdrop, we have ventured to explore a model toward the evaluation of protonation energy with an intention to overcome such problems as are found inherent in the methods already available.

Since we have found that the individual quantum chemical descriptors such as ionization potential (I), global softness (S), chemical potential (μ), and electrophilicity index (ω) to correlate with protonation energy, we have used these parameters as the components of our modeling.

In this project, we have modeled and given a mathematical relation with the above-mentioned quantum chemical descriptors for the evaluation of protonation energy. We have taken recourse to the method of multilinear regression (MLR) to obtain good parameters because, it is known that as the number of components (here descriptors) increased, the method were automatically reached to a good result.

10.8   PRESENT MODEL REGARDING PROTONATION

In this work, we have developed a model for the evaluation of PA in terms of some akin conceptual reactivity descriptors that can be conceptually linked and associated with the physicochemical process of protonation. The akin descriptors are the ionization energy (I), the global softness (S), the electronegativity (χ), and the global electrophilicity index (ω).

THE MODELING OF THE PHYSICOCHEMICAL PROCESS OF PROTONATION AND ALGORITHM FOR COMPUTING THE PROTON AFFINITY OF THE MOLECULES

The descriptors such as the ionization process of atoms and molecules, the physical property such as hardness, softness, the electronegativity, and the electrophilicity have close relation, that is, akin with each other in their operational significance and origin.

We have tried to posit above that the physicochemical process of protonation can be linked to the above akin descriptors: the ionization process, the hardness, softness, electronegativity, and electrophilicity. Recently, Ghosh et al. [80–88] have published good number of papers where they [80–88] have discussed that the three descriptors, the electronegativity, the hardness, and the electrophilicity index of atoms and molecules are fundamentally qualitative per se and operationally the same. All these three descriptors represent the attraction of screened nuclei toward the electron pair/bond. Thus, we can safely and reasonably conclude that the PA and the three descriptors have inverse relationship.

Thus, since the above four parameters have dimension of energy and can be linked to the process of charge rearrangement and polarization during the physicochemical process of protonation, they can be components of a probabilistic scientific modeling of PA. The physicochemical process of protonation has direct link to the charge polarization and alteration of electron distribution in the molecule.

The PA or the ability of donating the lone pair of a Lewis base and the ability for the deformation of electron cloud of a species, the softness, and/ or the tendency of the molecule to lose electron, the ionization potential, are fundamentally similar in physical appearance stemming from the attraction power of the nuclei of the atoms forming the molecule. The softness, the ionization energy, the electronegativity (chemical potential), and the electrophilicity index have direct link to the process of polarization and transfer of charge from a substrate and, hence, control the energetic effect—the protonation energy. Considering all the above-mentioned fundamental nature of the physicochemical process of protonation and its probable relationship with the quantum mechanical descriptors, we suggest an ansatz for the computation of the PA in terms of these theoretical descriptors. The physicochemical process and the energetic effect must entail the above-stated four parameters. To derive an explicit relation to compute the PA in terms of the above-stated descriptors, we suggest explicit interrelationships between the protonation energy and the descriptors relying upon their response toward the protonation.

$$PA \propto (-I) \tag{10}$$

$$PA \propto S \tag{11}$$

$$PA \propto 1/\chi \tag{12}$$

$$PA \propto 1/\omega \tag{13}$$

Combining the above four relations, we obtain

$$PA = C + C_1 (-I) + C_2 S + C_3 (1/\chi) + C_4 (1/\omega) \tag{14}$$

where PA is the proton affinity; C, C_1, C_2, C_3, and C_4 are the *regression coefficient*; I is ionization energy; S is global softness; χ is the electronegativity; and ω is the global electrophilicity index of the molecule.

In our model, we have invoked multilinear regression (MLR) to evaluate these *regression coefficient* (C, C_1, C_2, C_3, and C_4) and then we have combined these calculated *regression coefficient* (C, C_1, C_2, C_3, and C_4) with the aforesaid akin quantum chemical descriptors, the ionization energy (I), the global softness (S), the electronegativity (χ), and the global electrophilicity index (ω) according to the Eq. (14) to evaluate the PA of the individual molecule.

10.9 MATHEMATICAL FORMULAE OF THE GLOBAL REACTIVITY DESCRIPTORS INVOKED IN THE STUDY

According to Koopmans' theorem, the ionization potential (I) and the electron affinity (A) are computed as follows:

$$I = - \varepsilon_{HOMO} \tag{15}$$

$$A = - \varepsilon_{LUMO} \tag{16}$$

where ε_{HOMO} and ε_{LUMO} are the orbital energies of the highest occupied and the lowest unoccupied orbitals.

Parr et al. [89,90] defined the chemical potential, μ, electronegativity, χ, and hardness, η, in the framework of DFT [91] as follows:

$$\mu = (\partial E/\partial N)_{v(r)} = -\chi = (I+A)/2 \tag{17}$$

$$\eta = \tfrac{1}{2} \, [\partial \mu/\partial N]_{v(r)} = \tfrac{1}{2} \, [\partial^2 E/\partial N^2]_{v(r)} = \tfrac{1}{2} \, (I-A) \tag{18}$$

where E, N, $v(r)$, I, and A are the energy, the number of electrons, the external potential, the ionization energy, and the electron affinity of an atomic or molecular system, respectively.

Softness is a reactivity index and is defined as the reciprocal of hardness:

$$S = (1/\eta) \tag{19}$$

Parr et al. [92] defined electrophilicity index (ω) as follows:

$$\omega = (\mu)^2/(2\eta) \tag{20}$$

In this study, we have taken some hydrocarbons as Set 1; some alcohols, carbonyls, carboxylic acids and esters as Set 2; some aliphatic amines as Set 3; some aromatic amines as Set 4; some pyridine derivatives as Set 5; and some amino acids as Set 6 for which the experimental protonation [18,93–96] energy are known. The PQS Mol 1.2-20-win software (PQSMol) have been used to calculate the global descriptors by using the *ab initio* HF SCF method with the 6-31g basis set. The geometry optimization technique is adopted. The ionization energy, I, the electronegativity,

χ, the global softness, S, and the global electrophilicity index, ω, respectively, of the molecules are computed by invoking the Koopmans' theorem and Eqs. (15), (17), (19), and (20).

An MLR [97] is performed using Minitab15 to compute the correlation coefficients C, C_1, C_2, C_3, and C_4 by plotting experimental PA along the abscissa and the values of the quantum mechanical descriptors along the ordinate. The computed correlation coefficients C, C_1, C_2, C_3 and C_4, for all the sets are tabulated in Table (10.1).

TABLE 10.1   Correlation coefficients and R^2 value for the Set 1, Set 2, Set 3, Set 4, Set5, and Set 6

Sets	C	C_1	C_2	C_3	C_4	R^2
1	450	18.0	24100	−40539	8019	0.992
2	−113	−4.66	−1810	3561	−705	0.818
3	17.1	0.666	−0.1	−0.1	−0.15	0.995
4	−129	−7.94	147	167	−11.1	0.916
5	31.7	1.08	−31.4	−39.5	4.19	0.911
6	2.3	−0.308	89.1	−44.1	4.06	0.88

Thereafter, invoking the suggested ansatz, Eq (14), and putting the quantum mechanical descriptors and the correlation coefficients in the Eq (14), we have computed the PAs of six sets of carbon compounds. The comparative study of theoretically evaluated and experimentally determined PAs of the Set 1–Set 6 is performed in the Tables (10.2–10.7), respectively.

TABLE 10.2   Experimental PA (eV), calculated PA (eV), and R^2 for the Set 1

Molecule	Experimental PA	Calculated PA	R^2
Methane	5.63294	6.01418	0.99
Ethane	6.17932	6.56332	
Propane	6.48286	6.83883	
Butane*	6.83237	7.07331	
Isobutane	7.02491	7.34303	

TABLE 10.2 *(Continued)*

Molecule	Experimental PA	Calculated PA	R^2
Pentane*	6.86533	7.13276	
Hexane*	7.01407	7.37095	

Note: *PA calculated by Wróblewski et al. (2007)

TABLE 10.3 Experimental PA (eV), calculated PA (eV), and R^2 for the Set 2

Molecule	Experimental PA	Calculated PA	R^2
Formaldehyde	7.38916	7.90889	0.817
Formic acid	7.68837	8.13938	
Methanol	7.81846	8.57263	
Ketene	8.55564	8.96532	
Acetaldehyde	7.9659	8.34277	
Ethanol	8.04829	8.57857	
Acetic acid	8.12201	8.55023	
Acetone	8.41254	8.90774	
Propanol	8.15236	8.47112	
Propionic acid	8.26077	8.50291	
Methyl acetate	8.28679	8.61904	
Butanol	8.17838	8.46674	

TABLE 10.4 Experimental PA (eV), calculated PA (eV), and R^2 for the Set 3

Molecule	Experimental PA	Calculated PA	R^2

NH$_3$	8.846181	8.860042	0.995
CH$_3$NH$_2$	9.284153	9.341572	
CH$_3$CH$_2$NH$_2$	9.409908	9.399806	
(CH$_3$)$_2$CHNH$_2$	9.47929	9.499455	
(CH$_3$)$_2$NH	9.566017	9.583402	
(CH$_3$)$_3$CNH$_2$	9.57469	9.596479	
(CH$_3$)$_3$N	9.761153	9.794852	

TABLE 10.5 Experimental PA (eV), calculated PA (eV), and R^2 for the Set 4

MOLECULE	Experimental PA (eV))	Calculated PA (eV)	R^2
3-H$_3$C$_6$H$_4$N(C$_2$H$_5$)$_2$	9.925935	9.722904	0.91
4-H$_3$C$_6$H$_4$N(C$_2$H$_5$)$_2$	9.912926	9.706435	
C$_6$H$_5$N(C$_3$H$_7$)$_2$	9.912926	9.673925	
C$_6$H$_5$N(CH$_3$)(C$_2$H$_5$)	9.84788	9.522402	
C$_6$H$_5$NH(C$_2$H$_5$)	9.618053	9.592654	
C$_6$H$_5$NHCH$_3$	9.457608	9.44481	
C$_6$H$_5$CH$_2$NH$_2$	9.401235	8.976198	
2-(OH)C$_6$H$_4$NH$_2$	9.28849	9.197386	
3-(OH)C$_6$H$_4$NH$_2$	9.28849	9.197251	
4-CH$_3$C$_6$H$_4$NH$_2$	9.266808	9.06326	
3-CH$_3$C$_6$H$_4$NH$_2$	9.253799	9.04584	
3-CH$_3$C$_6$H$_4$N(CH$_3$)$_2$	9.253799	9.044886	
1,2-C$_6$H$_4$(NH$_2$)$_2$	9.22778	9.031081	
4-ClC$_6$H$_4$NH$_2$	9.045653	8.720894	
3-BrC$_6$H$_4$NH$_2$	9.023971	8.683775	
4-FC$_6$H$_4$NH$_2$	9.023971	8.763088	
3-CF$_3$C$_6$H$_4$NH$_2$	8.854853	8.674228	

TABLE 10.6 Experimental PA (eV), calculated PA (eV), and R^2 for the Set 5

Name	Experimental P.A	Calculated P.A	R^2
Pyridine	9.579025	9.70499435	0.911
3-Fluoropyridine	9.292825	9.45509615	
4-Trifluoromethylpyridine	9.227780	9.24233169	
2-Trifluoromethylpyridine	9.171407	9.27524221	
4-cyanopyridine/4-pyridinecarbo-nitrile	9.119371	9.11862912	
3-cyanopyridine/3-pyridinecarbo-nitrile	9.076007	9.16793132	
4-methoxypyridine	9.869562	9.91634082	
2-t-butylpyridine	9.860889	9.84251312	
2,4-dimethylpyridine	9.856553	9.97185252	
2-isopropylpyridine	9.852216	9.84129804	
2-ethylpyridine	9.808853	9.75667056	
2,3-dimethylpyridine	9.808853	10.0097702	
3,4-dimethylpyridine	9.808853	9.88622832	
2,5-dimethylpyridine	9.800180	9.89131007	
pyridine -2-methoxymethyl	9.800180	9.71229849	
4-tert-butylpyridine	9.795844	9.81876855	
3,5-dimethylpyridine	9.778498	9.76297831	
4-methylpyridine	9.765489	9.79359891	
2-methylpyridine	9.756816	9.84350118	
4-ethylpyridine	9.739471	9.7890431	
3-methylpyridine	9.717789	9.73935956	
3-ethylpyridine	9.709116	9.77988682	
3-methoxypyridine	9.696107	9.72770612	
4-vinylpyridine	9.678762	9.70246112	
2-methoxypyridine	9.622389	9.76651527	

TABLE 10.6 *(Continued)*

Name	Experimental P.A	Calculated P.A	R^2
2-(methylthio)-pyridine	9.626725	9.53136835	
2-chloro-6-methylpyridine	9.496634	9.5342994	
2-chloro-4-methylpyridine	9.479289	9.51421841	
4-chloropyridine	9.444598	9.43047573	
4-Fluoropyridine	9.392562	9.53212685	
2-chloro-6-methoxypyridine	9.362207	9.45240344	
3-bromopyridine	9.327516	9.45856933	
2-chloropyridine	9.297162	9.45612427	
3-chloropyridine	9.314507	9.44773003	
2-bromopyridine	9.310171	9.46820189	

TABLE 10.7 Experimental PA (eV), calculated PA (eV), and R^2 for the Set 6

Name	Experimental PA	Calculated PA	R^2
Glycine	9.175744	9.324845	0.88
Alanine	9.314508	9.33187	
Cysteine	9.292826	9.386151	
Serine	9.379553	9.445344	
Tryptophan	9.774162	9.822751	
Tyrosine	9.639735	9.639794	
Methionine	9.600708	9.660442	
glutamic acid	9.388226	9.391748	
(2S,3R) threonine	9.474953	9.431556	
aspartic acid	9.396899	9.340133	

For better visualization of the comparative study, the results of the theoretically computed and experimentally determined proton affinities of Set 1–Set 6 are depicted in the Figures (10.1–10.6), respectively.

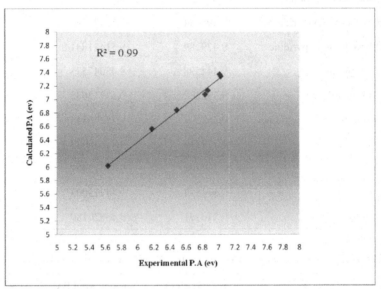

FIGURE 10.1 Plot of calculated PA Vs Experimental PA and PA calculated by Wróblewski et al. for Set 1.

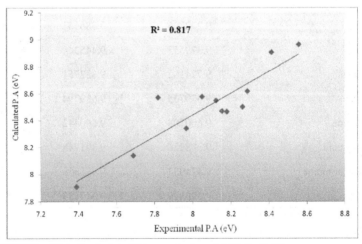

FIGURE 10.2 Plot of calculated PA vs experimental PA for Set 2.

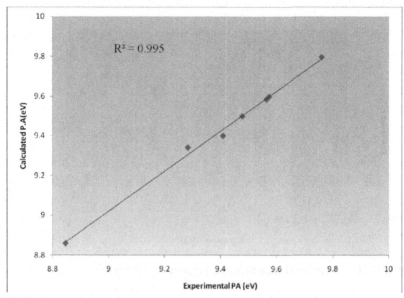

FIGURE 10.3   Plot of calculated PA Vs experimental PA for Set 3.

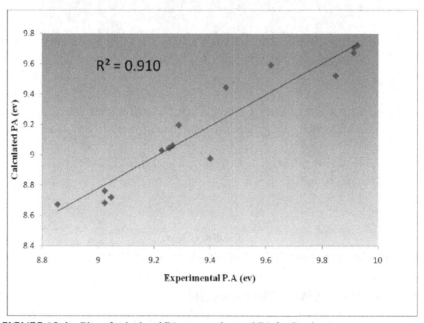

FIGURE 10.4   Plot of calculated PA vs experimental PA for Set 4.

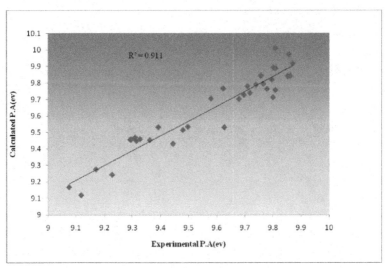

FIGURE 10.5 Plot of calculated PA vs experimental PA for Set 5.

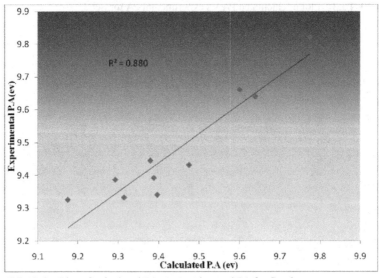

FIGURE 10.6 Plot of calculated PA vs experimental PA for Set 6.

10.10   RESULTS AND DISCUSSION

A deep look at Table (10.2) and Figure (10.1) (for Set 1); Table (10.4), and
Figure (10.3) (for Set 3); and Table (10.6) and Figure (10.5) (for Set 5)

reveals that there are excellent correlation between the theoretically computed PAs of the seven hydrocarbons (Set 1), seven aliphatic amines (Set 3), and 40 pyridine derivatives (Set 5), respectively. The R^2 value for correlation of Set 1, Set 3, and Set 5 are 0.99, 0.995, and 0.911, respectively. A close look at the Figures (10.1), (10.3), and (10.5) reveals that the two sets of PAs—experimental and theoretical of the three sets molecules viz the hydrocarbons (Set 1), the aliphatic amines (Set 3), and pyridine derivatives (Set 5) are so close to each other that one curve just superimposes upon the other.

A look at Table (10.3) and Figure (10.2) (for Set 2); Table (10.5) and Figure (10.4) (for Set 4); and Table (10.7) and Figure (10.6) (for set 6) reveals that there is fairly a good correlation between the theoretically computed and experimentally determined PAs of as many as 12 compounds containing alcohols, carbonyls, carboxylic acids and esters (Set 2), 17 aromatic amines (Set 4), and 10 amino acids (Set 6), respectively. The R^2 value for correlation of Set 2, Set 4, and Set 6 are 0.817, 0.91, and 0.88, respectively.

10.11   CONCLUSION

From the literature survey, it is understood that there is enough scope to model to calculate the protonation energy, and we have presented a scientific model for the evaluation of protonation energy of molecules in terms of four quantum theoretical descriptors—the ionization energy, the global softness, the electronegativity, and the global electrophilicity index. As a basis of scientific modeling, we have posited that these akin theoretical descriptors can be entailed in following and describing the alteration in geometrical parameters, the charge rearrangement, and polarization in molecules as a result of protonation. The suggested ansatz is invoked to calculate the PAs of as many as 93 carbon compounds of diverse physicochemical nature. The validity test of the model is performed by comparing theoretically computed protonation energies and the corresponding experimental counterparts. The close agreement between the theoretically evaluated and experimentally determined PA's suggests that the conceived modeling and the suggested ansatz for computing PA of molecules are efficacious and the hypothesis is scientifically acceptable.

In summary, it is clear that quantum chemical descriptors have tremendous applicability and potential in the study of protonation phenomenon.

KEYWORDS

- Calculation of proton affinity
- Correlation of quantum chemical descriptors
- Global descriptors
- Protonation

REFERENCE

1. Hartree, D. R.; Results of calculations of atomic wave functions. I. Survey, and self-consistent fields for Cl^{-} and Cu^{+}. *Proc. Roy. Soc. (London).* **1933**, *141*, 282–301.

2. Ghosh, D. C.; A theoretical study of some selected molecules and their protonation by the application of CNDO method. Premchand Roychand Research Studentship Award, University of Calcutta; **1976**.

3. Brønsted, J. N.; Einige bemerkungen über den begriff der säuren und basen. *Rec. Trav. Chim. Pays-Bas.* **1923**, *42*, 718–728.

4. Lewis, G. N.; Valence and the Structure of Atoms and Molecules. New York: Chemical Catalog; **1923**.

5. Bouchoux, G.; Gas-phase basicities of polyfunctional molecules. Part 1: Theory and Methods Mass Spectrometry Reviews. **2007**, *26*, 775–835.

6. Hehre, W. J.; Pople, J. A.; Molecular orbital theory of electronic structure of organic compounds. XV. The protonation of Benzene. *J. Am. Chem. Soc.* **1972**, *94*, 6901–6904.

7. Abdel–Halim, S. T.; Awed, M. K.; Effect of protonation on the molecular structure and reactivity of a typical merocyanine dye: experimental and theoretical investigation. *J. Phys. Chem.* **1993**, *97*, 3160–3165.

8. Anderson, A. B.; Derivation of the extended Hückel method with corrections: one electron molecular orbital theory for energy level and structure determinations. *J. Chem. Phys.* **1975**, *62*, 1187–1188.

9. Boyd, S. L.; Boyd, R. J.; Bessonette, P. W.; Kerdraon, D. I.; and Aucoin, N. T.; A theoretical study of the effects of protonation and deprotonation on bond dissociation energies. *J. Am. Chem. Soc.* **1995**, *117*, 8816–8822.

10. Grana, A. M.; and Mosquera, R. A.; Effect of protonation on the atomic and bond properties of the carbonyl group in aldehydes and ketones. *Chem. Phys.* **1999**, *243*, 17–26.

11. Kennedy, R. A.; Mayhew, Ch. A.; Thomas, R.; and Watts, P.; Reactions of H_3O^+ with a number of bromine containing fully and partially halogenated hydrocarbons. *Int. J. Mass Spectrum.* **2003**, *223*, 627–637.

12. Harris, T. K.; and Turner, G. J.; Structural basis of perturbed pKa values of catalytic groups in enzyme active sites. *Rev. Article.* **2002**, *53*, 85–98.

13. Stewart, R.; The Proton: Appellation to Organic Chemistry. New York: Academic Press; **1985**.

14. Carrol, F. A.; Perspectives on Structure and Mechanism in Organic Chemistry. New York: Brooks-Cole; **1998**.

15. Zhao, J.; Zhao, C. R.; Proton transfer reaction rate constants between hydronium ion (H3O+) andvolatile organic compounds. *Atmos. Environ.* **2004**, *38*, 2177.

16. Shan, Y.; et al. A conserved protonation-dependent switch controls drug binding in the Abl kinase. *PNAS.* **2009**, *106*, 139–144.

17. Rabenstein, B.; and Knapp, E.; *Biophys. J.* **2001**, *80*, 1141–1150.

18. Lias, S. G.; Liebman, J. F.; and Levine, R. D.; Evaluated gas phase basicity and proton afinity of molecules; heat of formation of protonated molecules. *J. Phys. Chem. Ref. Data.* **1984**, *13*, 695–808.

19. Munson, M. S. B.; and Franklin, J. L.; Energetics of some gaseous oxygenated organic ions. *J. Phys. Chem.* **1964**, *68*, 3191–3196.

20. Harrison, A. G.; Ivko, A.; and Raalte, D. V.; Energetics of formation of some oxygenated ions and the proton affinities of carbonyl compounds. *Can. J. Chem.* **1966**, *44*, 1625–1632.

21. Beauchamp, J. L.; and Buttrill, Jr. S. E.; Proton Affinities of H₂S and H₂O. *J. Chem. Phys.* **1968**, *48*, 1783–1789.

22. Haney, M. A.; and Franklin, J. L.; Mass spectrometric determination of the proton affinities of various molecules. *J. Phys. Chem.* **1969**, *73*, 4328–4331.

23. Aue, D. H.; Webb, H. M.; and Bowers, M. T.; Quantitative relative gas-phase basicities of alkylamines. Correlation with solution basicity. *J. Am. Chem. Soc.* **1972**, *94*, 4726–4728.

24. Watanabe, K.; Nakayama, T.; and Mottl, J. R.; Ionization potentials of some molecules. *J. Quantum. Spectrosc. Radiat. Transfer.* **1962**, *2*, 369–382.

25. Long, J.; and Munson, B.; Proton affinities of some oxygenated compounds. *J. Am. Chem. Soc.* **1973**, *95*, 2427–2432.

26. Aue, D. H.; Webb, H. M.; and Bowers, M. T.; Quantitative proton affinities, ionization potentials, and hydrogen affinities of alkylamines. *J. Am. Chem. Soc.* **1976**, *98*, 311–317.

27. Doiron, C. E.; Grein, F.; Mcmahon, T. B.; and Vasudevan, K.; An *abinitio* and ion cyclotron resonance study of the protonation of borazine. *Can. J. Chem.* **1979**, *57*, 1751–1757.

28. Lee, T. H.; Jolly, W. L.; Bakke, A. A.; Weiss, R.; and Verkade, J. G.; On correlating phosphorus core binding energies, phosphorus lone pai; ionization potentials, and proton affinities of tervalent phosphorus compounds. *J. Am. Chem. Soc.* **1980**, *102*, 2623–2636.

29. Eades, R. A.; Scanlon, K.; Ellenberger, M. R.; Dlxon, D. A.; and Marynlck, D. S.; The proton afflnity of ammonia. A theoretical determination. *J. Phys. Chem.* **1980**, *84*, 2840–2842.

30. Bene, J. E. D.; Frlsch, M. J.; Raghavacharl, K.; and Pople, J. A.; Molecular orbital study of some protonated bases. *J. Phys. Chem.* **1982**, *86*, 1529–1535.

31. Lohr, L. L.; Protonic counterpart of electronegativity as an organizing principle for acidity and basicity. *J. Phys. Chem.* **1984**, *88*, 3607–3611.

32. McAllister, T.; Ion—molecule reactions and proton affinities of methyl thio- and isothiocyanate. *Int. J. Mass Spectrom. Ion Phys.* **1974**, *15*, 303–310.

33. Karpas, Z.; Stevens, W. J.; Buckley, T. J.; and Metz, R.; Proton affinity and gas-phase ion chemistry of methyl isocyanate, methyl isothiocyanate, and methyl thiocyanate *J. Phys. Chem.* **1985**, *89,* 5274–5278.

34. Dewar, M. J. S.; and Dieter, K. M.; Evaluation of AM1 calculated proton affinities and deprotonation enthalpies. *J. Am. Chem. Soc.* **1986**, *108,* 8075–8086.

35. Nagy–Felsobuki, E. I. V.; and Kimura, K.; Ab initio proton affinities of HCOOH, CH3COOH, CH,OH, and CPH,OH. *J. Phys. Chem.* **1990**, *94,* 8041–8044.

36. Szulejko, J. E.; and McMahon, T. B.; Progress toward an absolute gas-phase proton affinity scale. *J. Am. Chem. Soc.* **1993**, *115,* 7839–7848.

37. McLoughlin, R. G.; and Traeger, J. C.; Heat of formation for tert-butyl cation in the gas phase. *J. Am. Chem. Soc.* **1979**, *101,* 5791–5792.

38. Meot–Ner, M.; and Sieck, L. W.; Proton affinity ladders from variable-temperature equilibrium measurements. 1. A reevaluation of the upper proton affinity range. *J. Am. Chem. Soc.* **1991**, *113,* 4448–4460.

39. Mulliken, R. S.; A new electroaffinity scale; together with data on valence states and on valence ionization potentials and electron affinities. *J. Chem. Phys.* **1934**, *2,* 782–793.

40. Reed, J. L.; Electronegativity: proton affinity. *J. Phys. Chem.* **1994**, *98,* 10477–10483.

41. Eekert–Maksic, M.; Klessinger, M.; and Maksic, Z. B.; Theoretical calculations of proton affinities in phenol. *Chem. Phys. Lett.* **1995**, *232,* 472–478.

42. Angelelli, F.; Aschi, M.; Cacace, F; Pepi, F.; and Petris, G. de.; Gas-phase reactivity of hydroxylamine toward charged electrophiles. A mass spectrometric and computational study of the protonation and methylation of H2NOH. *J. Phys. Chem.* **1995**, *99,* 6551–6556.

43. Smith, B. J.; and Leo, Radom; Calculation of proton affinities using the G2(MP2,SVP) procedure. *J. Phys. Chem.* **1995**, *99,* 6468–6471.

44. Wasada, H.; Tsutsui, Y.; and Yamabe, S.; Ab initio study of proton affinities of three crown ethers. *J. Phys. Chem.* **1996**, *100,* 7367–7371.

45. Meot–Ner (Mautner), M.; The ionic hydrogen bond. 2. Intramolecular and partial bonds. Protonation of polyethers, crown ethers, and diketones. *J. Am. Chem. Soc.* **1983**, *105,* 4906–4911.

46. Sharma, R. B.; Blades, A. T.; and Kebarle, P.; Protonation of polyethers, glymes and crown ethers, in the gas phase. *J. Am. Chem. Soc.* **1984**, *106,* 510–516.

47. Chandra, A. K.; and Goursot, A.; Calculation of proton affinities using density functional procedures: a critical study. *J. Phys. Chem.* **1996**, *100,* 11596–11599.

48. Josefredo, R. P. Jr.; and Almeida, W. B. De.; Absolute proton affinity and basicity of the carbenes CH_2, CF_2, CCl_2, $C(OH)_2$, FCOH, CPh_2 and fluorenylidene. *J. Chem. Soc. Faraday Trans.* **1997**, *93,* 1881–1883.

49. Maksic, Z. B.; Kovačevic, B.; and Kovaček, D.; Simple Ab initio model for calculating the absolute proton affinity of aromatics. *J. Phys. Chem. A.* **1997**, *101,* 7446–7453.

50. Eckert–Maksic, M.; Klessinger, M.; and Maksic, Z. B.; Theoretical study of the additivity of proton affinities in aromatics: polysubstituted benzenes. *Chem. Eur. J.* **1996**, *2,* 155–161.

51. Kovaček, D.; Maksić, Z. B.; and Novak, I.; Additivity of the proton affinity in aromatics: fluorinated naphthalenes. *J. Phys. Chem.* **1997**, *101,* 1147–1154.

52. Maksic, Z. B.; Eckert–Maksic, M.; and Klessinger, M.; Additivity of the proton affinity of polysubstituted benzenes: the ipso position. *Chem. Phys. Lett.* **1996**, *260*, 572–576.
53. Eckert–Maksic, M.; Klessinger, M.; Antol, I.; and Maksic, Z. B.; Additivity of proton affinities in disubstituted naphthalenes. *J. Phys. Org. Chem.* **1997**, *10*, 415–419.
54. Howard, S. T.; Foreman, J. P.; and Edwards, P. G.; Correlated proton affinities of arylphosphines. *Chem. Phys. Lett.* **1997**, *264*, 454–458.
55. Fernandez, M. T.; Williams, C.; Mason, R. S.; and Cabral, B. J. C.; Experimental and theoretical proton affinity of limonene. *J. Chem. Soc. Faraday Trans.* **1998**, *94*, 1427–1430.
56. Topola, I. A.; Burt, S. K.; Toscanob, M.; and Russob, N.; Protonation of glycine and alanine: proton affinities, intrinsic basicities and proton transfer path. *J. Molecular Struct. (Theochem).* **1998**, *430*, 41–49.
57. Jursic, B. S.; Complete basis set, Gaussian, and hybrid density functional theory evaluation of the proton affinities of water and ammonia. *J. Molecular Struct. (Theochem).* **1999**, *490*, 1–6.
58. Jursic, B. S.; Density functional theory and complete basis set ab initio evaluation of proton affinity for some selected chemical systems. *J. Mol. Struct. (Theochem).* **1999**, *487*, 193–203.
59. Pérez, P.; Toro–Labbé, A.; and Contreras, R.; HSAB analysis of charge transfer in the gas-phase acid-base equilibria of alkyl-substituted alcohols. *J. Phys. Chem. A.* **1999**, *103*, 11246–11249.
60. Vayner, E.; and Ball, D. W.; Ab initio and density functional optimized structures, proton affinities, and heats of formation for aziridine, azetidine, pyrrolidine, and piperidine. *J. Molecular Struct. (Theochem).* **2000**, *496*, 175–183.
61. Pérez, P.; Toro–Labbé, A.; and Contreras, R.; Global and local analysis of the gas-phase acidity of haloacetic acids. *J. Phys. Chem. A.* **2000**, *104*, 5882–5887.
62. Silva, C. O.; Silva, E. C. da; and Nascimento, M. A. C.; Ab initio calculations of absolute pK_a values in aqueous solution II. Aliphatic alcohols, thiols, and halogenated carboxylic acids. *J. Phys. Chem. A.* **2000**, *104*, 2402–2409.
63. Cerofolinia, G. F.; Marrone, A.; and Re, N.; Correlating proton affinity and HOMO energy of neutral and negatively charged bases. *J. Molecular Struct. (Theochem).* **2002**, *588*, 227–232.
64. Miller, C. E.; and Francisco, J. S.; A quadratic configuration interaction study of the proton affinity of acetic acid. *Chem. Phys. Lett.* **2002**, *364*, 427–431.
65. Betowski, L. D.; and Enlow, M.; A high-level calculation of the proton affinity of diborane. *J. Molecular Struct. (Theochem).* **2003**, *638*, 189–195.
66. Van Beelen, E. S. E.; Koblenz, T. A.; Ingemann, S.; and Hammerum, S.; Experimental and theoretical evaluation of proton affinities of furan, the methylphenols, and the related anisoles. *J. Phys. Chem. A.* **2004**, *108*, 2787–2793.
67. Rao, J. S.; and Sastry, G. N.; Proton affinity of five-membered heterocyclic amines: assessment of computational procedures. *Int. J. Quantum Chem.* **2006**, *106*, 1217–1224.
68. Dinadayalane, T. C.; Sastry, G. N.; and Leszczynskl, J.; Comprehensive theoretical study towards the accurate proton affinity values of naturally occurring amino acids. *Int. J. Quantum Chem.* **2006**, *106*, 2920–2933.

69. Morgon, N. H.; Calculation of proton affinity using the CR-CCSD[T]/ECP method. *Int. J. Quantum Chem.* **2006**, *106*, 2658–2663.

70. Danikiewicz, W.; How reliable are gas-phase proton affinity values of small carbanions? A comparison of experimental data with values calculated using Gaussian-3 and CBS compound methods. *Int. J. Mass Spectrometry.* **2009**, *285*, 86–94.

71. Rivera, A.; Moyano, D.; Maldonado, M.; and Reyes, J. R. A.; FT-IR and DFT studies of the proton affinity of small aminal cages. *Spectrochimica Acta Part A.* **2009**, *74*, 588–590.

72. Meot–Ner (Mautner) M.; Sieck, W. L.; Proton affinity ladders from variable-temperature equilibrium measurements. 1. A reevaluation of the upper proton affinity range. *J. Am. Chem. Soc.* **1991**, *113*, 4448–4460.

73. Hansel, A.; Oberhofer, N.; Lindinger, W.; Zenevich, V. A.; and Billing, G. B.; Vibrational relaxation of NO⁺ (v) in collisions with CH_4: Experimental and theoretical studies. *Int. J. Mass Spectr.* **1999**, *185/186/187*, 559–563.

74. Meot–Ner, M.; Ion thermochemistry of low-volatility compounds in the gas phase. 2. Intrinsic basicities and hydrogen-bonded dimers of nitrogen heterocyclics and nucleic bases. *J. Am. Chem. Soc.* **1979**, *101*, 2396–2403.

75. Dixon, D. A.; and Lias, S. G.; In: Molecular Structure and Energetics, Physical Measurements. Ed. Liebman, J. F.; Greenberg, A.; Deereld Beach, FL: VCH; **1987**, *2*.

76. Curtiss, L. A.; Raghavachari, K.; and Pople, P. A.; Gaussian-2 theory using reduced M(i)ller-Plesset orders. *J. Chem. Phys.* **1993**, *98*, 1293–1298.

77. Del Bene, J. E., Molecular orbital study of the protonation of DNA bases, J. Phys. Chem., **1983**, *87*, 367–371(1983).

78. Hammerum, S.; Heats of formation and proton affinities by the G3 method. *Chem. Phys. Lett.* **1999**, *300*, 529–532.

79. Fontaine, M.; Delhalle, J.; Defranceschi, M.; and Lecayon, G.; Preliminary theoretical study of perfluorodimethyl ether and its protonated form. *Int. J. Quant. Chem.* **1993**, *46*, 171–181.

80. Ghosh, D. C.; and Islam, N.; Whether electronegativity and hardness are manifest two different descriptors of the one and the same fundamental property of atoms—a quest. *Int. J. Quantum Chem.* **2011**, *111*, 40–51.

81. Ghosh, D. C.; and Islam, N.; A quest for the algorithm for evaluating the molecular hardness. *Int. J. Quantum Chem.* **2011**, *111*, 1931–1941.

82. Ghosh, D. C.; and Islam, N.; Determination of some descriptors of the real world working on the fundamental identity of the basic concept and the origin of the electronegativity and the global hardness of atoms, Part 1: Evaluation of internuclear bond distance of some heteronuclear diatomics. *Int. J. Quantum Chem.* **2011**, *111*, 1942–1949.

83. Ghosh, D. C.; and Islam, N.; Whether there is a hardness equalization principle analogous to the electronegativity equalization principle—a quest. *Int. J. Quantum Chem.* **2011**, *111*, 1961–1969.

84. Ghosh, D. C.; and Islam, N.; Determination of some descriptors of the real world working on the fundamental identity of the basic concept and the origin of the electronegativity and the global hardness of atoms. Part 2: Computation of the dipole moments of some heteronuclear diatomics. *Int. J. Quantum Chem.* **2011**, *111*, 2802–2810.

85. Ghosh, D. C.; and Islam, N.; Charge transfer associated with the physical process of hardness equalization and the chemical event of the molecule formation and the dipole moments. *Int. J. Quantum Chem.* **2011**, *111*, 2811–2819.
86. Islam, N.; and Ghosh, D. C.; A new algorithm for the evaluation of equilibrium inter nuclear bond distance of heteronuclear diatomic molecules based on the hardness equalization principle. *Eur. Phys. J D.* **2011**, *61*, 341–348.
87. Islam, N.; and Ghosh, D. C.; A new radial dependent electrostatic algorithm for the evaluation of the electrophilicity indices of the atoms. *Int. J. Quantum Chem.* **2011**, *111*, 3556–3564.
88. Islam, N.; and Ghosh, D. C.; A new algorithm for the evaluation of the global hardness of polyatomic molecules. *Mol. Phys.* **2011**, *109*, 917–931.
89. Parr, R. G.; Donnelly, R. A.; Levy, M.; and Palke, W. E.; Electronegatigity: the density functional view point. *J. Chem. Phys.* **1978**, *68*, 3801–3807.
90. Parr, R. G.; and Pearson, R. G.; Absolute hardness: companion parameter to absolute electronegativity. *J. Am. Chem. Soc.* **1983**, *105*, 7512–7516.
91. Parr, R. G.; and Yang, W.; Density functional theory of atoms and molecules. New York: Oxford University Press; **1989**.
92. Parr, R. G.; Szentpaly, L. V.; and Liu, S.; Electrophilicity index. *J. Am. Chem. Soc.* **1999**, *121*, 1922–1924.
93. Hunter, E. P. L.; and Lias, S. G.; Evaluated gas phase basicities and proton affinities of molecules: an update. *J. Phys. Chem. Ref. Data*, **1998**, *27*, 413–656.
94. National Institute of Standards and Technology. http://webbook.nist.gov/chemistry/pa-ser.html.
95. Wróblewski, T.; Ziemczonek, L.; Alhasan, A. M.; Karwasz, G. P.; www.fizyka.umk.pl/~karwasz/.../2007_Ab_initio_and_density_functional.pdf.
96. Lias, S. G.; Bartmess, J. E.; Liebman, J. F.; Holmes, J. L.; Levin, R. D.; and Mallard, W. G.; Gas phase ion and nutral thermochemistry. *J. Phys. Chem. Ref. Data.* **1988**, *17*, 1–861.
97. Nantasenamat, C.; Isarankura-Na-Ayudhya, C.; Naenna, T.; and Prachayasittikul, V.; A practical overview of quantitative structure –activity relationship. *EXCLI J.* **2009**, *8*, 74–88.

CHAPTER 11

ANALYSIS OF CASSON FLUID MODEL FOR BLOOD FLOW IN EXTERNALLY APPLIED MAGNETIC FIELD

RATAN KUMAR BOSE

CONTENTS

11.1 INTRODUCTION

The cause and development of many arterial diseases are related to the flow characteristics of blood and the mechanical behavior of the blood vessel walls. The abnormal and unnatural growth in the arterial wall thickness at various locations of the cardiovascular system is medically termed "stenosis." Its presence in one or more locations restricts the flow of blood through the lumen of the coronary arteries into the heart leading to cardiac ischemia. A systematic study on the rheological and hemodynamic properties of blood and blood flow could play a significant role in the basic understanding, diagnosis, and treatment of many cardiovascular, cerebrovascular, and arterial diseases. It is well known that stenosis (narrowing in the local lumen in the artery) is responsible for many cardiovascular diseases. The high blood pressure and the arterial constriction increase flow velocity and shear stress and decrease pressure substantially leading to thrombus formation. If this disease takes a severe form, it may lead to serious circulatory disorders, morbidity, or even fatality. The fact that the hemodynamic factors play a commendable role in the genesis and growth of the disease has attracted many researchers to explore modern approach and sophisticated mathematical models for investigation on flow through stenotic arteries. In most of the investigations relevant to the domain under discussion, the Newtonian behavior of blood (single-phase homogeneous viscous fluid) was accepted. Sankar et al. suggested that this model of blood is acceptable for high shear rate in case of a flow through narrow arteries of diameter ≤1,000 μm on the basis of experimental observations Bernett and White more [1] suggested that blood behaves like a non-Newtonian fluid under certain conditions. H-B fluid model and Casson fluid models are used in the theoretical investigation of blood flow through narrow arteries. Investigations have mentioned that blood obeys Casson fluid equation at low shear rates when flowing through a tube of diameter of 0.095 mm or less and represent fairly closely occurring flow of blood in arteries. In narrow arteries, at a time, the arterial transport becomes much larger as compared to axial transport, and it contributes to the development of atherosclerotic plaques, greatly reducing the capillary diameter. The problem of flow and diffusion becomes much more difficult through a capillary with stenosis at some region. The theoretical study of Scott Blair and Spanner [2] pointed out that blood obeys the Casson's equation only in the limited range, except at very high and very low shear rate and that there is no difference between the Casson's plots and the Herschel–Bulkley plots of experimental data over the range where the Casson's plot is valid. Also, he suggested that the assumptions included in the Casson's equation are unsuitable for cow's blood and that the Herschel–Bulkley equation represents fairly closely what is occurring in the blood. As the Herschel–Bulkley equation contains one more parameter than as compared to Casson's equation, it will be expected that more detailed information about blood properties could be obtained by the use of the Herschel–Bulkley equation. It has been demonstrated by Blair [3] and Copley [4] that the Casson fluid model is adequate for the representation of the simple shear behavior of blood in narrow arteries. Casson [5] examined the validity of Casson fluid model in his studies pertaining to the flow characteristics of blood and reported that at low shear rates the yield stress for blood is nonzero. It has been established by Merrill et al. [6] that the Casson fluid model predicts satisfactorily the flow behaviors of blood in tubes with the diameter of 130–1,000 μm. Charm and Kurland [7] pointed out in their experimental findings that the Casson fluid model could be the best representative of blood when it flows through narrow arteries at low shear rates and that it could be applied to human blood at a wide range of hematocrit and shear rates. Aroesty and Gross [8] developed a Casson fluid theory for pulsatile blood flow through narrow uniform arteries. Chaturani and Samy [9] analyzed the pulsatile flow of Casson fluid through stenosed arteries using the perturbation method. Misra and Chakraborty [10] developed a mathematical model to study unsteady flow of blood through arteries treating blood as a Newtonian viscous incompressible fluid paying due attention to the orthotropic material behavior of the wall tissues. The analysis explored the wall stress in the stenotic region and the shear stress at stenotic throat. The tapered blood vessel segment having a stenosis in its lumen is modeled as a thin elastic tube with a circular cross-section containing a non-Newtonian incompressible fluid. Nanda and Basu Mallik [11] presented a theoretical study for the distribution of axial velocity for blood flow in a branch capillary emerging out of a parent artery at various locations of the branch. The results are computed for various values of r and the angle made by the branch capillary with the parent artery. A mathematical analysis of MHD flow of blood in very narrow capillaries in the presence of stenosis has been studied by Jain et al. [12]. It is assumed that the arterial segment is a cylindrical tube with time-dependent multistenosis. In the proposed investigation, an attempt will be made to deal with a problem, considering hemodynamic and cardiovascular disorders due to non-Newtonian flow of blood in multistenosed arteries. The application of magneto hydrodynamics principles in medicine and biology is of growing interest in the literature of bio-mathematics [13–15]. Bali and Awasthi [16] suggested that by Lenz's law, the Lorentz's force will oppose the motion of conducting fluid. As blood is an electrically conducting fluid, the MHD principles may be used to decelerate the flow of blood in a human arterial system, and thereby, it is useful in the treatment of certain cardiovascular disorders and in the diseases that accelerate blood circulation, such as hemorrhages, hypertension, etc. [17]. This provides us an opportunity to consider the problem of blood flow through a stenosed segment of an artery where the rheology of blood is described by Casson fluid model under the influence of externally applied magnetic field. A quantitative analysis will be done based on numerical computations by taking the different values of material constants and other parameters. The variation of shear stress and skin-friction with different radial distance in the region of the stenosis is presented graphically with respect to externally applied magnetic field on stenosed arterial segment. The qualitative and quantitative changes in the skin-friction, shear stress, and volumetric flow rate at different stages of the growth of the stenosis have also been presented in the presence of an applied magnetic field.

Nomenclature

T	shear stress	z	axial coordinate
τ_H	yield stress	u	Axial average velocity of flow
τ_R	skin-friction	R_0	radius of the artery
M	Magnetization	R(z)	radius of the artery at stenosed portion
B	Applied magnetic field	L_0	length of the stenosis
Q	volumetric flow rate	p	pressure
R	radial coordinate	k	viscosity coefficient

11.2   THE PROBLEM AND ITS SOLUTION

Consider the motion of blood following Herschel–Bulkley equation through an axially symmetric stenosed artery under the influence of an external applied uniform transverse magnetic field, shown in Figure (11.2), whereas the apparent geometry shown in Figure (11.1).

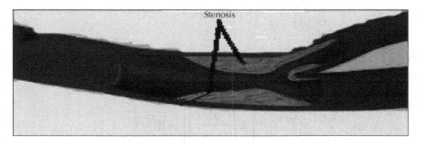

FIGURE 11.1   Geometry of stenosis.

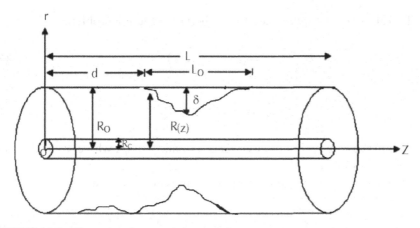

FIGURE 11.2   Geometry of composite stenosis in an artery.

In such a case, the radius of artery $R(z)$ can be written as

$$\overline{R}(z) = R_0\left[1 - A\left\{(\overline{l_0})^{(s-1)}(\overline{z}-\overline{d}) - (\overline{z}-\overline{d})^s\right\}\right], \text{ where } \overline{d} \le \overline{z} \le \overline{d} + \overline{l_0}$$

and radius of the artery is $R(z)$

$= R_0,$ otherwise   (1) where $A = \dfrac{\delta}{R_0 \bar{l}_0{}^s} \dfrac{s^{s/(s-1)}}{(s-1)}$

The Navier–Stoke equation is

$$-\frac{\partial \bar{p}}{\partial z} + \frac{1}{r}\frac{\partial}{\partial r}(\overline{r}\overline{z}) + \mu_0 M \frac{\partial \bar{B}}{\partial z} = 0 \qquad (2)$$

For Casson fluid model, the relation between shear stress and shear rate is given by Fung [18].

$$\bar{\tau}^{1/2} = \bar{\tau}_H{}^{1/2} + \left[\mu\left(-\frac{\partial \bar{u}}{\partial r}\right)\right]^{1/2} \text{ if } \bar{\tau} \geq \bar{\tau}_H$$

$$\frac{\partial \bar{u}}{\partial r} = 0 \text{ , if } \bar{\tau} \leq \bar{\tau}_H \qquad (3)$$

Therefore, the boundary conditions pertaining to the problem

$$\bar{u} = 0 \text{ at } \bar{r} = \overline{R(z)} \qquad (4)$$

$$\bar{\tau} \text{ is finite at } \bar{r} = 0 \qquad (5)$$

And in the core region of artery $\bar{u} = \bar{u}_c$ and $\bar{r} = \bar{R}_c$, where $\bar{u}_c$ is the core velocity of blood.

Therefore, the nondimensional schemes are as follows:

$$r = \frac{\bar{r}}{R_0}, z = \frac{\bar{z}}{l}, R = \frac{\bar{R}}{R_0}, p = \frac{\bar{p}}{\rho u_0{}^2}, u = \frac{\bar{u}}{u_0}, \tau = \frac{\bar{\tau}}{\rho u_0{}^2}, d = \frac{\bar{d}}{l}, l_0 = \frac{\bar{l}_0}{l}, B = \frac{\bar{B}}{B_0} \quad (6)$$

B_0 is the external transverse uniform constant magnetic field; now, the geometry is

$$R(z) = R_0\left[1 - A\{(l_0)^{(s-1)}(z-d) - (z-d)^s\}\right]; \ d \leq z \leq d + l_0$$

$$= 1, \text{ otherwise} \qquad (7)$$

where

$$A = \frac{\delta}{R_0 l_0^{\,s}} \frac{s^{s/(s-1)}}{(s-1)}$$

Now, Eqs. (2) and (3) reduce to

$$-\frac{\partial p}{\partial z} + \frac{1}{r}\frac{\partial}{\partial r}(r\tau) + \left(\frac{\mu_0 M B_0}{\rho u_0^{\,2}}\right)\frac{\partial B}{\partial z} = 0 \tag{8}$$

$$-\frac{\partial p}{\partial z} + \frac{1}{r}\frac{\partial}{\partial r}(r\tau) + m_1 \frac{\partial B}{\partial z} = 0 \tag{9}$$

$$\tau^{1/2} = \tau_H^{\,1/2} + m_2 \left(-\frac{\partial u}{\partial r}\right)^{1/2}, \text{ if } \tau \ge \tau_H \tag{10}$$

$$\frac{\partial u}{\partial r} = 0, \text{ where } \tau \le \tau_H$$

Where considering $m_1 = \left(\dfrac{\mu_0 M B_0}{\rho u_0^{\,2}}\right)$ and $m_2 = \sqrt{\dfrac{\mu}{\rho u_0 R_0}}$.

Now, from Eq. (10),

$$\left(\tau^{1/2} - \tau_H^{\,1/2}\right)^2 = m_2^{\,2}\left(-\frac{\partial u}{\partial r}\right)$$

$$\frac{1}{m_2^{\,2}}\left(\tau^{1/2} - \tau_H^{\,1/2}\right)^2 = \left(-\frac{\partial u}{\partial r}\right) = f(\tau) \tag{11}$$

We know the volumetric flow rate

$$Q = \int_0^{R(z)} 2\pi r u\, dr$$

$$= 2\pi \left\{ \left(u \cdot \frac{r^2}{2} \right)_0^R - \int_0^R \frac{du}{dr}\frac{r^2}{2}\, dr \right\}$$

$$Q = \frac{\pi R^3}{3m_2{}^2}\left(\tau^{1/2} - \tau_H{}^{1/2}\right)^2 \tag{12}$$

Again, from Eqs. (9) and (10),

$$\frac{1}{r}\frac{\partial}{\partial r}(r\tau) = \frac{\partial p}{\partial z} - m_1\frac{\partial B}{\partial z}$$

$$\frac{\partial u}{\partial r} = \frac{1}{m_2{}^2}\left(2\sqrt{\tau\tau_H} - \tau_H - \frac{r}{2}\left(\frac{\partial p}{\partial z} - m_1\frac{\partial B}{\partial z}\right)\right)$$

$$u = \left(\frac{1}{m_2{}^2}2\sqrt{\tau\tau_H}.r - \tau_H r - \frac{r^2}{4}\left(\frac{\partial p}{\partial z} - m_1\frac{\partial B}{\partial z}\right)\right) \tag{13}$$

Again, from volumetric flow rate and Eq. (13),

$$Q = \int_0^{R(z)} 2\pi r u\, dr = \pi R^2 u \tag{14}$$

$$Q = \pi R^2\left(\frac{1}{m_2{}^2}2\sqrt{\tau\tau_H}.r - \tau_H r - \frac{r^2}{4}\left(\frac{\partial p}{\partial z} - m_1\frac{\partial B}{\partial z}\right)\right) \tag{15}$$

When $r = R$, then $\tau = \tau_R$

$$Q = \pi R^2\left(\frac{1}{m_2{}^2}2\sqrt{\tau\tau_H}.R - \tau_H R - \frac{R^2}{4}\left(\frac{\partial p}{\partial z} - m_1\frac{\partial B}{\partial z}\right)\right) \tag{16}$$

Therefore, from Eqs. (11) and (14),

where $\tau = -\frac{r}{2}\frac{dp}{dz}$ and $\tau_R = -\frac{R}{2}\frac{dp}{dz}$ gives $dr = \frac{R}{\tau_R}d\tau$

$$Q = \pi \int_0^{\tau_R} f(\tau) R^2 \frac{\tau^2}{\tau_R{}^2}\frac{R}{\tau_R}d\tau$$

$$Q = \frac{\pi R^3 \tau_R}{m_2^{\,2}} \left(\frac{1}{4} + \frac{16}{49} \frac{\tau_H}{\tau_R} - \frac{4}{7} \sqrt{\frac{\tau_H}{\tau_R}} \right)$$

$$2\sqrt{\tau_R \tau_H} = Q^{1/2} 4 \sqrt{\frac{\tau_H}{\pi R^3}} + \frac{16}{7} \tau_H \tag{17}$$

Equations (16) and (17) give the volumetric flow rate

$$Q = \left[\left(\frac{4\pi^2 R^3 \tau_H}{m_2^{\,2}} + \frac{16}{7} \cdot \frac{R \tau_H}{m_2^{\,2}} - \tau_H R - \frac{R^2}{4} \left(\frac{\partial p}{\partial z} - m_1 \frac{\partial B}{\partial z} \right) \right)^{1/2} + \frac{2\pi R^2}{m_2} \sqrt{\frac{\tau_H}{\pi R}} \right]^2 \tag{18}$$

Therefore, from Eqs. (18) and (14), the velocity of flow is

$$u = \frac{1}{\pi R^2} \left[\left(\frac{4\pi^2 R^3 \tau_H}{m_2^{\,2}} + \frac{16}{7} \cdot \frac{R \tau_H}{m_2^{\,2}} - \tau_H R - \frac{R^2}{4} \left(\frac{\partial p}{\partial z} - m_1 \frac{\partial B}{\partial z} \right) \right)^{1/2} + \frac{2\pi R^2}{m_2} \sqrt{\frac{\tau_H}{\pi R}} \right]^2 \tag{19}$$

Shear stress is considered as τ,

Thus,
$$\tau = -k \left(\frac{\partial u}{\partial r} \right)_{r=R} \tag{20}$$

where
$$k = \mu$$

Therefore,
$$\tau = -\mu \left(\frac{\partial u}{\partial r} \right)_{r=R} \tag{21}$$

Differentiating Eq. (19) with respect to r and substituting the value in Eq. (22), we obtain shear stress

$$\tau = -\mu \left[\left(\frac{4\pi^2 R^3 \tau_H}{m_2^{\,2}} + \frac{16}{7} \cdot \frac{R \tau_H}{m_2^{\,2}} - \tau_H R - \frac{R^2}{4} \left(\frac{\partial p}{\partial z} - m_1 \frac{\partial B}{\partial z} \right) \right)^{1/2} + \frac{4}{m_2} \sqrt{\frac{\tau_H}{\pi R^3}} + \frac{72 \tau_H}{7 m_2^{\,2}} - \tau_H - \frac{R}{2} \left(\frac{\partial p}{\partial z} - m_1 \frac{\partial B}{\partial z} \right) \right] \tag{22}$$

11.3   NUMERICAL RESULTS AND DISCUSSION

To obtain an estimate of the quantitative effects of the various parameters involved in the analysis, it is necessary to evaluate the analytical results obtained for dimensionless shear stress to flow, τ. It is based on area-axial average velocity of flow on constant tube diameter, stenosis height considered as $\dfrac{\delta}{R_0} = (0.1, 0.2, 0.3, 0.4, 0.5)$, $u = (0.5, 2.5, 4.5, 8.5)$, $\tau_H = 0.05$, then $k = 3$, when $\tau_H = 0.10$ then $k = 4$, because the viscosity of blood at 37°C is $(3 - 4) \times 10^{-3}$ Pa.S [19]. It is seen that the shear stress increases as the axial distance z increases from 0 to 0.5, and then it decreases as z increases from 0.5 to 1. This is due to large velocity gradient, and therefore, the severity of the stenosis significantly affects the shear stress characteristics [20]. Here, we have considered that the magnetic intensity assumed the values as $B = (1.1 \times 10^4, 2.1 \times 10^4, 4.1 \times 10^4)$ [21, 22] and $B_0 = 8$ tesla. Measurement has also been performed for the estimation of the magnetic susceptibility of blood, which was found to be 3.5×10^{-6} and -6.6×10^{-7} for the venous and arterial blood, respectively [20]. Approximately considering the density of blood in stenosed artery is $\rho = 1$ (1.060 approx).

To obtain an estimate of the quantitative effects of various parameters involved in this analysis, the relevant computational work has been performed for some specific cases using available experimental data. The purpose of this numerical computation is to bring out the effects of magnetic field intensity, slip velocity, stenotic height, shear stress, and radial distance on the rheology of blood through stenosed artery taking the non-Newtonian (Casson fluid model) for blood.

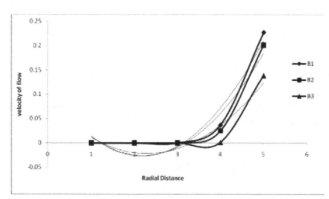

FIGURE 11.3   Variation of velocity of flow with respect to different increasing magnetic field intensity and radial distance.

In the above theoretical analysis, Figure (11.3), variation of velocity of flow with respect to different increasing magnetic field intensity and radial distance, where we observe that increasing magnetic field intensity affects the blood flow in a significant way, increases after a significant point of radius, which is nearly equal to the midpoint of radius.

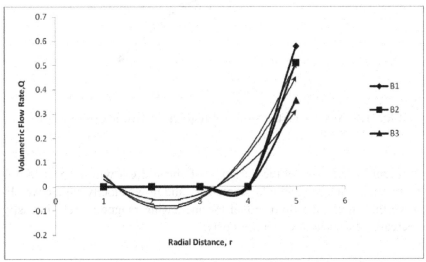

FIGURE 11.4   Variation of volumetric flow rate with respect to different increasing magnetic field intensity and radial distance.

And in Figure (11.4), variation of volumetric flow rate with respect to different increasing magnetic field intensity and radial distance of the stenosed artery is shown; after a certain range, the volumetric flow rate increases with a small quantity.

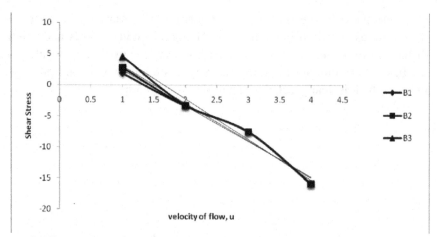

FIGURE 11.5   Variation of shear stress with respect to different increasing magnetic field intensity and flow velocity.

Figure (11.5) shows the variation of shear stress with respect to different increasing magnetic field intensity and flow velocity, where we observe that in Casson fluid model the increasing magnetic field intensity decreases the shear stress enormously.

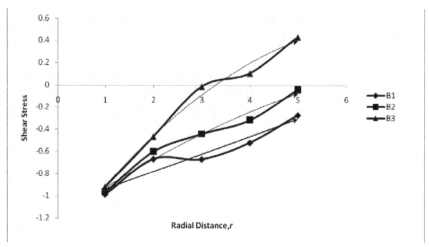

FIGURE 11.6   Variation of shear stress with respect to different increasing magnetic field intensity and radial distance.

Figure (11.6) shows that with respect to the different rheological parameters in Casson fluid model, the different increasing magnetic field intensity and radial distance of artery affect the shear stress of blood in atherosclerosis significantly and increase mildly with the parameters.

11.4   CONCLUSION

The rheology of blood through narrow stenosed arterial segments with an externally applied magnetic field has been studied in this analysis, treating blood as a Casson fluid. It is observed that the magneto hydrodynamic parameter, radius of stenosis, flow velocity, and Casson fluid parameters are the strong parameters influencing the flow and flow characteristics qualitatively and quantitatively. It is interesting to note that the different increasing magnetic field intensity and radial distance of artery affects the shear stress, volumetric flow rate, and velocity of flow. As expected, axial velocity and flow rate both reveal an increasing tendency with the increasing magnetic field intensity but shear stress decreases due to MHD effects. This study is more useful for the purpose of simulation and validation of different models in different conditions of arteriosclerosis. Also, it is expected that the analytical study will help the physicians to estimate the severity of stenosis and its consequences. Thus, this may help in taking decisions regarding the treatment of the patients. This study can be further extended by the introduction of more rheological and physical parameters in the analysis. Thus, the model developed in this chapter will throw light on the clinical treatment of the obstruction of fluid movement due to formulation of multiple stenoses in the arterial system.

KEYWORDS

- **Casson fluid**
- **MHD effect**
- **Volumetric flow rate**
- **Stenosis**
- **Slip velocity**
- **Shear stress**

REFERENCES

1. Whitmore, R. L.; Rheology of the Circulation, **xii** +. New York: Oxford Pergamon Press; **1968**.
2. Blair, G. W. S.; and Spanner, D. C.; An Introduction to Biorheology. Oxford UK: Elsevier Scientific; **1974**.
3. Blair, G. W. S.; An equation for the flow of blood, plasma and serum through glass capillaries. *Nat.* **1959**, *183(4661)*, 613–614.
4. Copley, A. L.; Apparent Viscosity and Wall Adherence of Blood Systems, in Flow Properties of Blood and Other Biological Systems. Ed. Copley, A. L. and Stainsly, G.; Oxford UK: Pergamon Press; 1960.
5. Casson, N.; Rheology of disperse systems, in flow equation for pigment oil suspensions of the printing ink type. Rheology of Disperse Systems. Ed. Mill, C. C.; London UK: Pergamon Press; **1959**, 84–102.
6. Merrill, E. W.; Benis, A. M.; Gilliland, E. R.; Sherwood, T. K.; and Salzman, E. W.; Pressure-flow relations of human blood in hollow fibers at low flow rates. *J. Appl. Physiol.* **1965**, *20(5)*, 954–967.
7. Charm, S.; and Kurland, G.; Viscometry of human blood for shear rates of 0-100,000 sec−1, *Nat.* **1965**, *206(4984)*, 617–618.
8. Aroesty J.; and Gross, J. F.; Pulsatile flow in small blood vessels. I. Casson theory. *Biorheol.* **1972**, *9(1)*, 33–43.
9. Chaturani, P.; and Samy, R. P.; Pulsatile flow of Casson's fluid through stenosed arteries with applications to blood flow. *Biorheol.* **1986**, *23(5)*, 499–511.
10. Mishra J. C.; and Chakravorty, S.; Flow in arteries in the presence of stenosis. *J. Biomech.* **1986**, *19(11)*, 1907–1918.
11. BasuMallik, B.; and Nanda S. P.; A non-Newtonian two-phase fluid model for blood flow through arteries under stenotic condition. *Int. J. Pharm. Bio. Sci.* **2012**, *2*, 237–247.
12. Jain, M.; Sharma, G. C.; and Kumar, A.; Performance modeling and analysis of blood flow in elastic artery. *Math. Comp. Modelling.* **2004**, *39*, 1491–1499.
13. Suri, P. K.; and Pushpa, R.; Effect of static magnetic field on blood flow in a branch. *J. Pure Appl. Math.* **1981**, *12(7)*, 907–918.
14. Amos, E.; Magnetic effect of pulsatile flow in a con-stricted axis symmetric tube. *J. Pure Appl. Math.* **2003**, *34(9)*, 1315–1326.
15. Elnaby, M. A.; Eldabe, M. T. N.; Abou Zied M. Y.; and Sanyal, D. C.; Mathematical analysis on MHD pulsatile flow of a non-Newtonian fluid through a tube with varying cross-section. *J. Inst. Math. Comp. Sci.* **2007**, *20(1)*, 29–42.
16. Bali, R.; and Awasthi, U.; A casson fluid model for multiple stenosed artery in the presence of magnetic field. *Appl Math.* **2012**, *3*, 436–441.
17. Das, K.; and Saha, G. C.; Arterial MHD pulsatile flow of blood under periodic body accelaration. *Bull. Math. Soc.* **2009**, *16*, 21–42.
18. Fung, Y. C.; Mechanical properties of living tissue. *Biomechan.* **1986**, *4(2)*, 68–81.
19. Sankar, D. S.; Two-fluid nonlinear mathematical model for pulsatile blood flow through stenosed arteries. *Bull. Malaysian Math. Sci. Soc.* **2012**, *35(2A)*, 487–498.

20. Mandal, P. K.; Ikbal, Md. A.; Chakravarty, S.; Wong, b.; Kelvin. K. L.; and Mazumdar, J.; Unsteady response of non-Newtonian blood flow through a stenosed artery in magnetic field. *J. Comput. Appl. Math.* **2009,** *230,* 243–259.
21. Haik, Y.; Pai, V.; and Chen, C. J.; Biomagnetic Fluid Dynamics: Fluid Dynamics at Interfaces. Ed. Shyy, W.; Narayanan, R.; Cambridge: Cambridge University Press; **1999,** 439–452.
22. Motta, M.; Haik, Y.; Gandhari, A.; and Chen, C. J.; High magnetic field effects on human deoxygenated hemoglobin light absorption. *Bioelectrochem. Bioenerg.* **1998,** *47,* 297–300.

INDEX

Printed in the United States
by Baker & Taylor Publisher Services